SAP SRM7 Technical Principles

A Technical Guide for SRM Developer

SELVA LAKSHMANAN

&

MOORTHY MAHADEVAN

ISBN: 0692382275
ISBN-13: 978-0692382271

Preface

This Book is intended for SAP SRM Technical Team, focusing primarily on Technical and Techno Functional Consultants who work on SRM component. Technical development and enhancements are very different from one SAP component to other. This book gives a complete understanding of simple to very complex changes involved in a SAP SRM implementation. Understanding the technical architecture is important for a technical developer who is involved in large SRM projects. This book provides wide coverage on SRM component and brings the reader's technical knowledge to higher levels.

Each SAP components is technically architected in different style. For example, HR uses macros and index tables in their most of codes, SD/MM uses very vast coding due to greater number of transactions and database tables. Understanding the technical principles of the component is very vital for a successful technical consultant. SRM uses basic CRM technical framework and developed in a very high structured way of programming. Up until SRM version 5.5 it uses PD/PDO layer as their main technical component. SRM7.0 uses Web application server instead of ITS and uses floor plan manager, which increases the complexity of SRM7 technical framework.

In our experience we have come across developers working on SRM solutions without understanding technical framework and it makes their solution difficult to maintain and makes further enhancements very hard. There are a number of books available for SRM but it covers most of functional and small part of technical details like BADIs.

Technical challenges and possible solutions are explained in all chapters. The book explains Functional solution or technical solution or a mix of both for approaching a requirement. Functional solution is usually achieved by IMG configuration. Technical solution will resolve issues by code. Each challenge is discussed with an optimal solution and with sample code wherever possible. Author's technical tips and insights are available throughout the book. This style benefits the reader by helping in approaching solutions for real life problems. The reader will be better prepared to give solution to customers. The solution provided is proposed only and it may not cover all your requirements. Use the solution with your discretion.

How this book is organized

The book is divided into eight chapters which cover's basic and advanced technical solutions. Each chapter gives more insights to SRM technical development

- Chapter 1 provides details of technical architecture framework and helps user understand how the technical objects can be used. ECC integration is explained with possible technical challenges and solutions.
- Chapter 2 explains basic SRM document components, version management, audit trail and authorization objects. It also explains about GUI document display utility tool.
- Chapter 3 provides complete insights into SRM 7.0 technical Layers and provides detail technical Function Modules and ABAP Objects which are frequently used in SRM. Details about SRM 7 Web Dynpro and Floor plan manager concepts are also covered.
- Chapter 4 provides insight into basic and advanced enhancements available in SRM 7.0. SRM Technical developers' role is to provide solution through development of enhancement of SRM component and this chapter discusses these enhancements in detail.
- Chapter 5 explains the master data particularly about business partners and product master. The chapter discuss about vendor synchronization and material master replication and custom fields.
- Chapter 6 explains business objects used in business scenarios and related technical challenges with solutions. It covers Portal Integration, Alert Management, External requirements, Sourcing, Shopping Cart Transfer, Bid Invitation and Responses, Purchase Order and Contract.
- Chapter 7 explains about introduction to POWL and Advanced Search tools. It also discusses configuration and enhancements of advanced search tool.
- Chapter 8 explains SRM7 Workflow includes process controlled workflow and business rule framework. It discusses BRF configuration and enhancements with possible technical challenges and troubleshooting techniques.

This book will be an invaluable guide for all SRM consultants whether Technical or Functional. This book aims to advance the consultants skill set to the next level in their career as a SRM Consultant.

Any Questions or Comments, visit us at sapsrmtechbook.com.

TABLE OF CONTENTS

Supplier Relationship Management is a fast growing SAP product. Overview includes Technical Architecture, Technical Scenarios and Business Scenarios of SRM. Technical layers provide detailed technical insight.

1. SRM Overview

Supplier Relationship Management (SRM) is a new dimension product and it is a part of SAP Business suite applications. SAP SRM automates, simplifies and accelerates the procure-to-pay process for goods and services. SAP SRM provides integrated offerings for procurement processes and includes best business practices and software. The goal of SRM is to streamline and provide more effective processes between an enterprise and its supplier.

The SAP SRM processes integrate Supplier Qualification, Negotiation, Contract Management, Sourcing and Awarding more tightly and cost effectively with other enterprise functions and their suppliers' processes. SRM provides support from simple self-service procurement to strategic sourcing and supplier enablement. SRM can be integrated tightly with existing SAP back-end systems.

This chapter explains the more technical side of SRM application. The chapter explains the basic Architecture, Technical Scenarios and the SRM/ECC Integration model. The Technical Scenarios explain different types of SRM deployment scenarios used in SRM. Few SRM implementations use a combination of deployment options.

1.1 Architecture

SRM7 uses state-of-the-art NetWeaver Web Dynpro User Interface technology along with NetWeaver Enterprise portal. In the previous major version SRM 5.0, ITS User Interface technology has been used. The NetWeaver Enterprise Portal is a mandatory component for SAP SRM7.0. SAP ECC is used as a back-end system and integrated highly. All SRM reporting are available in SAP BW system. Catalog and Pricing can be integrated with external systems. See details in the figure.

Components: The components of SRM7 are as of following:

- **NetWeaver Enterprise Portal** – The SAP NetWeaver Portal serves as a single point of entry to applications, services and information. The portal provides a role-based and secure access to all types of application. The portal facilitates a single point of login for all applications. In previous SRM versions, the portal was always optional which meant that most of tasks could be processed with the ITS. In SRM7.0, the portal is mandatory and fully integrated with the solution.

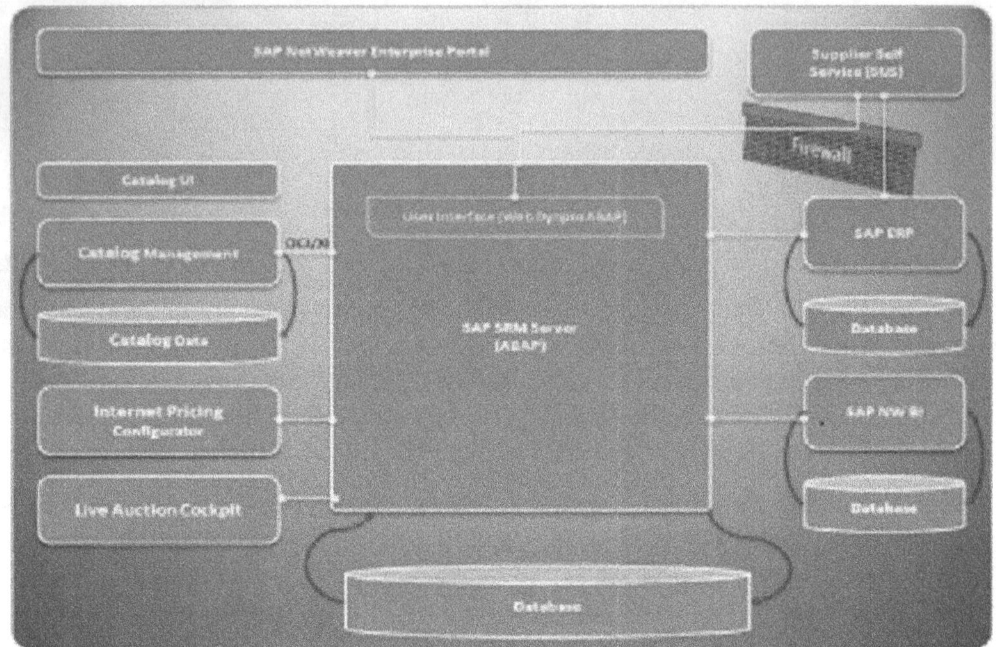

SAP NetWeaver is SAP's integrated technology computing platform and is the technical foundation for many SAP applications. SAP NetWeaver is a service-oriented application and integration platform. SAP NetWeaver facilitates the development and run time environment for SAP applications and can be used for custom development and integration with other applications and systems. SAP NetWeaver primarily uses ABAP programming language but it uses C, C++, and Java also. It also employs open standards and provides industry standard extensions to inter operate with Microsoft .NET, Java EE, and IBM WebSphere.

Supplier Self Service (SUS) – Supplier Self Service is an Add-on component of SAP SRM. SUS is offered as portal for the suppliers to manage their functions. SUS is integrated to the SAP Back-end systems using XI Integration with standard components.

Supplier Enablement consists of document exchange, the supplier portal, and supplier collaboration. SAP SUS is a web-based application that provides full processing capabilities for goods and service orders and integrates into the procurement process.

Some of the benefits of using SUS:

- Supplier Self-registration
- Ability to update vendor organization data via the web portal
- Offers full document exchange capabilities without any third-party intervention

- Ability to respond to RFx for Spot buys
- Receive timely e-mail notifications

User Interface (WD ABAP) – User interface uses the floor plan manager concept. The number of Web Dynpro applications is provided by the SRM system. Web Dynpro for ABAP is the SAP standard user interface technology for developing web applications in the ABAP environment. It consists of a run time environment and a graphical development environment with special Web Dynpro tools that are integrated in the ABAP Workbench.

It offers following advantages for application developers:

- Use of declarative and graphical tools which significantly reduces implementation effort
- Web Dynpro supports a structured design process
- Strict separation between layout and business data
- Reuse and better maintainability by using components
- Layout and navigation easily changed using Web Dynpro tools
- Stateful application support to access webpage data throughout the application context
- Automatic data transport using data binding
- Automatic input check
- Full integration in the reliable ABAP development environment

Live Auction Cockpit (LAC) – LAC is a front-end tool for the reverse auction process. The real time user interface is provided to do online bid submission for suppliers and administration user interface for the purchases. LAC can be installed on the Enterprise Portal.

Internet Pricing Configurator – IPC is a separate component that allows users to configure product online and compare prices across different catalogs and marketplaces. IPC can be installed separately or as part of SRM. SRM Pricing uses the IPC component to determine prices. SRM uses the condition technique to determine prices. SRM uses IPC when the procurement document is being created. For example, when a shopping cart or purchase order is generated, the system automatically determines the gross price and surcharges/discounts that apply to a certain vendor according to defined conditions and computes Net Price. Pricing can be calculated without IPC. BADI BBP_PRICEDATA_READ_DATA can generate the simplified pricing.

BI Content – Business Intelligence is based on BW. All SRM reporting business contents are available in BI. BW is a SAP data warehouse tool. RFC technology is used to integrate between SRM and BW system.

Catalog Management – SRM catalog management is Master Data Management (MDM) for Product and Service catalogs. SRM-MDM is available with pre-configured content. An MDM catalog provides a search engine to finds products and services. You can pull pricing and availability from a supplier catalog. A catalog can be categorized into an Internal and External Catalog.

Open Catalog Interface – SAP SRM OCI is used to describe the data exchange between SRM and external catalog applications. The integration supports the procurement processes for SAP solutions and enables the transmissions of selected products from an external catalog, which can be located on the Internet or intranet, to SAP SRM. OCI is the standard format used by SAP SRM when connecting to external punch-out catalogs. OCI is used to define field mapping between suppliers catalog and SAP SRM Shopping cart. Using OCI, you can select products and transfer them to the SRM shopping cart. The catalog can be hosted on a catalog marketplace or on a supplier based catalog system. SAP Provides catalog content management system as add-on.

ECC – SAP Back-end system has MM/FI modules. The ECC integration is part of Classic and Extended Classic technical scenarios.

1.2 SRM Technical Scenarios

SRM supports a number of business scenarios (explained in later sections). SRM provides three different technical scenarios to deploy the business scenarios. For example, you can implement self-service procurement using one of three technical solutions. There are few core programs written based on the technical scenarios. Each technical scenario has pros and cons. The choice of technical scenarios is based on customer requirements and business scenarios. In a few instances, you can run technical scenarios in parallel.

1.2.1 Classic Scenario

The Classic Scenario relies on ECC back-end system(s). All the MM documents such as purchase order, goods receipts, and invoices are in the back-end system. The shopping cart is created and approved in the SAP SRM system. The remainder of the procurement process takes place in the back-end ERP system(s), and all other follow-on documents, such as the purchase order, goods receipt, or service entry sheet and invoice, are located there. With *SAP Supplier Self-Services*, you have supplier involvement for the operational procurement business scenarios.

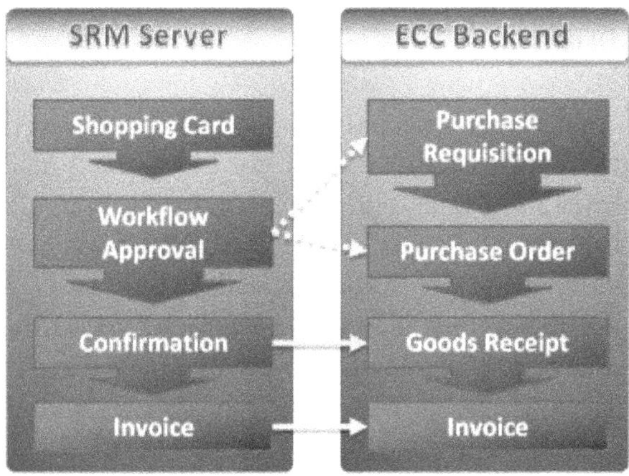

1.2.2 Extended Classic Scenario

The Extended Classic Scenario is an extension of the Classic Scenario. The procurement process takes place in SRM system. The SRM purchasing order is a leading purchase order. The shopping cart is created in the SAP SRM system. The purchase order and follow-on documents are also created there and then replicated to the back-end system.

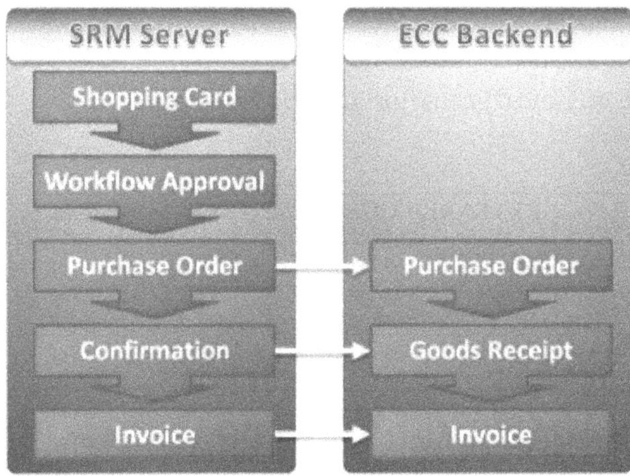

The purchase order in the SAP SRM system is the leading purchase order and cannot be changed in the back-end system. Goods receipts and invoices can be pre-entered in the SAP SRM system or entered directly in the back-end system. With *SAP Supplier Self-Services*, you have partial supplier involvement for all your operational procurement scenarios. In these scenarios, you have supplier involvement for the purchase order and the purchase order response.

1.2.3 Standalone Scenario

The entire purchasing process occurs on the SRM side. All PO, GR and Invoices are processed in the SRM system. FI will not be handled in the SRM system. The invoice can be replicated to ECC back-end system. The shopping cart and purchase order are processed directly in the SAP SRM system. You have no materials management functions in your ERP system and, instead, use those in SAP SRM for all procurement processes. The final invoice is sent to a back-end accounting system. With *SAP Supplier Self-Services*, you have complete supplier involvement for all your operational procurement scenarios.

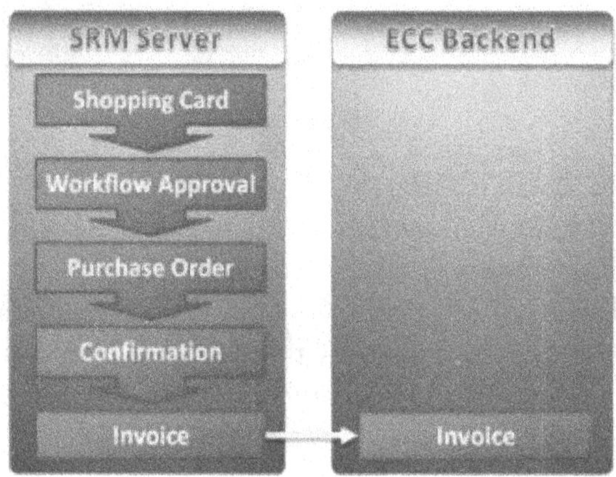

The following table provides the technical scenarios and the SRM processes.

PROCESS	CLASSIC	EXTENDED CLASSIC	STANDALONE
Shopping Cart	SAP SRM System	SAP SRM System	SAP SRM System
Approval	SAP SRM System	SAP SRM System	SAP SRM System
Purchase Order	Back-end system	SAP SRM System (leading system) and back-end system	SAP SRM System
Goods Receipt	Back-end system (can be pre-entered in SAP SRM System)	Back-end system (can be pre-entered in SAP SRM System)	SAP SRM System
Invoice	Back-end system (can be pre-entered in SAP SRM System)	Back-end system (can be pre-entered in SAP SRM System)	SAP SRM System (accounting information sent to back-end system)

SRM provides flexibility to choose between the Extended Classic Scenario and the Classic Scenario when the Extended Classic Scenario is chosen. The BADI BBP_EXTLOCAL_PO_BADI can override the extended classic scenario settings to control the technical scenarios between extended classic and classic scenario.

Technical Challenge: - Override Extended Classic Scenario (Controlled Extended Classic Scenario or Decoupled Scenario). The extended classic technical scenario is set active but POs with transaction type ZCLS should follow the Classic Scenario.

Solution: There is a BADI BADI BBP_EXTLOCALPO_BADI available. You can implement the BADI and the following code provides the solution. There is one more method on the BADI and it can be used for shopping cart.

There is one more method on the BADI and it can be used for shopping cart.

Name: BBP_EXTLOCALPO_BADI	Multiple Use: No	Filter: No

Description: Exit function for overwriting the extended classic scenario flag.

Method: DETERMINE_EXTPO_CREATE

Description: Control the extended classic scenario settings for the PO. Method can also change the FI (Back-end) logical system.

Parameters:

Name	**Type**	**Data Type**	**Description**
IV_PROC_ORG	Import	BBP_PROC_ORG	Purchase Org
IV_TRANS_TYPE	Import	BBP_PROC_TYPE	Business Transaction type
BBP_EXTPO_GL	Change	BBP_EXTPO_GL	Global control
IV_LOGSYS_FI	Change	BBP_LOGSYS_FI	Logical system

Sample code: The sample code is for technical solution.

```
if iv_trans_type = 'ZCLS'.
  clear bbp_extpo_gl-bbpexpo.
endif.
```

There is one more method on the BADI and it can be used for shopping cart.

Method: DETERMINE_EXTPO

Description: Control the extended classic scenario settings for the shopping carts.

Parameters: The method is used only for Shopping carts.			
Name	**Type**	**Data Type**	**Description**
ITEM_DATA	Import	BBPS_EXTPO_BADI	Item data
BBP_EXTPO_GL	Change	BBP_EXTPO_GL	Global control

1.3 Business Scenarios

SRM offers a number of Business Scenarios. In this section, you can view each SRM business scenario briefly. You can provide a better technical solution by understanding basic business scenarios. Based on client's business scenario, the technical solutions may vary.

1.3.1 Self-Service Procurement

The self-service procurement scenario is allows employee to create and manage your own requisitions. This reduces purchasing department responsibilities. The self-service procurement can be implemented at both Classic and Extended-Classic technical scenarios. The sequences of business processes for Classic scenarios are as follows:

- Processing Shopping Carts
- Processing ERP Purchasing Requisitions
- Processing ERP Purchase Orders
- Inbound Processing and Receipt Confirmations with Warehouse Management
- Verifying Invoices
- The business processes of the extended classic scenarios are as follows:
- Processing Shopping Carts
- Searching for Sources of Supply
- Processing SRM Purchase Orders
- Inbound Processing and Receipt Confirmations with Warehouse Management
- Confirming SRM Goods Receipts
- Processing SRM Invoices
- Verifying Invoices

1.3.2 Plan-Driven Procurement

Plan-driven procurement supports the automated procurement of goods, which is especially important for the procurement of direct materials. In a highly integrated procurement process, demand for materials can come from several different planning applications that reside outside of SAP SRM. The planning applications may include Material Requirement Planning (MRP), APO, Plant Maintenance and Repair Planning. Demands from production are transferred to SAP SRM using Open XML interface. The plan driven procurement can be integrated with Plant Maintenance or Supplier.

1.3.3 Service Procurement

Services procurement is often seen as complex and not standardized, because the requirement of a service is typically undefined in quantity, duration, and price at the point of purchase. This assumption implies that the service is not specified until the supplier confirms it. This ambiguity is one reason that, while other categories of spend have uncovered significant cost-saving potential in the purchasing process, services have generally not been considered part of cost-saving measures.

You can manage resources and monitor costs over the entire range of services. SRM supports analytics, sourcing, contract management, and supplier collaboration so you can optimize services procurement processes. Functionality covers a wide range of procured services, such as planned and unplanned maintenance, temporary labor, and construction.

- Purchase Requisition with Service Directories
- Searching for Sources of Supply Centrally
- Processing RFx Events
- Evaluating RFx Responses
- Processing Follow-On Documents
- Processing Purchase Orders in SAP ERP
- Processing Sales Orders in SUS
- Entering Services in SAP RM
- Entering Services in SAP ERP
- Processing Invoices
- Verifying Logistics Invoices in Background
- Verifying Logistics Invoices Online

- Processing Evaluated Receipt Settlements (ERS) in SAP ERP
- Analyzing Service Procurement

1.3.4 Strategic Sourcing

You can use this business scenario to source goods using RFx (request for information, request for proposal, and/or request for quotation). You can use this business scenario with or without integration of the sourcing cockpit. The sourcing cockpit helps you, as a professional purchaser, to process your requirements and to determine the best source of supply. You can also integrate document storage functionality – maintained in cFolders – in the RFx. After you have received bids from suppliers, you can create a purchase order or contract (local or global outline agreement) directly from the sourcing cockpit or in SAP Bidding Engine as a result of the RFx.

The Strategic Sourcing with RFx business scenario comprises these process steps:

- Processing Shopping Carts
- Processing Purchase Requisitions in SAP ERP
- Searching for Sources of Supply Centrally
- Negotiating Contracts
- Processing Bidding Events
- Processing Collaborative Bidding Events Using cFolders
- Evaluating Bids
- Processing Follow-On Documents
- Analyzing Sourcing with RFx

1.3.5 Analytics

SRM Analytics has two scenarios viz., Spend Analysis and Supplier Evaluation. This is part of SRM-BI component. You can use Spend Analysis business scenario to analyze the expenditure of your company, using data from a wide range of heterogeneous systems as well as from all relevant business units and areas. You can configure SRM system to capture of spend and harmonization of master data for reporting purposes.

You can use Supplier Evaluation business scenario to evaluate your suppliers on the basis of Web-based surveys. You can configure individual surveys and questionnaires. Once the data transferred to BI system, several reports are available to analyze the results. SRM provides Supplier Survey Cockpit to create and distribute surveys. You can monitor incoming responses and send reminders to those did not reply.

1.3.6 Contract Management

The contract management allows you to maintain contract features such as Contract Hierarchies, Discount and Grouping Logic. You can create a central contract in SRM and it can be used as a source of supply in both SRM and ECC. You can create and change central contracts and re-negotiate existing contracts directly with a supplier or through creation of RFx.

- Define Usage of Central Contracts
- Developing Contracts
- Processing Contracts and Sourcing Rules in SAP ERP
- Negotiating Contracts
- Process Delivery Schedules
- Searching for Sources of Supply Centrally
- Monitoring Contracts

1.4 SRM and ECC Integration

There is back-end SAP (ECC) system involved. For example, in extended classic scenario, the replication of SRM PO to ECC requires the communication process. SAP SRM system uses a number of communication processes like RFC, IDOC and XML. The synchronous communication uses RFC function call. All back-end systems must be configured in SRM.

1.4.1 Back-end Logical Systems

The ECC back-end system should be defined as part of logical system. Configuration of back-end system is part of basis process. The back-end logical system definition can be configured using the following IMG path. IMG: Supplier Relationship Management → SRM Server → Technical Basic Settings → Define Back-end Systems or you can use transaction SM59 to define back-end systems.

You can configure back-end logical system based product category and it can be invoked under Technical Basic Settings->Define Back-end System for Product Category. The logical systems for the product category are available in BBP_DET_LOGSYS DB table. Note that all back-end destination information is store in BBP_BACK-END_DEST table. This information is configured in IMG under Define System Landscape.

SRM provides the BADI BBP_DETERMINE_LOGSYS to determining the back-end system based on Item data and/or account data criteria. The BADI has two methods CONTRACT_LOGSYS_DETERMINE (for contract) and DETERMINE_LOGSYS. This BADI overwrites Logical system configured product category level back-end system.

Technical Tips: You can use different RFC destination for custom RFC ECC call. It will help you to make difference between the standard and custom program execution.

The following function modules are useful to get logical system list and detail.

Function Module	Description
BBP_LOGICAL_SYSTEM_GETLIST	Lists all the back-end systems
BBP_LOGICAL_SYSTEM_GETDETAIL	Gets detail about the back-end system using logical system name.

1.4.2 Business Function Map

Most of the integration between SRM and SAP ECC is done by RFC functions. These RFC function is part of the business and technical process. These processes and RFC functions are mapped in the SRM system. The mapping has flexibility to enhance the integration. The SRM system uses Meta BAPIs to execute the RFC call in ECC system. For example, a PO creation in ECC system will be done by function module META_PO_CREATE. The Meta function module first identifies the driver function module and executes the FM META_BAPI_DISPATCH. Then driver function module will execute RFC function module which transfers SRM document to back-end system.

The driver function between the SRM and ECC is stored in BBP_FUNCTION_MAP table. It stores the object, method, type of external system and driver function module. SAP provides different function module based on the type of the ECC system and the technical scenario defined. The function mapping defines Object, Method, Server type and its BAPI function module. The function module META_BAPI_DISPATCH fetches function name for given object and method. Standard SAP provided driver function BAPIs can be replace with new (custom) BAPI using the BADI BBP_DRIVER_DETERMINE. Using this exit, you can use the custom function module to handle business needs.

In some cases, the BBP_FUNCITON_MAP has ABAP class name instead of function module name. The META program will handle the ABAP class information. Make sure that your BADI implementation should fall by the META program logic.

Technical Challenges: In Vendor (Supplier) Synchronization program BBP_VENDOR_SYNC, it uses ECC RFC function module BBP_VENDOR_GET_LIST2. The customer requirement is add some more filters to vendor synchronization between SRM and ECC.

Solution: The supplier synchronization uses get vendor list using Meta FM META_VENDOR_GET_LIST2. In Meta BAPI dispatch function module uses Object BUS10006200 and method GetVendorList2. Instead of changing the standard FM BBP_VENDOR_GET_LSIT2, the new custom function module ZFM_VENDOR_GET_LIST2 is developed. Implement the BADI BBP_DRIVER_DETERMINE with new function module name for the object and method.

Note that business object used in this META_BAPI_DISPATCH is same as in ECC system (not SRM system). In SRM system, the business object for PO is BUS2201 but it in ECC, PO business object is BUS2012. You can see the back-end object types are defined in /SAPSRM/IF_PDO_OBJ_TYPES_C with prefixed with 'GC_PDO_BE_'.

1.4.3 XI Integration

SRM uses XI integration to integrate with SUS, MDM and ECC (back-end system). SUS and MDM use only XI integration. SAP NetWeaver XI consists of core components to model, design, automate, and integrate the processes of one or more application systems. XI will incorporate all functions for integration of internal and cross company processes. XI is now known as PI (Process Integration). The Integration Proxy and Integration Engine is part of SRM component. It will communicate with PI integration engine using XML structure. SRM provides a pre-defined content to integrate with SUS and MDM components.

Integration Engine Monitoring

You can monitor the processing XML messages using the transaction SXMB_MONI (or SXMB_ADMIN). You can view the data of XML message. Also, you can restart the XML process again. This can be very useful while testing. Instead of creating new data, you can change XML data and reprocess the data.

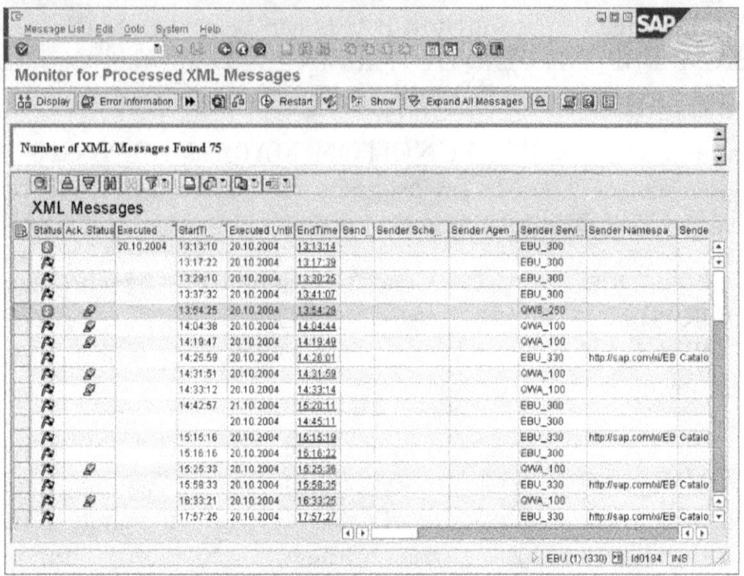

Proxy Generation

The proxy generation converts the WSDL interface description into executable interfaces as Proxies. You can communicate web service infrastructure (XI) using the proxy. SRM uses ABAP proxy generation. You can access these proxies using the transaction code SPROXY.

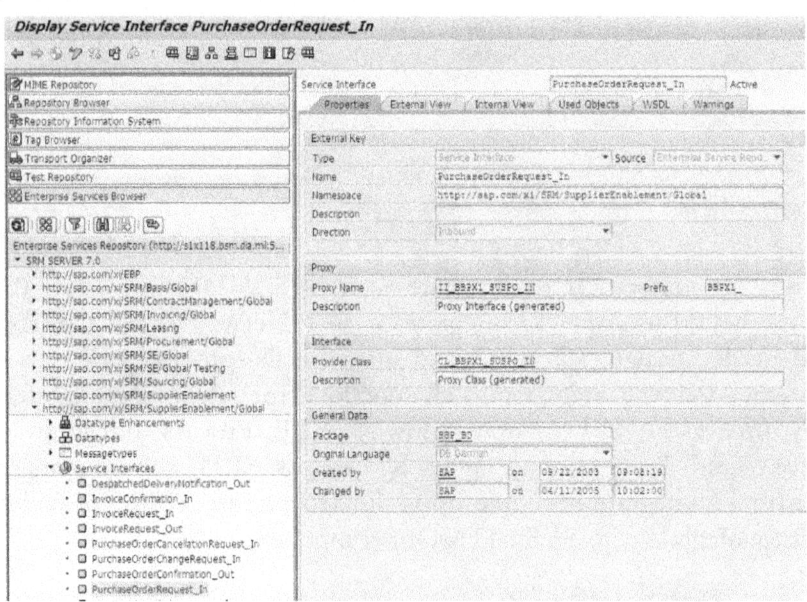

The transaction is very powerful that you can test the interface manually without XI. You can execute (test) the interface by hot key F8 or clicking test button in toolbar. The execution allows you to set few manual options.

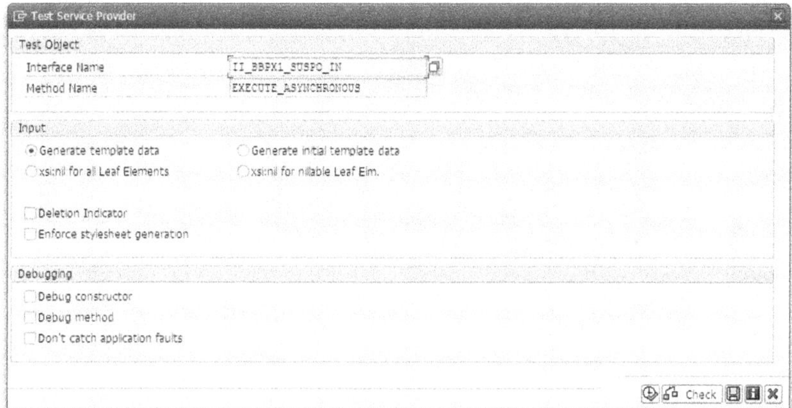
Test Service Provider
Test Object
Interface Name
II_BBPX1_SUSPO_IN
Method Name
EXECUTE_ASYNCHRONOUS
Input
Generate template data
Generate initial template data
xsi:nil for all Leaf Elements
xsi:nil for nillable Leaf Elm.
Deletion Indicator
Enforce stylesheet generation
Debugging
Debug constructor
Debug method
Don't catch application faults
Check

You can edit the XML content using XML editor. Also, you can download and upload XML content on the proxy service provider. You can pretty printer option for better readability.

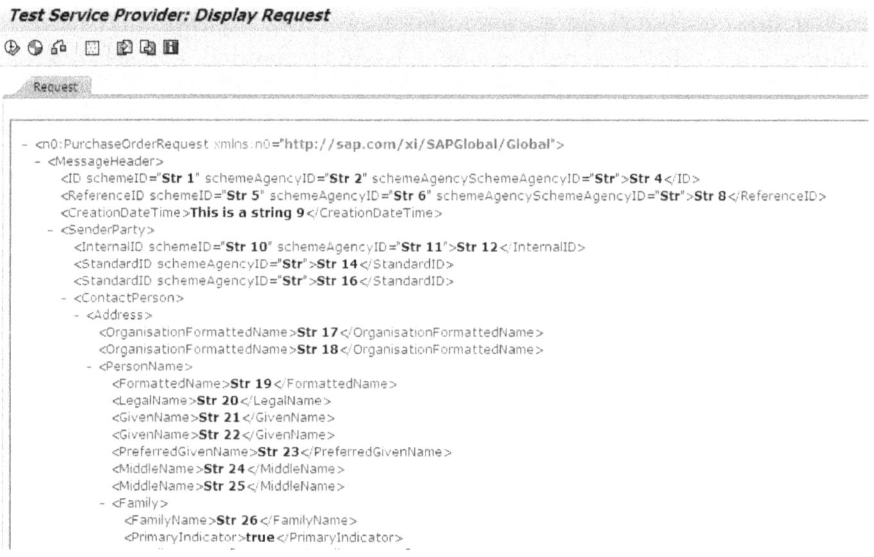
Test Service Provider: Display Request
Request
- <n0:PurchaseOrderRequest xmlns:n0="http://sap.com/xi/SAPGlobal/Global">
- <MessageHeader>
<ID schemeID="Str 1" schemeAgencyID="Str 2" schemeAgencySchemeAgencyID="Str">Str 4</ID>
<ReferenceID schemeID="Str 5" schemeAgencyID="Str 6" schemeAgencySchemeAgencyID="Str">Str 8</ReferenceID>
<CreationDateTime>This is a string 9</CreationDateTime>
- <SenderParty>
<InternalID schemeID="Str 10" schemeAgencyID="Str 11">Str 12</InternalID>
<StandardID schemeAgencyID="Str">Str 14</StandardID>
<StandardID schemeAgencyID="Str">Str 16</StandardID>
- <ContactPerson>
- <Address>
<OrganisationFormattedName>Str 17</OrganisationFormattedName>
<OrganisationFormattedName>Str 18</OrganisationFormattedName>
- <PersonName>
<FormattedName>Str 19</FormattedName>
<LegalName>Str 20</LegalName>
<GivenName>Str 21</GivenName>
<GivenName>Str 22</GivenName>
<PreferredGivenName>Str 23</PreferredGivenName>
<MiddleName>Str 24</MiddleName>
<MiddleName>Str 25</MiddleName>
- <Family>
<FamilyName>Str 26</FamilyName>
<PrimaryIndicator>true</PrimaryIndicator>

You can execute the SPROXY to test XI XML interface.

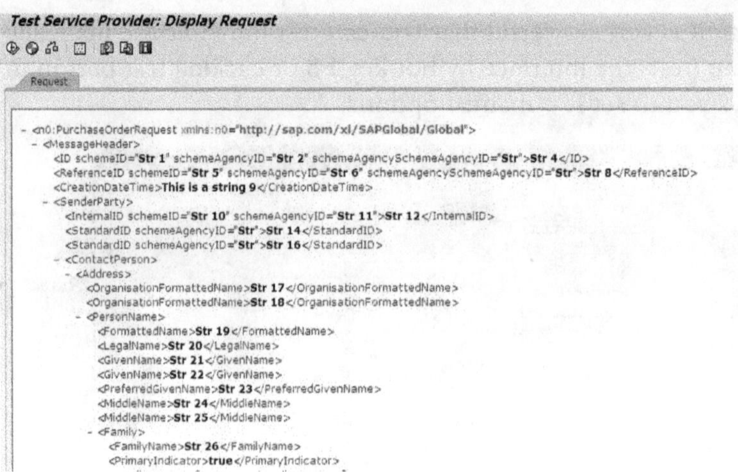
Test Service Provider: Display Request
Request
- <n0:PurchaseOrderRequest xmlns:n0="http://sap.com/xi/SAPGlobal/Global">
- <MessageHeader>
<ID schemeID="Str 1" schemeAgencyID="Str 2" schemeAgencySchemeAgencyID="Str">Str 4</ID>
<ReferenceID schemeID="Str 5" schemeAgencyID="Str 6" schemeAgencySchemeAgencyID="Str">Str 8</ReferenceID>
<CreationDateTime>This is a string 9</CreationDateTime>
- <SenderParty>
<InternalID schemeID="Str 10" schemeAgencyID="Str 11">Str 12</InternalID>
<StandardID schemeAgencyID="Str">Str 14</StandardID>
<StandardID schemeAgencyID="Str">Str 16</StandardID>
- <ContactPerson>
- <Address>
<OrganisationFormattedName>Str 17</OrganisationFormattedName>
<OrganisationFormattedName>Str 18</OrganisationFormattedName>
- <PersonName>
<FormattedName>Str 19</FormattedName>
<LegalName>Str 20</LegalName>
<GivenName>Str 21</GivenName>
<GivenName>Str 22</GivenName>
<PreferredGivenName>Str 23</PreferredGivenName>
<MiddleName>Str 24</MiddleName>
<MiddleName>Str 25</MiddleName>
- <Family>
<FamilyName>Str 26</FamilyName>
<PrimaryIndicator>true</PrimaryIndicator>

1.5 Summary

In this chapter, you learned the basic SRM architecture and components. Understanding the technical scenarios and business scenarios are basic of SRM implementation. You have gone through Classic, Extended Classic and standalone technical scenarios. You are also learned the RFC integration between SRM and ECC through RFC function and XI technologies. You have learned how business map function is implemented in SRM to integrate ECC system through RFC function module. The chapter 2 explains about the SRM procurement document.

Procurement document is base document for SRM. The basic structure of Procurement, Version Management, Audit Trail and Authorization are discussed. Back-end display utility tool is discussed.

2 SRM Procurement Document

The SRM Procurement Document explains the basic structure of SRM business documents. SRM technical functionality revolves around SRM procurement documents. Understanding the structure of procurement document is vital for technical programming. This chapter explains the technical details with respect to each component in the structure a procurement document. This chapter summarizes each component with possible sample technical code.

SAP SRM supports version management for purchasing documents. The version management of a procurement document is explained with respect to business objects and technical challenges are explained. Version management kicks in when a posted document is changed. This could be a change to a Posted Purchase Order or change to a released contract. Change documents are discussed to track the changes to procurement documents in the Audit Trail section. Authorization objects of procurement document and BADI exit is discussed. The lock objects are discussed with technical object information.

The document display utility program (BBP_PD) is explained to show the table level relationships of SRM documents and issued from SAP GUI. All objects of SRM document are stored in centralized database tables. Common technical objects are used for database access. The utility tool will provide all segments of the SRM document and related database table name.

2.1 SRM Document

The SRM document is a procurement document. SRM document is categorized by the object type, such as Shopping Cart, PO, Contract etc. Each SRM document type is associated with a business object. The SRM document has components and associated technical information. The developer needs to understand the components of a SRM document to make programming easier. Procurement documents are divided into two components, Header and Item data. Header data includes organizational data, tax and payment data and partner relevant data. Item data includes part/material information, account assignment and conditions, and item level partner data.

Base SRM document can be accessed using a set of technical objects. Each business transaction has a separate set of wrapper technical objects which uses the base set of technical objects.

2.1.1 Object Type

Object Type is one of the attributes of SRM document. Business object type is equivalent to a business object. The list of business objects types are as follows:

BBP_PDC_PROCTYPE_FOR_OBJTYPE - Get list of the process type for given the business object type

BBP_PDC_PROCTYPE_GETDETAIL – Get the process type details of the process type. The associated database table is BBPC_PROC_TYPE

2.1.2 Object Id

Each SRM Object refers to an object ID and it has been based on Number Range configuration for the document type. The number ranges can be configured and it is associated with transaction type of the object type. This is unique number for the document type. The object ID is based on the transaction type of the object type.

Note that based on version management, an object ID can have one or more CRMD_ORDERADM_H records (GUIDs) and only one active version.

Object Type	Description
BUS2000113	EBP Purchase Contract
BUS2121	EBP Shopping Cart
BUS2200	EBP Bid Invitation
BUS2201	EBP Purchase Order
BUS2202	Vendor Bid (EBP)
BUS2203	EBP Confirmation of Goods/Service
BUS2205	EBP Incoming Invoice

BUS2206	EBP Vendor List
BUS2208	EBP Auction
BUS2209	EBP Purchase Order Response
BUS2210	EBP Invoice Default
BUS2230	SUS Purchase Order
BUS2231	SUS Shipping Notification (ASN)
BUS2232	SUS Purchase Order Confirmation
BUS2233	SUS Confirmation of Goods/Service
BUS2234	SUS Invoice

2.1.3 Transaction Types

Each procurement document object type can be categorized into further by transaction types. The transaction type can be configured in IMG. The transaction type controls number range and status profile. Configuration can be accessed at IMG path SRM Server->Cross Application Settings->Define Transaction Types.

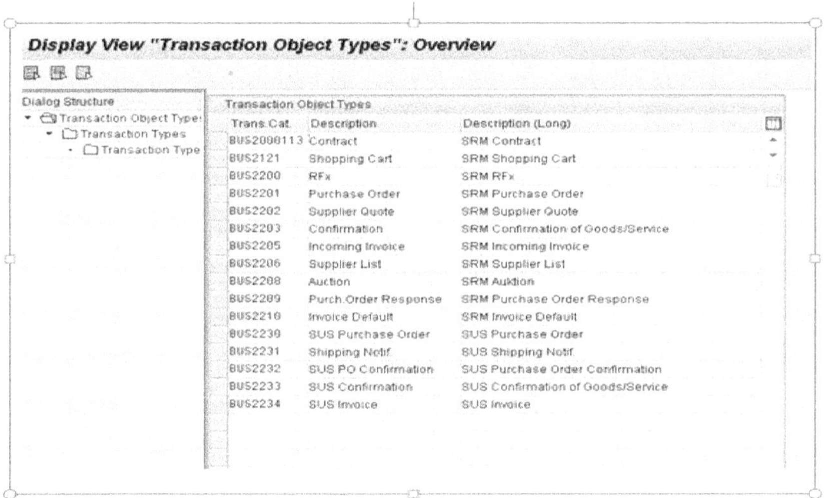

Display View "Transaction Object Types": Overview

Dialog Structure
- Transaction Object Types
  - Transaction Types
    - Transaction Type

Transaction Object Types

Trans.Cat.	Description	Description (Long)
BUS2000113	Contract	SRM Contract
BUS2121	Shopping Cart	SRM Shopping Cart
BUS2200	RFx	SRM RFx
BUS2201	Purchase Order	SRM Purchase Order
BUS2202	Supplier Quote	SRM Supplier Quote
BUS2203	Confirmation	SRM Confirmation of Goods/Service
BUS2205	Incoming Invoice	SRM Incoming Invoice
BUS2206	Supplier List	SRM Supplier List
BUS2208	Auction	SRM Auktion
BUS2209	Purch.Order Response	SRM Purchase Order Response
BUS2210	Invoice Default	SRM Invoice Default
BUS2230	SUS Purchase Order	SUS Purchase Order
BUS2231	Shipping Notif.	SUS Shipping Notif.
BUS2232	SUS PO Confirmation	SUS Purchase Order Confirmation
BUS2233	SUS Confirmation	SUS Confirmation of Goods/Service
BUS2234	SUS Invoice	SUS Invoice

You can configure transaction types for each SRM object type.

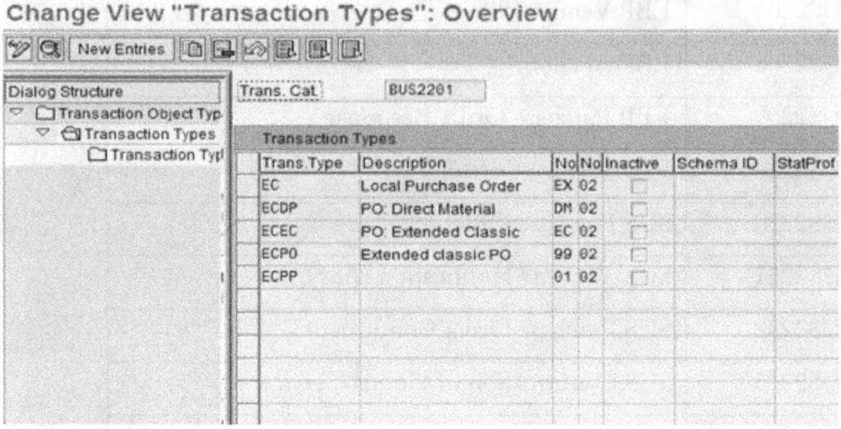

Change View "Transaction Types": Overview

New Entries

Dialog Structure
- Transaction Object Typ
  - Transaction Types
    - Transaction Typ

Trans. Cat. BUS2201

Transaction Types

Trans.Type	Description	No	No	Inactive	Schema ID	StatProf
EC	Local Purchase Order	EX	02			
ECDP	PO: Direct Material	DM	02			
ECEC	PO: Extended Classic	EC	02			
ECPO	Extended classic PO	99	02			
ECPP		01	02			

2.1.4 GUID

GUID is commonly used in the SRM (CRM) technical world. GUID means Globally Unique Identifier and is a 128-bit object identifier calculated using an algorithm defined by the Open Software Foundation. It serves as the primary key for all tables in the SRM (all new dimension SAP products tables). A The GUID is generated by a special algorithm using certain hardware information of the host computer, the current system time, and a randomly generated number. The GUID can be represented in two formats: a 32-byte character field or a 16-byte raw sequence. It is globally unique in the sense that two GUIDs produced on any two computers (or even on the same one) at any time can never be the same.

Technical Info:

The GUID is created using the function module GUID_CREATE. The FM GUID_CONVERT can be used to convert between RAW 16, Characters 22 and Characters 32.

```
 CALL METHOD cl_srm_fm_call_handler_admin=>build_guid
  IMPORTING
*   EV_GUID_16 =
    ev_guid_22 = lv_guid.

Or

  CALL FUNCTION 'GUID_CREATE'
    IMPORTING
     ev_guid_22 = lv_queue_guid.
```

2.1.5 SRM Document Components

An SRM document is commonly stored in database. The procurement document consists of a number of components which refer a group of set information. Each component either refers to database normality or by business process of the document. In this section, you can see procurement document components and possible technical information. The procurement document consists of the following information.

- Header
- Dynamic Attributes
- Account Assignment
- Tax
- Attachment
- Custom Fields
- Long Text
- Header relations
    - Item
        - Dynamic Attributes
        - Custom Fields
        - Account Assignment
        - Long Text
        - Conditions
        - Schedule Line
        - Attachment
        - Item relations
- Partner
- Organizational Units
- Versions
- Status
- Messages
- Historical Archives

Header

SRM Document has header information like GUID, Object Id, Object Type, Transaction Type, Currency and other information. The information is stored in CRMD_ORDERADM_H. The header is uniquely identified by GUID. PDO layer get detail FM has option to get total value of the procurement document. You can derive the total value using function module BBP_PDH_TOTAL_VALUE_CALC. Base SRM technical core is from CRM technical. So, you can see CRM kind of tables like CRMD_ORDERADM_H and CRMD_ORDERADM_I. The following SRM tables are associated with header detail:

- BBP_PDHGP -Business Transaction Purchasing Information
- BBP_PDHSB - RFx Related Information and it is applicable only for Bid Invitation
- BBP_PDBEH - Back-end Specific Header Data. It stores back-end follow-on document information.
- BBP_PDPSET - Further Procurement Information.
- BBP_PDHSC - Header level Customer Field Extensions
- BBP_PDHSS - Header level SAP Internal enhancements. Public Sector fields are defined in this table.

Organization Data

HR organizational management is used as SRM organizational management. SRM Business Workflow uses organization structure to determine which agents are responsible for approving SRM documents. In the SRM document, organizational data includes purchasing organization and purchasing group. The organizational data of the SRM document is stored in DB table BBP_PDORG.

The transaction BBP_PD_OM_INTEGRATION is a tool to validate the consistency of objects in Organizational structure. The tool provides you a variety of select options like Central Person, Employee, Positions, Users, Org Units, etc. Another important tool in SRM Org data is USERS_GEN transaction. The transaction can be used to manage user and employee data.

Partner

The business partners are associated with the SRM document by the partner function. The business partners are described in detail at the chapter on master data. There is a separate function module BBP_PDBUP_GETDETAIL to read the partners for the SRM document. The partner is associated with both header and item level. SRM document uses the object kind for the partner association with the header and item level.

Partner Function

Partner function describes the business about the business partners like Goods Recipient or Bill to Party. The partner function should be configured in SAP IMG. The custom partner function will be defined the partner function type above 500. Partners will be associated with the SRM business transaction based on the partner functions. Each SRM business transaction will have a possible list of partner functions.

Partner functions are configured in IMG using the menu path SRM Server->Cross Application Basic Settings->Define Partner Functions.

The function module BBP_PARTNER_TYPE_TO_FUNCTION provides the partner function for the given partner type and Usage (sub type). The partner type has been predefined in the SRM system. The list of constants are defined in the include BBP_PD_CON_CL. For example, to get the partner functions for the bidder.

```
CALL FUNCTION 'BBP_PARTNER_TYPE_TO_FUNCTION'
 EXPORTING
  iv_partner_pft   = c_bidder      "value is 0011
  iv_partner_subtype = c_subtype_b2b       "B2B
 IMPORTING
  et_partner_fct   = t_partner_function.
```

Note that one partner type and sub type can have more than one partner functions. The partner function can be determined by the description and abbreviation. The function module will not return the description and abbreviation. The partner function information is stored in the table BBPC_PARTNERFUNC. There is a reverse function module BBP_PARTNER_FUNCTION_TO_TYPE will provide the partner type for the given partner function.

The function module BBP_PARTNER_FUNCTION_EXISTENCE returns the list of possible partner functions (with type and description) for given object type and reference kind. The partner type to partner function is used for Invoice partner FM BBP_IV_PARTNER_FUNCTIONS_GET and the SUS partner FM BBP_SUS_PARTNER_FUNCTIONS_GET.

Status

The status of the SRM document explains current position of the SRM document. The core SRM component handles the status of the SRM document. The status involves alert management and workflow management. The SRM uses the CRM status management.

The Status Management functionality provides two types of status management options.

- System Status: This is the status set by the system to inform the user what process steps (business transactions) have been completed for a document
- User Status: This is an additional status which can be maintained in addition to system status and informs the user about the business specific step that has been executed.

The FM BBP_PD_STATUS_GETDETAIL will return the system status for the give GUID. To fetch the item level status, the item GUID must be passed. Include program BBP_PD_CON_STATUS lists all the status information. Include program is used in most of PD programs. The ABAP object /SAPSRM/IF_PDO_STATUS_C does have all status related constants. The user status has been used in public sector for the close-out function. The user status is used in Closeout Functionality of Procurement for Public Sector (PPS). You can use FM BBP_PROCDOC_STATUS_CHANGE to change the status of the procurement document. Also you can use FM BBP_PROCDOC_STATUS_CHANGE_DIRE update status directly to database.

Dynamic Attributes

The dynamic attributes are applicable for the Bid Invitation and Bid Response (Quote). The dynamic attribute is the question and answer associated with Bid Invitation. The dynamic attributes can be added at Bid Invitation and answers will be at Bid Response. The dynamic attributes will be copied from the Bid Invitation to Bid Response automatically. The dynamic attributes can be associated with header or item level.

Dynamic attributes can be configured in IMG path SRM Server->RFx->Questions. In IMG, you can define data types, Question Group, Dynamic Attributes (Questions), Assigning Group to Product Category, and Assigning Dynamic Attributes to Groups. The dynamic attributes of the Bid Invitation item can be populated based on the product category. The dynamic attributes are stored in the BBP_PDDYN database table. The function module BBP_PDDYN_GETDETAIL can fetch the information. The BADI BBP_DETERMINE_DYNATR controls determination of the attributes in the Bid Invitation. The BADI works only when proposal button is clicked.

Technical Challenges: Custom dynamic attributes are configured in IMG. The dynamic attributes are automatically populated in the Bid Invitation based on Product Category. The custom dynamic attributes must be populated with supplier information and their previous PO history.

Solution: Custom dynamic attributes can be populated by implementing the BADI BBP_DETERMINE_DYNATR.

Name: BBP_DETERMINE_DYNATR		Multiple Use: Yes	Filter: No
Description: Determine Dynamic Attributes			
Method: DETERMINE_ATTRIBUTES *Description*: Determine the attributes for Header and Item level. Parameters:			
Name	Type	Data Type	Description
IV_DOC_GUID	Import	BBP_GUID	Document GUID
IS_HEADER	Import	BBP_PDS_HEADER	Header
IS_ITEM	Import	BBP_PDS_ITEM	Item
CT_ATTRIBUTES	Change	BBPT_PDS_DYNATTRIB UTE	Dynamic Attributes
Sample code: The sample code is for technical solution. * Get detail of Quote			

Long Text

Long text can be stored at Header and Item level. The Text category must be configured. The function module BBP_PDLTX_GETDETAIL can fetch the long text. The long text is stored in the long text with object type as BBP_PD and name as GUID of the object. That means you can use standard text function modules READ_TEXT, SAVE_TEXT using the object type and object name.

Text schemas, Text types, and relationship between text schema and Business Transaction types can be configured. The IMG path is SRM Server->Cross-Application Basic Settings->Text Schema. The text object BBP_PD is used for the text types. Using the configuration, you can define default fixed values. So, it will populate automatically.

Technical Tips: The BADI BBP_LONGTEXT_BADI is used to change text schema and other long text related changes. You can this BADI text scheme and enrich your long text. This BADI has a default implementation BBP_LONGTEXT_BADI_I.

Account Assignment

Account assignment (FI/CO) related information is associated with the header and item level. The account assignment includes G/L account, Cost center, Business area, FM related information, etc. The function module BBP_ACCOUNT_GETDETAIL will fetch the account assignment details for given SRM document GUID and object Kind (Header or Item level). There is possible line item can have one or more Account assignments. The data is stored in the table BBP_PDACC.

Tax

Tax information is stored in the table BBP_PDTAX. You can configure Tax calculation in IMG. The path is SRM Server->Cross-Application Basic Settings->Tax Calculation. IMG configuration provides tax determination procedure.

Change View "Defining System for Tax Calculation": Overview

New Entries

Defining System for Tax Calculation

System for tax calculation	Choose
No Tax Calculation	○
Tax Calculation Occurs in Backend	◉
Customer-Specific Implementation	○
Tax Calculation Occurs via External T...	○
Tax Calculation Occurs via TTE	○

You can use FM BBP_PROCDOC_CALC_TOTAL_TAX to compute total tax for the procurement document. There are three BADIs in Tax calculation procedure.

- BBP_DET_TAXCODE_BADI – Determine tax code which can be extended further from the table
- BBP_FREIGHT_BADI - Identify the freight Partner
- BBP_TAX_MAP_BADI – Change supplement table entries used in tax calculation.

Conditions

The SRM pricing function determines prices using the condition techniques. These pricing conditions are associated with the item level. The function module BBP_PDCND_GETDETAIL can be used to read the pricing conditions. The scale information is part of the structure BBP_PDS_CND. Pricing Conditions has scale information. Based on the quantity range, price can be defined. The program BBP_CND_CUSTOMIZING_CHECK can be used to view custom settings for conditions check.

Attachment

The attachment of the SRM document can be at Header and/or Item Level. The attachment is stored in the table BBP_PDATT. The attachment can be retrieved using the FM BBP_ATTACH_GETDETAIL. The following is the sample code to add an attachment to PO.

```
DATA:
  lv_funcname     TYPE funcname,
  lv_size         TYPE i,
  lv_phio_size    TYPE sdok_fsize.
  li_binary_tab   TYPE bbpt_att_cont,
  lt_attach       TYPE bbpt_pds_att_t,
  li_messages     TYPE TABLE OF bbp_pds_messages,
  lv_po_header_u  TYPE bbp_pds_po_header_u, "PO Update str
  lv_po_header_e  TYPE bbp_pds_po_header_d, "PO Display Hdr
  lv_xstring      TYPE xstring.
 lv_xstring = get_xstring_from_PDF().  "Get PDF Xstring Info
 IF lv_xstring IS NOT INITIAL.
  CALL FUNCTION 'SCMS_XSTRING_TO_BINARY'
   EXPORTING
    buffer          = lv_xstring
    append_to_table = c_yes
   IMPORTING
    output_length   = lv_size
   TABLES
    binary_tab      = li_binary_tab.
* Create Entry in Attachment Table
  lv_phio_size          = lv_size.
  wa_attach-p_guid      = is_bid_header-guid.
  wa_attach-internal_ind = c_yes.

  wa_attach-description = 'Description'."Define your own
  wa_attach-phio_fname = 'test.pdf'."Define yr own file name
  wa_attach-phio_ext = '.pdf'.
  wa_attach-phio_fsize   = lv_phio_size.
  wa_attach-phio_content = li_binary_tab[].
  APPEND wa_attach TO lt_attach.
*  Get PO header and update Header_u variable
 REFRESH lt_messages.
 CALL FUNCTION 'BBP_PD_PO_UPDATE'
  EXPORTING
   i_header   = lv_po_header_u
   it_attach  = lt_attach
   i_save     = c_yes
  IMPORTING
   es_header  = lv_po_header_d
  TABLES
   e_messages = lt_messages.
 CALL FUNCTION 'BAPI_TRANSACTION_COMMIT'
  EXPORTING
   wait   = 'X'
  IMPORTING
   return = lv_return.
```

Document Flow

The document flow of the SRM document can be found in the header relation and item relation. Any preceding and succeeding documents are associated in the document flow. The document flow can be possible both in Header and Item level. The header level and item level uses the structures BBP_PDS_HREL and BBP_PDS_ILREL respectively.

The document flow can be retrieved using the FM BBP_PROCDOC_GETDETAIL or PDO Get detail Function modules. The header relation can be related by the relationship PDHL and item relation can be related by the relationship PDIL. The function module BINARY_RELATION_CREATE can be used to create relationship between the SRM documents. The function module BINARY_RELATION_DELETE can be used to delete relationship between the SRM documents.

The following sample code provides how to create relationship between Shopping Cart Line item and Bid Invitation Line. If the relationship is between header levels then use the relationship PDHL.

```
LS_OBJ_B-OBJKEY    = WA_REV_RESULT-ZZPRITM_GUID.
LS_OBJ_B-OBJTYPE    = 'BUS2121001'.
LS_OBJ_B-LOGSYS    = LC_LOGSYS.
LS_OBJ_A-OBJKEY    = WA_REV_RESULT-ZZBIDINVITM_GUID.
LS_OBJ_A-OBJTYPE    = 'BUS2200001'.
LS_OBJ_A-LOGSYS    = LC_LOGSYS.
LC_RELTYPE        = 'PDIL'.
CLEAR LC_HDR_GUID.
CALL FUNCTION 'BINARY_RELATION_CREATE'
 EXPORTING
  OBJ_ROLEA     = LS_OBJ_B
  OBJ_ROLEB     = LS_OBJ_A
  RELATIONTYPE   = LC_RELTYPE
  FIRE_EVENTS    = ''
 EXCEPTIONS
  NO_MODEL      = 1
```

```
      INTERNAL_ERROR = 2
      UNKNOWN       = 3
      OTHERS        = 4.
    CALL FUNCTION 'BAPI_TRANSACTION_COMMIT'
     EXPORTING
      WAIT = 'X'.
  ENDIF.
ENDLOOP.
```

Technical Challenges: Create a Shopping Cart programmatically.

Solution: The following sample code provides basic idea to create the shopping cart programmatically. GUID is one of important information need to be populated at header, Items, Account Assignment and other set information. The FM BBP_PD_SC_CREATE will create shopping cart and return message table lists all error and warning message. The parameters i_save and i_park settings make sure that when there is error message then it will park the shopping cart.

```
DATA:
  ls_i_header   TYPE  bbp_pds_sc_header_ic,
  ls_e_header   TYPE  bbp_pds_sc_header_d,
  ls_item       TYPE  bbp_pds_sc_item_icu,
  lt_item       TYPE  TABLE OF bbp_pds_sc_item_icu,
  lt_acc        TYPE  TABLE OF bbp_pds_acc,
  lt_partner    TYPE  TABLE OF bbp_pds_partner,
  lt_org        TYPE  TABLE OF bbp_pds_org,
  lt_longtext   TYPE  TABLE OF bbp_pds_longtext.
   " Fill header info
" Either guid can be populated using FM or just assign
" like ls_i_header-guid = '1'.
  CALL FUNCTION 'GUID_CREATE'
   IMPORTING
     ev_guid_32 = ls_i_header-guid.
  ls_i_header-currency      = con_usd.
  ls_i_header-process_type  = c_prc_typ.
  ls_i_header-description   = 'description'.
* Populate all required standard & custom fields
*** Populate Line Item
  CALL FUNCTION 'GUID_CREATE'
   IMPORTING
     ev_guid_32 = ls_item-guid.
 " Link between Header and Item
  ls_item-header     = ls_i_header-guid.
```

```
" Populate line item info like product, qty, price
append ls_item-header INTO lt_item.
" Populate all line items, Partner, Org data, Acc data
" Partner requires Partner function information
  " Create Shopping Cart
  CALL FUNCTION 'BBP_PD_SC_CREATE'
   EXPORTING
    i_save    = 'X'
    i_park    = 'X'
    i_header  = ls_i_header
   IMPORTING
    e_header  = ls_e_header
   TABLES
    i_item     = lt_item
    i_account  = lt_acc
    i_partner  = lt_partner
    i_orgdata  = lt_org
    e_messages = lt_messages.
" lt_messages will provide error and success info
  CALL FUNCTION 'BBP_PD_SC_SAVE'.
" Do commit work
```

2.2 Version Management

The SRM supports the version management for the object types Contract, PO, Invoice, Bid Invitation and Auction. IMG customization (SRM Server->Cross-Application Basic Settings-> Switch on Version Control for Purchasing Documents) is available to switch on version control for purchasing document. The version handling customizing information is stored in the table BBP_CT_VERSION.

Version management has been handled in the FM BBP_PROCDOC_SAVE. Version management is applicable to Contract, PO, Invoice, Bid Invitation, SUS PO and Quotation.

SRM Object	Description
PO	PO is ordered and any change.
Contract	Contract is released and any change.
Bid Invitation	Bid Invitation is published and any change
Quote	Quote is published and any change

SAP provides BADI BBP_VERSION_CONTROL to set change version management flag. The BADI method has Object type, GUID, current status and old status. Note that the BADI will work only for SRM documents applicable for version management.

Technical Info

The version management uses the following function modules to fetch the versions:

- BBP_PD_ALL_VERSION_GETLIST – List out all versions associated with GUID or table of GUID.
- BBP_PROCDOC_VERSION_GETLIST - Get list of the versions of SRM document by GUID.
- BBP_PD_<BO>_GETDETAIL returns version information.
- ***Tips***: Do not use CRMD_ORDERADM_H selection field with Object ID for these objects. There is always possible to have more than one record for the object ID. Use PDO get detail function module to active version of GUID.

Technical Challenge – Disabling PO versioning

The PO version should not be allowed for the process type is ZTST. We should not allow to creating the version control.

Solution: In version management, the version control is supported for the new objects only. The functional team can configure whether the total object be in version control or not. In configuration, there is no possible to determination of the version control based on the data in the PO header.

Version management cannot be implemented when it is not listed in the configuration. The version management involves screen object and alert management.

Implement the BADI BBP_VERSION_CONTROL for the PO object type BUS2201.

<table>
<tr><td colspan="2">Name: BBP_VERSION_CONTROL</td><td>Multiple Use: No</td><td>Filter: Yes</td></tr>
<tr><td colspan="4">Description: Exit function for version control based on BBP_SEARCH_OBJTYP filter. Accepted values are in the domain BBP_SEARCH_OBJTYP.</td></tr>
<tr><td colspan="4">Method: BBP_VERSION_CREATE_CONTROL

Description: Set the version control flag based on the header GUID, new statuses and old statuses.

Parameters:</td></tr>
<tr><td>Name</td><td>Type</td><td>Data Type</td><td>Description</td></tr>
<tr><td>IV_HEADER_GUID</td><td>Import</td><td>CRMT_OBJECT_GUID</td><td>Object GUID</td></tr>
</table>

IT_X_STATUS	Import	BBPT_STATUS	New status list
IT_Y_STATUS	Import	BBPT_STATUS	Old status list
EV_CREATE_VERSION	Change	C	Flag for creation of version

Sample code: The sample code is for technical solution.

```
data: ls_header type bbp_pds_po_header_d.
* Get PO Details
CALL FUNCTION 'BBP_PD_PO_GETDETAIL'
  EXPORTING
    i_guid          = iv_header_guid
  IMPORTING
    e_header        = ls_header.
* If the process type condition then set version control
if ls_header-process_type = 'ZTST'.
    clear ev_create_version.
else.
    ev_create_version = 'X'.
endif.
```

You can use the function module BBP_PD_ALL_GET_DIFF to get differences between two versions for an object type. The function module provides option what are sets do you want compare or get all differences. There are smart forms available to compare the versions. The details are discussed in smart form section.

2.3 Audit Trail

Audit Trail is one of important concept required to track the changes done by the user. Also, an audit trails require you to log the important changes. Too many field change traces will slow down the basic operation. SAP provides the change document concept and it is used wide through all modules.

A change document logs changes to a technical object. The document is created independently of the actual database change. The change document structure is as follows:

- Change document header - The header data of the change to an object ID in a particular object class are stored in the change document header. The change document number is automatically issued.
- Change Document Item - The change document item contains the old and new values of a field for a particular change, and a change flag type. The flag can be Update, Insert or Delete.

The change documents are stored under the object class BBP_PRODOC and object ID of the GUID. Change documents can be read using the standard SAP function module BBP_CHANGE_DOC_GET_NEW.

How to Read Change Documents

Change documents can be accessed in SAP GUI. In the PO screen, you can view the change document logs in the tab "track changes". SAP provides a set of FM modules to read the change documents. The SRM change document can be viewed using the transaction BBP_PD. At the end of BBP_PD document record, the change document links are provided.

```
lessages:
)bject was not Checked
—> Check Again

:hange Document:
:hange document has not been read
—> Read Change Document (sorted by time)
—> Read Change Document (sorted by table)
—> Read Change Document (sorted by user)
```

Change documents Information

hange Document:

able	Key (first 40 characters)	Changenr	Field	Date	Time	User	Ind	Old value (first 49 characters)	New
RM_JEST	800084CC195DCA8084FB1E162DA0DB01102I1015	154314	INACT	19.09.2002	16:44:00	WF-BATCH	U		X
RM_JEST	800084CC195DCA8084FB1E162DA0DB01102I1129	154314	INACT	19.09.2002	16:44:00	WF-BATCH	U	X	
BP_PDBEI	800D877B2C885BCAA468E5175A360F86EA3	154315	BE_OBJECT_ID	19.09.2002	16:44:14	WF-BATCH	U		1000
BP_PDBEI	800D877B2C885BCAA468E5175A360F86EA3	154315	BE_OBJECT_TYPE	19.09.2002	16:44:14	WF-BATCH	U		BUS2
BP_PDBEI	800D877B2C885BCAA468E5175A360F86EA3	154315	BE_OBJ_ITEM	19.09.2002	16:44:14	WF-BATCH	U		0000
RM_JEST	800D877B2C885BCAA468E5175A360F86EA3I1111	154315	INACT	19.09.2002	16:44:14	WF-BATCH	U		X
RM_JEST	800D877B2C885BCAA468E5175A360F86EA3I1113	154315	INACT	19.09.2002	16:44:14	WF-BATCH	U	X	

The change document object of SRM document is ***BBP_PROCDOC***. The change document is applicable for the data element is defined for the change document. A new customer field's data element should be set as "change document flag" if the custom field needs to be in the change document value.

The change document object can be accessed by the transaction SCDO.

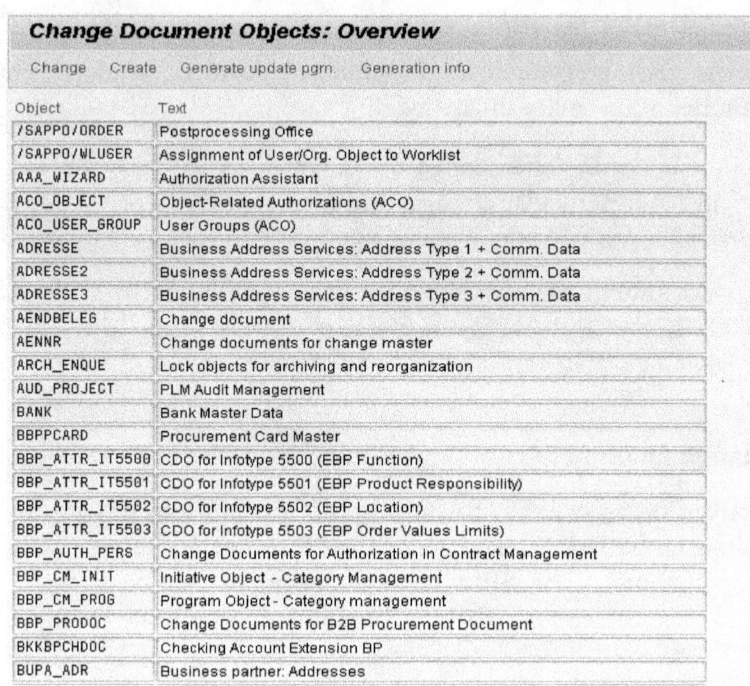

Change Document Objects: Overview

Change Create Generate update pgm. Generation info

Object	Text
/SAPPO/ORDER	Postprocessing Office
/SAPPO/WLUSER	Assignment of User/Org. Object to Worklist
AAA_WIZARD	Authorization Assistant
ACO_OBJECT	Object-Related Authorizations (ACO)
ACO_USER_GROUP	User Groups (ACO)
ADRESSE	Business Address Services: Address Type 1 + Comm. Data
ADRESSE2	Business Address Services: Address Type 2 + Comm. Data
ADRESSE3	Business Address Services: Address Type 3 + Comm. Data
AENDBELEG	Change document
AENNR	Change documents for change master
ARCH_ENQUE	Lock objects for archiving and reorganization
AUD_PROJECT	PLM Audit Management
BANK	Bank Master Data
BBPPCARD	Procurement Card Master
BBP_ATTR_IT5500	CDO for Infotype 5500 (EBP Function)
BBP_ATTR_IT5501	CDO for Infotype 5501 (EBP Product Responsibility)
BBP_ATTR_IT5502	CDO for Infotype 5502 (EBP Location)
BBP_ATTR_IT5503	CDO for Infotype 5503 (EBP Order Values Limits)
BBP_AUTH_PERS	Change Documents for Authorization in Contract Management
BBP_CM_INIT	Initiative Object - Category Management
BBP_CM_PROG	Program Object - Category management
BBP_PRODOC	Change Documents for B2B Procurement Document
BKKBPCHDOC	Checking Account Extension BP
BUPA_ADR	Business partner: Addresses

The function module BBP_PRODOC_WRITE_DOCUMENT is generated by change document object to write the changes into change document changes.

Technical Challenges: You need audit trail on a set of custom fields. The header level custom fields should track the audit trail log.

Solution: Make sure that BBP_PDHSC (Header custom fields) and BBP_PDISC (Item custom fields) are included in the BBP_PROCDOC Change document. If not then choose it and generate the program. Also, make sure the data element of the custom fields change document flag is set.

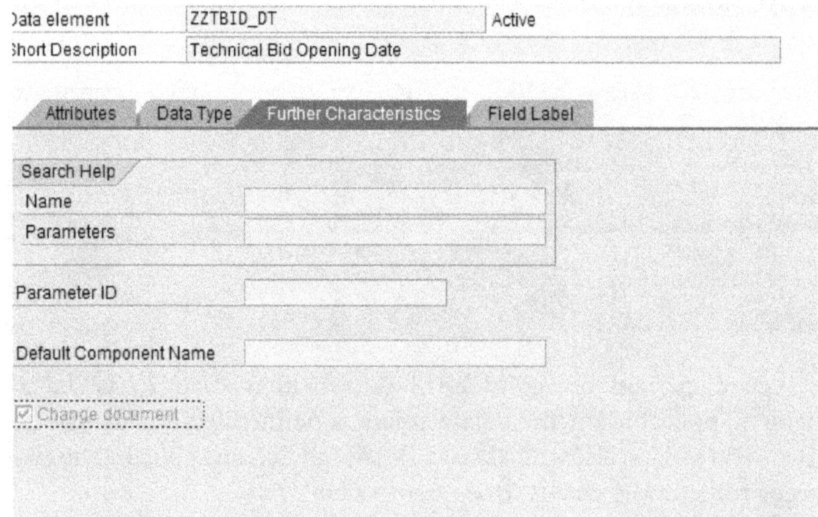

This will activate the audit trail on the data element and if it is not one of procurement document fields then you can see change document on the fields.

2.4 Authorization Object

SRM provides a set of authorization objects to control activities on the SRM document. The authorization objects can be viewed and maintained using the transaction code SU21. The few of standard basic authorization objects for the SRM business transactions are listed as below.

Authorization Object	Description
BBP_PD_AUC	Live Auction
BBP_PD_BID	Bidding
BBP_PD_CNF	Confirmation
BBP_PD_INV	Invoice
BBP_PD_PO	Purchase Order
BBP_PD_PCO	PO Confirmation
BBP_PD_QUO	Quotation
BBP_PD_VL	Vendor List
BBP_PD_SC	Shopping cart
BBP_SUS_P2	Accesses to SUS documents
BBP_PD_AC	SUS Action
BBP_BUDGET	Budget display
M_BBP_PC	Procurement

Each PD Authorization object like BBP_PD_PO, BBP_PD_CTR etc has field names BBP_PURORG (Purchase Organization), BBP_PURGRP (Purchase Group), BBP_PROCTYP (Transaction Types) and ACTVT (Activities). The list of activities is based on the SRM object type. The following activities are based on the PO:

Activity	Description
01	Create Or Generate

02	Change
03	Display
04	Print, Edit Messages
06	Delete
33	Read
C4	Close Out
C5	Reopen
G7	Reverse

Technical Info

The function module BBP_PDSEC_AUTHORITY_CHECK – Authority check can be validated for the following object types.

- Auction
- Bid Invitation
- Confirmation
- Contract
- Invoice
- Purchase Order
- Purchase Order Confirmation
- Quotation
- Vendor List
- Shopping Cart

The list of authorization objects is defined in the previous section. The additional authority check can be implemented in the BADI BBP_PD_AUTH_CHECK.

BBP_PDSEC_SUS_AUTH_CHECK – Authority check can be validated against the SRM SUS objects. It uses the authorization object BBP_SUS_P2 and It supports the following objects.

- SUS Purchase Order
- SUS Shipping Notification (ASN)

- SUS Purchase order response
- SUS Purchase order confirmation
- SUS Invoice
- SUS Message

Note that the BADI BBP_PD_AUTH_CHECK is an additional authorization check that can be implemented.

<table>
<tr><td colspan="2">Name: BBP_AUTHORITY_CHECK</td><td>Multiple Use: No</td><td>Filter: No</td></tr>
<tr><td colspan="4">Description: Determine Authority Check.</td></tr>
<tr><td colspan="4">Method: AUTHORITY_CHECK_PRODOC
Description: Authorization check for the procurement Document
Parameters:</td></tr>
<tr><td>Name</td><td>Type</td><td>Data Type</td><td>Description</td></tr>
<tr><td>IV_USERNAME</td><td>Import</td><td>SY-UNAME</td><td>User Name</td></tr>
<tr><td>IS_AUTH_CHECK</td><td>Import</td><td>BBP_PDS_SEC_ICOM</td><td>Data Information. Contains Object type, GUIDs, etc.</td></tr>
<tr><td>ET_MESSAGES</td><td>Export</td><td>BBPT_PD_MESSAGES</td><td>Error Message Information</td></tr>
<tr><td>EV_SUBRC</td><td>Export</td><td>SY-SUBRC</td><td>Return value. 0-Authorized and > 0 – not authorized</td></tr>
</table>

Technical Info:

This BADI is an additional authorization check. If the authorization failed by the authorization object, the BADI will not be executed. If the authorization is successful then this BADI will be executed.

Run the program ***BBP_AUTH_DISPL*** to list out all authorization information for given user and object. The user input is exact user name. If you want to list all objects then do not enter the value in the object parameter.

Report BBP_AUTH_DISPL

```
Report BBP_AUTH_DISPL

User Authorization Profile                    SELVA
Display of all BBP Authorization Objects

   Profile:  SAP_ALL
                         ( Type=   C )

      Profile:  &_SAP_ALL_00
                            ( Type=   G )

         Object:     BBP_ADVS

            Authorization:   &_SAP_ALL
            Values:
                             BBP_ADVS   *

         Object:     BBP_BID_EV

            Authorization:   &_SAP_ALL
            Values:
                             BBP_BID_EV*

         Object:     BBP_BUDGET

            Authorization:   &_SAP_ALL
            Values:
                             ACTVT      *
                             BBPACCOBJ  *
                             BBPACCTYPE*

         Object:     BBP_BUYER

            Authorization:   &_SAP_ALL
            Values:
                             ACTVT      *

         Object:     BBP_CMS

            Authorization:   &_SAP_ALL
```

2.5 Document Display

One of important transaction in SRM is used to view the data from the back-end SAP GUI. The transaction (and program) BBP_PD will display SRM document information with full details when the selection parameters match only one SRM business transaction. Or it will provide the list of the records matching the selection criteria. The item GUID will result in the fetching the header business transactions. If selection parameters match with more than one business transaction then it will list the GUID, description, object ID and changed by & Date. The business transaction can be navigated further using the GUID.

The technical person can use this transaction to verify the data instead of going multiple tables in the database. The functional team always uses this transaction to compare their data. Based on the selection criteria, the program returns associated records. Drill down facility is available to drill down the header, item and related objects.

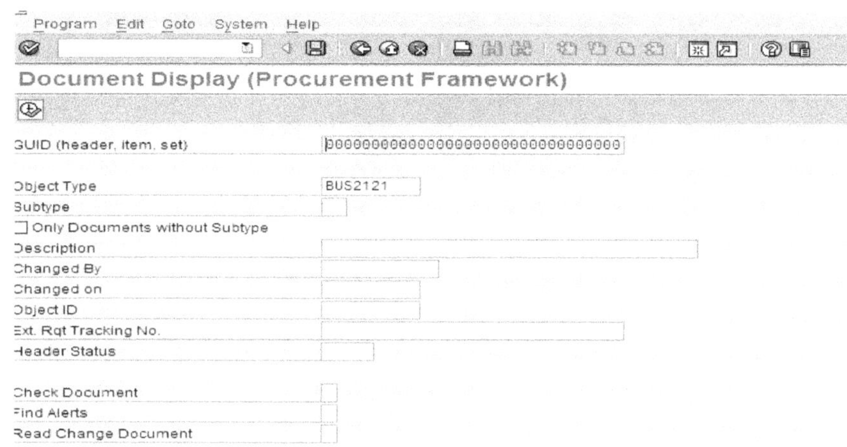

The list of SRM documents will be displayed with base information GUID, Object ID and 'Changed At' & 'Changed By'. When there is only one record then it will display the document. The result list can be drill down by the GUID.

Drill down the SRM document display:

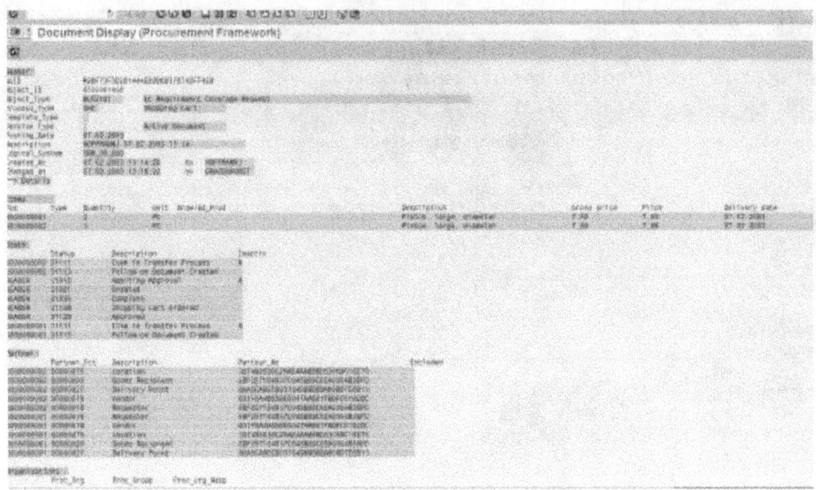

Details

The base Header is displayed in front screen and further details can be displayed by clicking the details hyperlink.

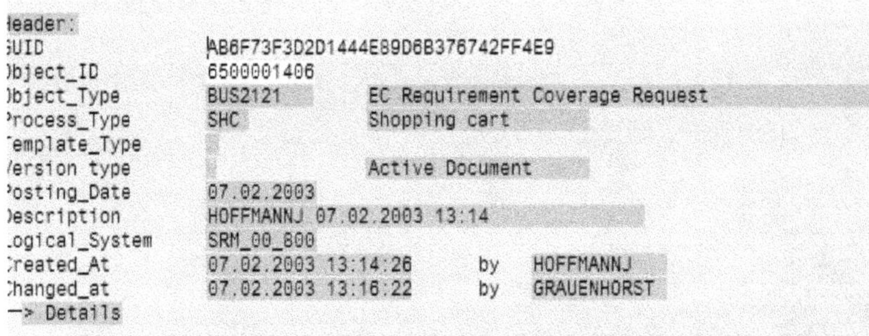

Header:				
GUID	AB6F73F3D2D1444E89D6B376742FF4E9			
Object_ID	6500001406			
Object_Type	BUS2121	EC Requirement Coverage Request		
Process_Type	SHC	Shopping cart		
Template_Type				
Version type		Active Document		
Posting_Date	07.02.2003			
Description	HOFFMANNJ 07.02.2003 13:14			
Logical_System	SRM_00_800			
Created_At	07.02.2003 13:14:26		by	HOFFMANNJ
Changed_at	07.02.2003 13:16:22		by	GRAUENHORST
--> Details				

The header detailed information shows the details of the table information CRMD_ORDERADM_H, BBP_PDHGP, BBP_PDHSB, BBP_PDBEH, BBP_PDPSET, BBP_PDHSC, BBP_PDHSS, Customer Include and Index Table for Search.

Table CRMD_ORDERADM_H		
CLIENT	800	Client
GUID	AB6F73F3D2D1444E89D6B376742FF4E9	GUID of a CRM Order Object
OBJECT_ID	6500001406	Transaction Number
PROCESS_TYPE	SHC	Business Transaction Type
POSTING_DATE	07022003	Posting Date for a Business Transaction
DESCRIPTION	HOFFMANNJ 07.02.2003 13:14	Transaction Description
DESCR_LANGUAGE	E	Language Key of Description
LOGICAL_SYSTEM	SRM_00_800	Logical System
CRM_RELEASE		SAP Release
SCENARIO		Scenario Identity
TEMPLATE_TYPE		Template Type of CRM Transaction
CREATED_AT	20030207121.426	Created At (Output in User Time Zone)
CREATED_BY	HOFFMANNJ	User that Created the Transaction
CHANGED_AT	20030207121.622	Changed At (Output in User Time Zone)

Table BBP_PDHGP		
CLIENT	800	Client
GUID	AB6F73F3D2D1444E89D6B376742FF4E9	Globally Unique identifier
REF_DOC_NO		Reference Document Number
POSTING_DATE_FI	00000000	Transaction Posting Date in Accounting
GR_GI_SLIP_NO		Goods receipt/issue slip number
BILL_OF_LADING		Bill of Lading Number
CO_CODE		Company Code in FI System
LOGSYS_FI		Logical System of FI System
CURRENCY	USD	Currency Key
GROSS_AMOUNT	0.00	Gross invoice amount in document currency
TOTAL_VALUE	22.80	Total Value of Shopping Cart / Target Value of Contract
TOTAL_TAX	0.00	Tax Amount

Items overview can be viewed at front screen and item can be drilled downed for further information like CRMD_ORDERADM_I, BBP_PDIGP, BBP_PDISB, BBP_PDBEH, BBP_PDPSET, BBP_PDISC, BBP_PDISS, Customer Include, Conditions and Index Table for Search.

Status Information provides detail about what are statuses handled in the document.

;tats:

	Status	Description	Inactiv
)000000002	I1111	Item in Transfer Process	X
)000000002	I1113	Follow-on Document Created	
HEADER	I1015	Awaiting Approval	X
HEADER	I1021	Created	
HEADER	I1038	Complete	
HEADER	I1106	Shopping cart ordered	
HEADER	I1129	Approved	
)000000001	I1111	Item in Transfer Process	X
)000000001	I1113	Follow-on Document Created	

Partners and partner function information are displayed and partner can be drilled downed to list out the table information CRMD_PARTNER, BBP_PDGBP, BUT000 and ADDR3_DATA.

'artner:

	Partner_Fct	Description	Partner_No	Excluded
)000000002	00000075	Location	3D7498530C25AE4AA666D53059C18E78	
)000000002	00000020	Goods Recipient	EBF257184937C045B89CEEA0304B3BFD	
)000000002	00000027	Delivery Point	B0A5CA9ECB037849B9B6DA609D7E6B13	
)000000002	00000019	Vendor	631F5A4655BE5047AA601FBDFCE192DC	
)000000002	00000016	Requester	EBF257184937C045B89CEEA0304B3BFD	
)000000001	00000016	Requester	EBF257184937C045B89CEEA0304B3BFD	
)000000001	00000019	Vendor	631F5A4655BE5047AA601FBDFCE192DC	
)000000001	00000075	Location	3D7498530C25AE4AA666D53059C18E78	
)000000001	00000020	Goods Recipient	EBF257184937C045B89CEEA0304B3BFD	
)000000001	00000027	Delivery Point	B0A5CA9ECB037849B9B6DA609D7E6B13	

You can drill down further on organization data.

2.6 Summary

In this chapter, you have learned SRM document structure and database orientation. Version management is one of prominent features of the SRM document and you have learned the basics and how to read the version management. Also, you have learned audit trail and authorization concept of the SRM document. The back-end document display utility tool is very powerful tool and you learned how to use it with technical perspective.

SRM Technical overview provides very vital details of SRM7 Technical layers and UI concepts. SRM7 new feature floor plan manager is discussed in details.

3 SRM Technical Overview

From UI interface to database update, SAP SRM has a number of technical objects to UI contextual object update, business object operations and database maintenance. The technical objects include ABAP objects like Web Dynpro components, ABAP objects, ABAP function modules and database components. These objects are vital for the SRM application

The technical design of SAP modules is different from each other. The aspects of technical design are based on time developed, module volume and complexity, etc. SRM technical design is based on the technical framework of the base CRM. SRM evolves independently from CRM.

The SRM technical objects are generally categories into UI Layer, Channel Logic Layer, PDO Layer, BBP Layer and Database objects. In new dimension SAP product like SRM, high level wrapper functions are utilized instead of reading and writing the database table directly. SRM7 uses Web Dynpro Applications to handle user interface technology. SRM 5 uses ITS user interface technology. The topics discuss only SRM 7.0 related technical layers. SRM 7.0 provides the wrapper classes for the PDO layers in ABAP objects.

This chapter explains the detailed SRM technical overview. The following figure can give an overall picture of the SRM technical components. The chapter explains technical objects based on the layers defined in the figure.

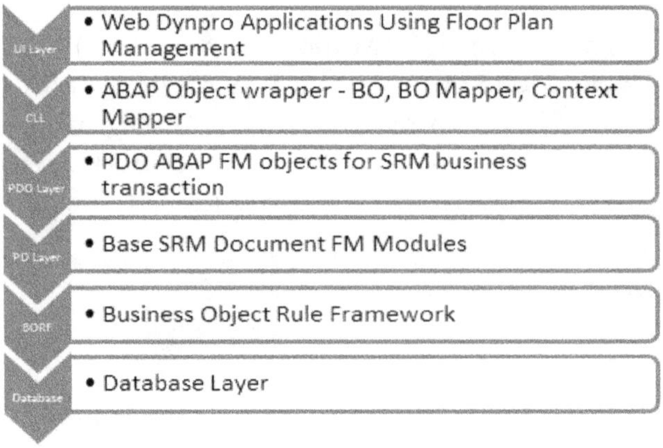

UI Layer
- Web Dynpro Applications Using Floor Plan Management

CLL
- ABAP Object wrapper - BO, BO Mapper, Context Mapper

PDO Layer
- PDO ABAP FM objects for SRM business transaction

PD Layer
- Base SRM Document FM Modules

BORF
- Business Object Rule Framework

Database
- Database Layer

3.1 Database Layer

The database layer is layer where all data is stored in the database. The GUID is the key to all SRM database tables. The database tables are discussed in BBP PD layer function modules. SRM is based on the procurement document. All procurement documents e.g., Shopping Cart, PO, RFX are stored in same set of tables. Based on the procurement document and business data, the data are stored in the database tables. Note that not all objects are associated with direct transparent tables. Object such long text is stored in text index table and links are stored in the CRMD_LINK DB table. Most of SRM procurement database tables can be listed using the document display tool using the transaction code BBP_PD.

3.2 Business Object Rule Framework

Business Object rules framework (BORF) is framework provided by SAP as an extension of BADI's (Business-Add-In) as transition from technical driven approach towards business driven approach. BORF has fast processing technique for business logic and validation. BORF is mainly used for validation purposes. With BORF, business logic is written and extended for use in SRM for validation by creating rules that contain additional business logic and then registering these rules to events.

BORF provides internal SAP BADI /SAPPSSRM/BO_RULES. That means you cannot implement any new implementations. SRM7.0 uses BORF for SAP standard validations. BORF will be future for document validation. The BORF is part of the Procurement for Public Sector (PPS) component.

3.2.1 PD Layer

The Procurement Development (PD) layer is a set of ABAP function modules to handle base SRM document object. The object is applicable for all types of SRM documents like PO, Shopping Cart, Contract, etc. BBP function is part of all SRM versions. BBP function modules are base of SRM development. In the initial SRM7 version, BORF is not part of GET_DETAIL. Latest version uses BORF concept. BBP Layer can be categorized into the following categories:

- Fetching details – The details can be fetched from the database for overall SRM document or a particular section of SRM document. The section includes Header, Item, and Account Assignment etc. Please refer the chapter SRM document for full details of those sections.

- Handling Actions – Actions related to SRM document like Create, Update, Delete or Check. The handling actions can be document level or a particular level of section.

The following table provides the list of procurement document category and its corresponding database table and BBP function module to get the details.

Category	DB Table	BBP Function Module
Header	CRMD_ORDERADM_H	BBP_HDRADM_GETDETAIL
Item	CRMD_ORDERADM_I	BBP_ITMADM_GETDETAIL
Organizational data	BBP_PDORG	BBP_PDORG_GETDETAIL
Dynamic Attributes	BBP_PDDYN	BBP_PDDYN_GETDETAIL
Conditions	PRCD_ITEM, PRCD_COND	BBP_PDCND_GETDETAIL
Attachment	BBP_PDATT	BBP_PDATT_GETDETAIL
Partners	BBP_PDVIEW_BUP	BBP_PDBUP_GETDETAIL
Limits	BBP_PDLIM	BBP_PDLIM_GETDETAIL
Status	CRM_JEST	BBP_PD_STATUS_GETDETAIL
Freight	BBP_PDFRT	BBP_PDFRT_GETDETAIL
Tax	BBP_PDTAX	BBP_PDTAX_GETDETAIL
Long Text	STXH	BBP_PDLTX_GETDETAIL
Account	BBP_PDACC	BBP_ACCOUNT_GETDETAIL
Weighting Set	BBP_PDWGT	BBP_PDWGT_GETDETAIL
Depending Attributes	BBP_PDDEP	BBP_PDDEP_GETDETAIL
Header Custom Fields	BBP_PDHCF	BBP_PDHCF_GETDETAIL
Exchange Rates	BBP_PDEXR	BBP_PDEXR_GETDETAIL
Item Custom Fields	BBP_PDICF	BBP_PDICF_GETDETAIL

The database table information provides the basic information. Getting the data from direct table may cause a number of data integration issues. Using the function module is best method to get data. You can get details of the document using the FM BBP_PROCDOC_GETDETAIL. The FM will fetch appropriate the categories detail using the input parameter i_read_flag (structure BBPS_DETAIL_REQUESTED). Unless the flag is set, the information will not be fetched so it will not hit the database. The FM BBP_PROCDOC_ITEM_GETDETAIL can be used for get details of item level.

Event handling function modules at document level are defined as follows.

- BBP_PROCDOC_CHECK – Do all validations on the SRM document. You can implement this BADI to do your customized checks. You can implement the BADI only once per filter type. The filter type is based on SRM document object type.
- BBP_PROCDOC_UPDATE – Update SRM documents based on the parameters. You can implement this BADI to do your customized update logic.
- BBP_PROCDOC_SAVE – Save SRM document into database. You can implement this BADI to do your customized update. Note that all updates are within same Logical unit of Work (LUW).

Most of enhancements are surrounded by these BADIs. The BADI can be implemented with object type filter. You need to write a clear code and proper documentation helps best implementation of these BADIs.

PD Buffer

The PD layer uses buffer cache to increase performance like not reading same object from database. You can reset the PD layer buffer using the FM BBP_PROCDOC_RESET_BUFFER. It clears all cache from PD layer for all SRM documents in the buffer. If you want to reset only one SRM document then use FM BBP_PROCDOC_RESET_DBBUFFER_SG. You can pass the GUID as the input parameter. There are a number of function modules to reset buffer at set types like Account, Long Text, Attributes, etc. The function module can be identified by BBP_<SET>_RESET_DBBUFFER. The set level reset requires the range of GUID as input parameter.

3.2.2 PDO Layer

PDO is the short form for Procurement Document Layer. PDO Layer is available in all SRM versions. PDO Layer helps developer highly to write clear and very specific SRM document level coding. PDO Layer is a wrapper of BBP Functions for each SRM business transaction type like PO, Shopping Cart, etc. Each PDO layer uses specific header, item and other structures for the SRM business transaction. The PDO layer level function modules execute the base associated BBP function module and map into PDO specific structure.

For each PDO object type, SRM provides a set of data structures and function modules. These data structures are very specific to the PDO object type. For example, PO header detail uses specific structure BBP_PDS_PO_HEADER_D for display purpose and BBP_PDS_PO_HEADER_U for update purpose. The BBP function module uses common header detail structure BBP_PDS_HEADER for both display and update purposes.

The standard function module has read flag parameter that determines what information is fetched from the database. The PDO get detail function module is not using i_read_flag structure instead the flag is set based on the FM parameters are supplied. The PDO GET detail function modules defaults its parameter i_with_itemdata as 'X'. That means it will fetch the item level even the item data is requested in the function module. If the item data is not required then it explicitly defines the parameter i_with_itemdata as blank. It is very useful tips of SRM performance tuning. You can set the parameter `I_WITHOUT_HEADER_TOTALS` as blank when you do not require header total. The header total may not be part of all PDO get detail function modules.

Performance Tips

Pass i_with_itemdata as blank in BBP_PD_<BO>_GETDETAIL FM when there is no item data required. Also, pass parameter i_without_header_totals as empty (Default is true) when there is no total at header is not required.

The PDO level function modules are listed in below table with BBP function module and PDO level function modules. The PDO layer function module for each object types are defined in the following section. There are a lot of PDO function modules and the table lists only important function modules.

Action	Function Module	PDO Layer
Check	BBP_PROCDOC_CHECK	BBP_PD_<BO>_CHECK

Create	BBP_PROCDOC_CREATE	BBP_PD_<BO>_CREATE
Get Detail	BBP_PROCDOC_GETDETAIL	BBP_ PD_<BO>_GETDETAIL
Get List	BBP_PROCDOC_GETLIST	BBP_ PD_<BO>_GETLIST
Item Get Detail	BBP_PROCDOC_ITEM_GETDETAIL	BBP_ PD_<BO>_ITEM_GETDETAIL
Lock	BBP_PROCDOC_LOCK	BBP_ PD_<BO>_LOCK
Save	BBP_PROCDOC_SAVE	BBP_ PD_<BO>_SAVE
Unlock	BBP_PROCDOC_UNLOCK	BBP_ PD_<BO>_UNLOCK

The standard naming convention is used for PDO Function. BBP_PD_PO_GETDETAIL is function module for get detail of the PO document. The <BO> abbreviation list is as follows:

BO Abbreviation	**Description**
AUC	Auction
AVL	Supplier List
BID	Bid Invitation (RFx)
CONF	Confirmation
CTR	Contract
INV	Invoice
PCO	PO Confirmation
PO	Purchase Order
QUOT	Quotation/Bid Response
SC	Shopping cart
SUSASN	SUS Advance Notification
SUSCF	SUS Confirmation
SUSINV	SUS Invoice
SUSPCO	SUS PO Confirmation
SUSPO	SUS PO

You can use the FM BBP_PD_<BO>_GETLIST to facilitate search on SRM documents. SAP uses this function in most of their SRM search services. You can see that each business object GETLIST will have different import and export parameters based on the business object. You can add filter on the Header and Item level custom fields.

Note for performance tuning, support package 5 uses BORF concept to get detail instead of BBP function. SAP recommends that use PDO layer instead of BBP get details information.

SRM provides lock object EBBP_PD that is based on the database table CRMD_ORDERADM_H with lock parameters of client and GUID. The lock will be based on GUID.

```
CALL FUNCTION 'ENQUEUE_EBBP_PD'
 EXPORTING
  mode_crmd_orderadm_h = c_enqueue_exclusive "E - Exclusive
  guid             = iv_guid
  _scope             = c_dequeue_after_commit " 2- Dequeue   EXCEPTIONS
  foreign_lock        = 1
  system_failure       = 2
  OTHERS            = 3.
```

3.2.3 Channel Logic Layer

The Channel Logic Layer is a wrapper on PDO Layer based on the ABAP objects. CLL layer is from SRM6 and it is not available at SRM 5 versions. CLL Layer prepares the business data for UI Layer and DO (Dependent Object) specific operations of the SRM business object. The following are type of objects is available in CLL.

- Business Object (BO) - Business object represents business contents, for example, PO or Shopping Cart. It has all basic operations on the SRM document.
- Dependent Object (DO) - Dependent Object is associated business contents like Account Assignment and Exchange Rate.
- Mapper Object – Mapper object is used to map between UI screens and business data.

3.2.4 Business Objects

The business object is based on the ABAP class object. The business object implements the interface classes like /SAPSRM/IF_PDO_BASE and its PDO business object level interfaces. The methods of PDO_BASE interface refer to basic business operations on the SRM document. The table lists the interface classes for each SRM business object. Note that objects suffixed with _ADV refer the object with workflow.

SRM BO	Interface Class
Auction	/SAPSRM/IF_PDO_BO_AUC
Contract	/SAPSRM/IF_PDO_BO_CTR_ADV
PO	/SAPSRM/IF_PDO_BO_PO_ADV
Quote	/SAPSRM/IF_PDO_BO_QTE_ADV
Bid Invitation	/SAPSRM/IF_PDO_BO_RFQ_ADV
Shopping Cart	/SAPSRM/IF_PDO_BO_SC_ADV

The following table lists the implemented ABAP class for the SRM business objects.

SRM BO	Implemented Class
Auction	/SAPSRM/CL_PDO_BO_AUC
Contract	/SAPSRM/CL_PDO_BO_CTR_ADV
PO	/SAPSRM/CL_PDO_BO_PO_ADV
Quote	/SAPSRM/CL_PDO_BO_QTE_ADV
Bid Invitation	/SAPSRM/CL_PDO_BO_RFQ_ADV
Shopping Cart	/SAPSRM/CL_PDO_BO_SC

Note that PO object has two implemented classes with and without workflow viz., /SAPSRM/CL_PDO_BO_PO_ADV and /SAPSRM/CL_PDO_BO_PO.

Factory Objects

Factory is an ABAP object for creating other object instances. Factory Objects are static objects. These are very useful ABAP Objects for CLL. Object instances are buffered and reduce the database accesses. It improves the performance. You can see the following methods in the CLL factory object.

Method	Description
GET_INSTANCE	Get instance from buffer. If not, get instance from database. It will add to buffered instance.
GET_BUFFERED_INSTANCE	Get instance from buffer. If not, return nothing.
GET_NEW_INSTANCE	Destroy instance from buffer if any and create new instance and add it to buffered instance.
CREATE_NEW_INSTANCE	Create new instance.

The CLL factory classes are listed as below.

Business Object	**Factory Class**
Auction	/SAPSRM/CL_PDO_FACTORY_AUC
Contract	/SAPSRM/CL_PDO_FACTORY_CTR_ADV
PO	/SAPSRM/CL_PDO_FACTORY_PO_ADV
Quote	/SAPSRM/CL_PDO_FACTORY_QTE_ADV
Bid Invitation	/SAPSRM/CL_PDO_FACTORY_RFQ
Shopping Cart	/SAPSRM/CL_PDO_FACTORY_SC_ADV

The following is sample code to using the Factory class to get instance.

```
DATA lo_pdo_qte      TYPE REF TO /sapsrm/if_pdo_bo_qte.
CALL METHOD /sapsrm/cl_pdo_factory_qte_adv=>get_instance
 EXPORTING
   iv_header_guid = is_header-guid
  RECEIVING
   ro_instance    = lo_pdo_qte.
```

The get instance will get the instance from factory instance table. If there is no entry then it will fetch data from database and insert the instance into instance table. Based on GUID, model access object returns base record. The following simple example is a wrapper for BBP_PROC_GETDETAIL function module.

```
DATA lo_pdo_qte      TYPE REF TO /sapsrm/if_pdo_bo_qte,
    ls_qte_header   TYPE bbp_pds_quot_header_d.
   lo_pdo_qte->get_header_detail( IMPORTING
     es_header = ls_qte_header ).
```

There are a number of methods are available at CLL Business object. You can use these methods based on your requirements.

3.2.5 Dependent Object

CLL objects support a wide range of dependent objects to get associated section of the data. The dependent class objects interfaces associated interface class. The following table lists few of Dependent Object Classes. Each DO object interfaces the corresponding DO interface /SAPSRM/IF_PDO_DO_ <DO>, /SAPSRM/IF_PDO_BO_BASE and /SAPSRM/IF_PDO_XO. The dependent object uses basic BBP function. The business object invokes DO objects. These dependent objects are part of attributes in the business object.

SRM DO	Implemented Class
Condition	/SAPSRM/CL_PDO_DO_CND
Dynamic Attributes	/SAPSRM/CL_PDO_DO_DYNATTRI
Exchange Rate	/SAPSRM/CL_PDO_DO_EXR
Freight	/SAPSRM/CL_PDO_DO_FREIGHT
History	/SAPSRM/CL_PDO_DO_HISTORY
Limit	/SAPSRM/CL_PDO_DO_LIMIT
Long Text	/SAPSRM/CL_PDO_DO_LONGTEXT
Org data	/SAPSRM/CL_PDO_DO_ORGDATA
Partner	/SAPSRM/CL_PDO_DO_PARTNER
SOS	/SAPSRM/CL_PDO_DO_SOS

Status	/SAPSRM/CL_PDO_DO_STATUS
Tax	/SAPSRM/CL_PDO_DO_TAX
Version	/SAPSRM/CL_PDO_DO_VERSION
Weight	/SAPSRM/CL_PDO_DO_WEIGHT

3.2.6 Mapper Object

The mapper object creates a connection between the UI and business object. This is specifically designed for Web Dynpro Application. SRM provides a list of BOM (business object mapper) and each object type refers to a Business Object Mapper (BOM). The BOM has been instantiated in the Web Dynpro application using the object /SAPSRM/CL_CH_WD_TASKCONTAINER. The BOM mapper instance is created using the ABAP object /SAPSRM/CL_CH_WD_MAP_FACTORY. The factory class has a separate method for each SRM object type.

Object	SRM BO Mapper
Auction	/SAPSRM/CL_CH_WD_BOM_AUC
Confirmation	/SAPSRM/CL_CH_WD_BOM_CONF
Contract	/SAPSRM/CL_CH_WD_BOM_CTR
Invoice	/SAPSRM/CL_CH_WD_BOM_INV
Purchase confirmation	/SAPSRM/CL_CH_WD_BOM_PC
Purchase Order	/SAPSRM/CL_CH_WD_BOM_PO
Quota Arrangement	/SAPSRM/CL_CH_WD_BOM_QTA
Quote	/SAPSRM/CL_CH_WD_BOM_QTE
Bid Invitation	/SAPSRM/CL_CH_WD_BOM_RFQ
Shopping Cart	/SAPSRM/CL_CH_WD_BOM_SC
SUS ASN	/SAPSRM/CL_CH_WD_BOM_SUSASN
SUS Confirmation	/SAPSRM/CL_CH_WD_BOM_SUSCONF
SUS Invoice	/SAPSRM/CL_CH_WD_BOM_SUSINV
SUS PO	/SAPSRM/CL_CH_WD_BOM_SUSPO

All above objects implements inherits from the super class /SAPSRM/CL_CH_WD_BO_MAPPER Also, objects interface the interfaces /SAPSRM/IF_CLL_MAPPER, /SAPSRM/IF_CLL_BO_MAPPER and other related mapper interfaces. For each CLL BOM has its own interface /SAPSRM/IF_CLL_BOM_<BO>. For PO mapper object interfaces /SAPSRM/IF_CLL_BOM_PO.

Identification Mapper

Identification Mapper is class configured at the FPM configuration level. The base identification mapper is /SAPSRM/CL_CH_WD_IDEN_MAP and it has been inherited further. Each SRM business object has an identification mapper /SAPSRM/CL_CH_WD_MAP_IDENT_<BO> inherited from base identification mapper. The identification mapper will handle all basic actions like Save, Check, Edit, Delete, etc. Also, you can enhance handle event method instead of using FPM_OIF_COMPONENT handle event option. The FPM component uses a generic object (TYPE ANY) and you have handle code based on the object type. When you are enhancing this method, the structures are very particular to the object type. There is a BADI /SAPSRM/BD_FPM_IDR_FIELD_DEF for the Identification Mapper to define fields at IDR level.

3.3 UI Layer

Web Dynpro Applications are used for SRM7 UI. SRM 5 uses ITS application. SRM7 uses Web Dynpro Applications based on the Floor Plan Manager (FPM). FPM is a Web Dynpro Application Framework for developing new Web Dynpro application interfaces consistent with SAP UI guidelines. SRM provides a set of Web Dynpro components using FPM framework.

3.3.1 Web Dynpro Components

SAP provides a number of Web Dynpro components to support their UI layer. UI layer integrates the Web Dynpro components using the floor plan manager and discussed in the next section. The list of basic Web Dynpro Applications is listed in the following table. Each Web Dynpro Application is associated with Mapper Object and CLL objects.

Mapper objects are used at each Web Dynpro Application. For example, PO header overview Web Dynpro Application /SAPSRM/WDC_PO_DOFC_OV_HD uses a separate mapper class and interface for the dependent object mapper. The object mapper class is /SAPSRM/CL_WD_DODM_PO_OV_H. The class will handle particular functionalities applicable to that screen and dependent object.

Error Message Handling

The error messages and/or information messages are displayed using the message manager. Using this message manager, you can display messages in the Web Dynpro component. The check BADI error/warning messages will be automatically showed in the message container. The following sample code provides idea how to add string as a message-to-message center in your custom code. This message handling can be used in any new action.

```
DATA:
  lo_api_controller    TYPE REF TO if_wd_controller,
  lo_message_manager   TYPE REF TO if_wd_message_manager.
 lo_api_controller ?= wd_this->wd_get_api( ).
 lo_message_manager = lo_api_controller->get_message_manager( ).
 lo_message_manager->report_message(
   EXPORTING message_type         = 0
             message_text         = lv_message ).
```

You can use report_message_from_t100 (from message class). Message types are used in this message manager as follows:

- 0 – Informational
- 1 – Warning
- 2 – Error
- 3 - Stop error.

3.3.2 Floor Plan Manager

Floor Plan Manager (FPM) is a framework, which can be highly configurable and easy for efficient application development and adaptation. The FPM can be developed using Web Dynpro applications with either ABAP or Java. SRM7 developed FPM applications using ABAP Web Dynpro applications.

FPM provides consistency across applications and UI compliance are guaranteed with pre-defined elements like toolbar, action buttons and UI look and feel. FPM provides wide range of enhancements and configurations to ease your development efforts. FPM automatically implements Identification area, Message area, Navigation region and Content area. FPM supports you in creating and configuration application-specific views with the following User Interface Building Blocks (UIBB).

- Form Component
- List Component
- Tabbed Component
- Search Component
- Hierarchical List Component

SRM supports the following types of floor plan:

- Object Instance Floor plan (OIF) – OIF can contain multiple tabs and its contents are determined by the business objects. Most SRM document uses the OIF type of Web Dynpro application. The basic Web Dynpro Application for FPM OIF is FPM_OIF_COMPONENT. SAP SRM provides a set of Web Dynpro configurations under the WD Application. The configuration starts with prefix /SAPSRM/WDCC_FPM.

- Guided Activity Floor plan (GAF) – GAF divides the activity into a logical sequence of steps. A good example on SRM is Souring Application. The basic Web Dynpro Application for FPM GAF is FPM_GAF_COMPONENT. SAP SRM provides a set of Web Dynpro configuration prefixes with /SAPSRM/WDCC_GAF.

Object Instance Floor Plan

In this section, you can see OIF usage in SRM document PO. The SRM OIF components have the following components. OIF is used in all procurement document applications. In the OIF application, you can organize all Web Dynpro Applications and Views in the Tab Screen. SRM connects all the WD application views by context objects and Mapper classes.

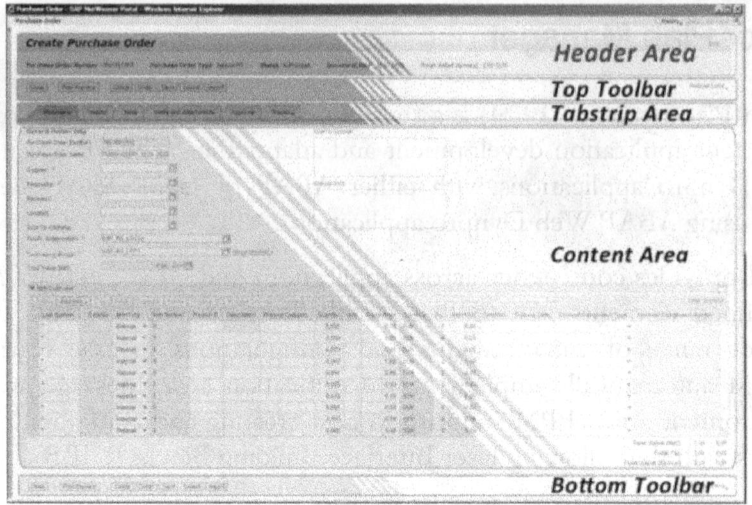

- **Header Area** - Title of the document and some basic information
- **Top Toolbar and Bottom Toolbar** - Contain available actions of the business object. Bottom Toolbar is copy of the Top toolbar.
- **Tabstrip Area** – If an object has several sub-screens, the sub-screens can be accessed by the Tabstrip.
- **Content Area** – Content Area contains the actual information and it is made from standard Web Dynpro Application.

Guided Activity Floor Plan

Guided Activity is step-by-step screen flow of activities. Each activity can be pointed to different Web Dynpro Application and View. SRM Sourcing is one of good example GAF Web Dynpro application used in SRM. SRM uses GAF only on few applications GAF screen has following components:

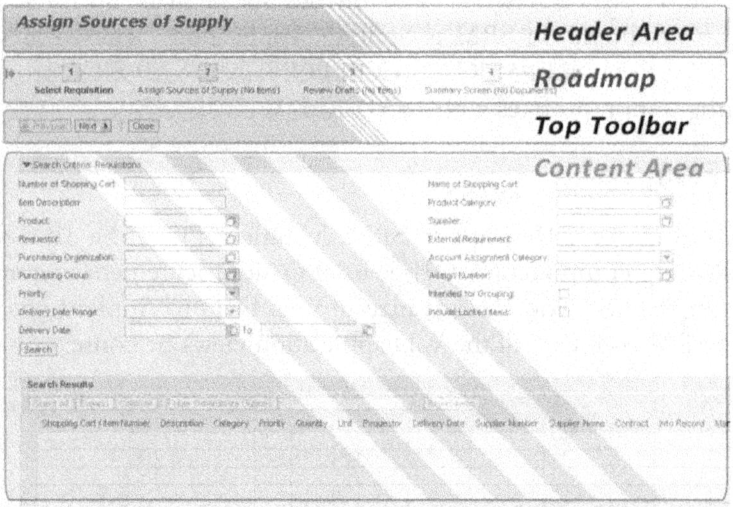

- **Header Area** - Contains the step description
- **Roadmap –** Provides an overview of steps
- **Top Toolbar and Bottom Toolbar** – Contains buttons to navigate steps and contains same set of buttons.
- **Content Area –** Web Dynpro component associated with the step.

The screen shot of SOCO configuration of GAF Web Dynpro component:

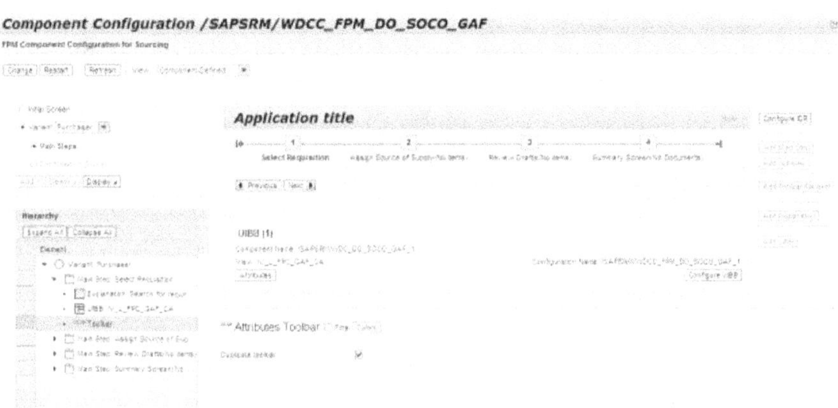

Technical Tips: SAP provides the set of WD components that are used by OIF and GAF applications. The following table is some sample set of Web Dynpro Applications. Note that your version may use different WD application. You can get Web Dynpro application by right click on UI screen.

Business Object	Scope	Web Dynpro Application
Common	Header Notes and Attachments	/SAPSRM/WDC_DODC_NA
	Notes And Attachment	/SAPSRM/WDC_UI_CTR_CA_NAT
	Header Table Extensions	/SAPSRM/WDC_DODC_CT
	Account Assignment	/SAPSRM/WDC_UI_DO_ACC
	Pricing Arrangements	/SAPPSSRM/WDC_DO_PA_TAB
	Delivery/Ship-to Address	SAPSRM/WDC_UI_DO_SHIPTO

	Source of Supply	/SAPSRM/WDC_DODC_SC_I_SOS
	Related Doucment/History	/SAPSRM/WDC_UI_DO_HISTORY
SC	Header General Data	/SAPSRM/WDC_UI_SC_DOFC_HD
	Item Data	/SAPSRM/WDC_DODC_SC_I_BD
Contract	Overview	/SAPSRM/WDC_UI_CTR_CA_OVR
	Header Basic Data	/SAPSRM/WDC_CTR_DODC_H_BD
	Header Condition	/SAPSRM/WD_CTR_DODC_CND
	Header Exchange Rate	/SAPSRM/WD_UI_DO_EXR
	Header Hierarchy	/SAPSRM/WD_CTR_DOTC_HIER
	Items	/SAPSRM/WDC_UI_CTR_CA_ITM
	Items Basic Data	/SAPSRM/WDC_CTR_DODC_I_BD
	Notes and Attachments	/SAPSRM/WDC_UI_CTR_H_NA
	Conditions	/SAPSRM/WDC_UI_CTR_CA_CND
PO	Overview	/SAPSRM/WDC_UI_PO_CA_OV
	Header General Data	/SAPSRM/WDC_DODC_PO_H_BD1
	Item	/SAPSRM/WDC_UI_PO_CA_ITM
	Approval	/SAPSRM/WDC_UI_PO_DODC_AP
	Tracking	/SAPSRM/WDC_UI_PO_CA_TRK

FPM Configuration

You can control the behavior of each individual component using a Web Dynpro application. A Web Dynpro application can have special parameters that can steer the behavior of the component. Configuration is defining the parameters and defines the behavior. You can create any number of configurations for a Web Dynpro component. Note that configuration is different from personalization. The personalization is a function available to user and provides option of adjusting the application. Personalization is limited to UI settings which never limit the running ability of the application. Also, personalization is available at runtime of an application.

SAP provides FPM configuration editor that configure Web Dynpro component configurations. You can view the FPM configurations into Attributes, Component-defined and Web Dynpro Built-in views.

Editor for the Web Dynpro ABAP Component Configuration

Change | Display | Cancel | Create | Copy | Delete | Other Functions

Which component do you want to configure?

Component Name: FPM_OIF_COMPONENT   Configuration ID: * /SAPSRM/WDCC_FPM_CTR

FPM configuration editor has the following work areas:

- Navigation Area - This is left side of configuration editor. It has two sub regions viz., control area and hierarchy area. You can use the Change or Display buttons to display or change the application global settings and variant parameters. You can see configuration elements in hierarchy view.
- Preview Area - It shows the user interface of application. You can use the preview function to navigate within the user interface.
- Action Area - You can see links to all actions that you can execute for the selected application user interface. You can configure the actions based on your requirements.
- Attribute Area - In this area, the attributes of these user interface elements are displayed. You can change the attributes depend on the user interface element selected. You can see any changes made in the preview.
- Message Area - Any potential conflicts in the configuration (like duplicate name) are immediately displayed.

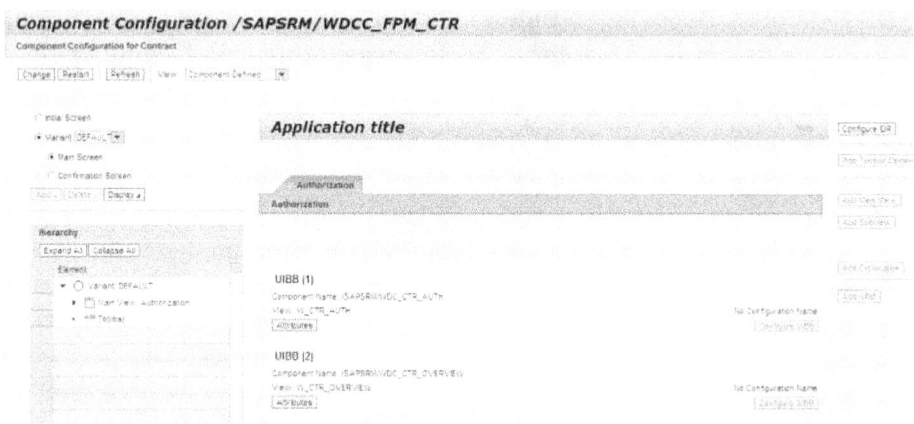

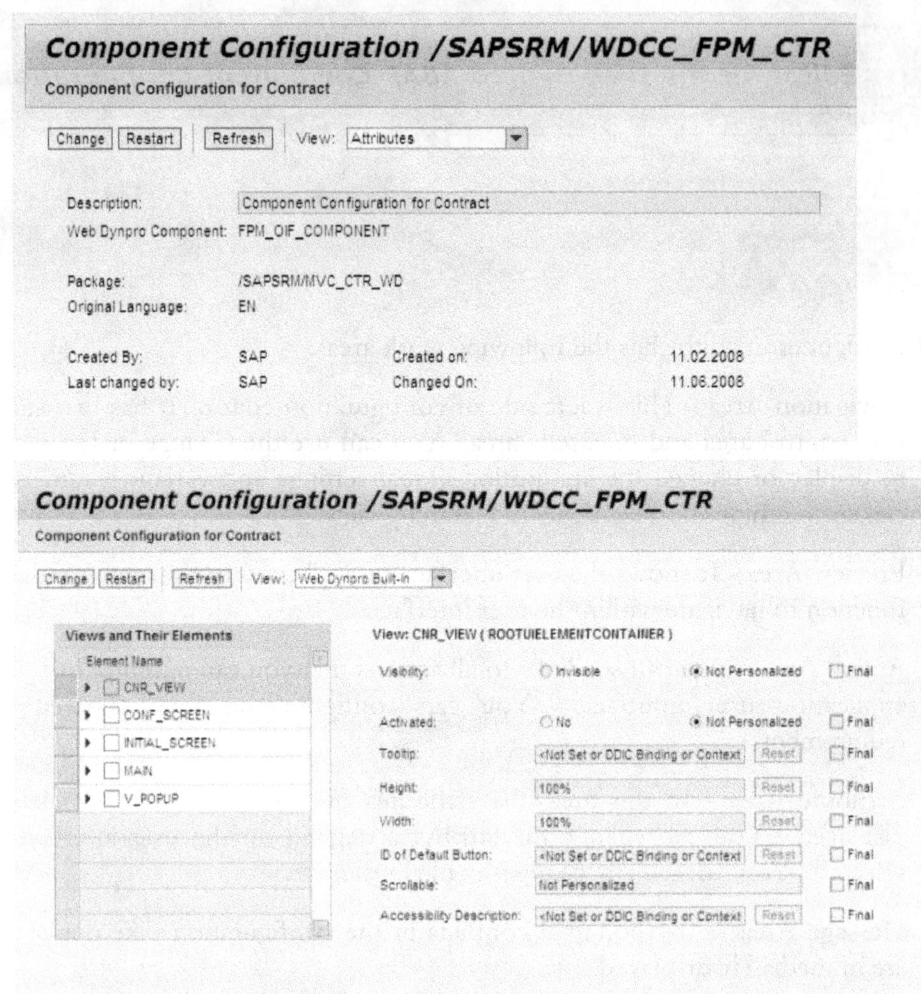

SRM provides a number of FPM component configurations to cover the different SRM object types and business conditions. You can see the FPM configuration name in the technical help screen. The following some FPM configurations used in SRM7.

Configuration	Description
/SAPSRM/WDCC_FPM_BEV_AUC	OIF Auction
/SAPSRM/WDCC_FPM_BEV_RFQ	OIF Bid Invitation
/SAPSRM/WDCC_FPM_CTR_PURCH	OIF Contract
/SAPSRM/WDCC_FPM_OIF_INV_PURCH	OIF Invoice
/SAPSRM/WDCC_FPM_OIF_SC_PROF	OIF Shopping Cart
/SAPSRM/WDCC_FPM_OIF_PO_PURCH	OIF Purchase Order

/SAPSRM/WDCC_FPM_DO_SOCO_GAF	GAF Sourcing
/SAPSRM/WDCC_FPM_GAF_CTR_MASS	Contract Mass Changes

3.4 PO Save Flow

In this section, you can see the technical flow when the PO save button is clicked in PO document screen.

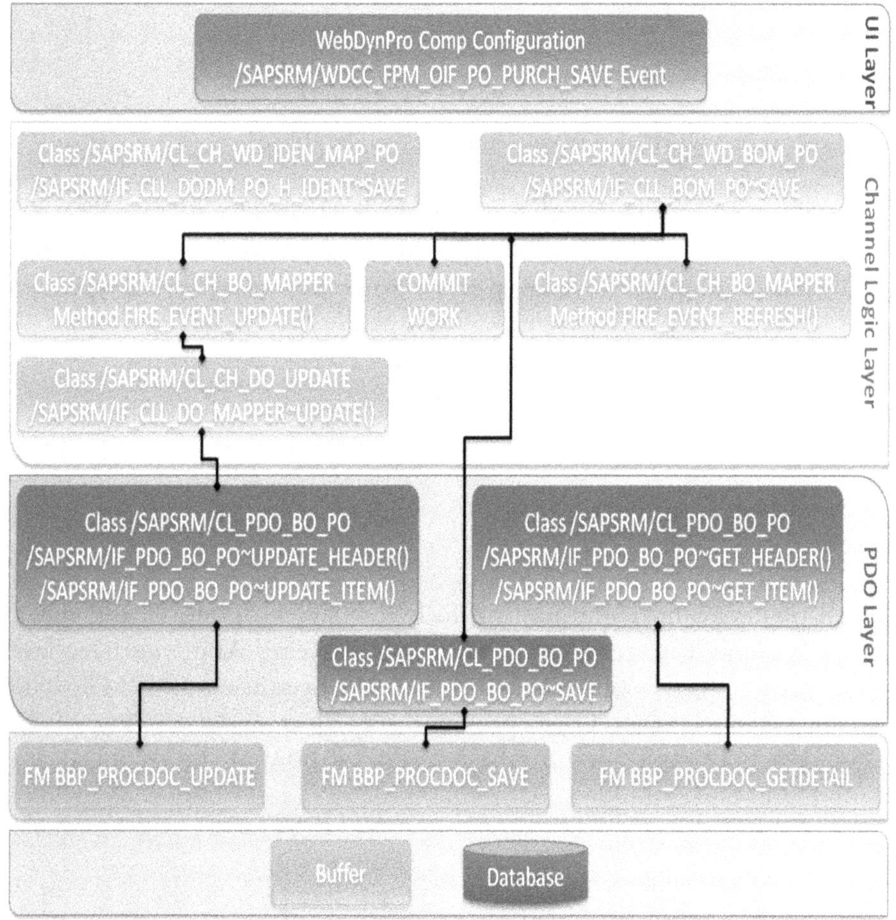

- Raises the event SAVE of the Web Dynpro configuration /SAPSRM/WDCC_FPM_OIF_PO_PURCH
- Executes the method /SAPSRM/IF_CLL_DODM_PO_H_IDENT~SAVE of the ABAP class /SAPSRM/CL_CH_WD_IDEN_MAP_PO.
- Executes the method /SAPSRM/IF_CLL_BOM_PO~SAVE of the ABAP class /SAPSRM/CL_CH_WD_BOM_PO.

- Executes the method /SAPSRM/IF_CLL_DO_MAPPER~UPDATE of the ABAP class /SAPSRM/CL_WD_DO_UPDATE.
- Executes the method /SAPSRM/IF_PDO_BO_PO~UPDATE_HEADER and/or /SAPSERM/IF_PDO_PO~UPDATE_ITEM of the ABAP class /SAPSRM/CL_PDO_BO_PO based on changes.
- Executes the function module BBP_PROCDOC_UPDATE.
- Changes applied to PD buffer.
- Executes the method /SAPSRM/IF_PDO_BO_PO~SAVE of the ABAP class /SAPSRM/CL_PDO_BO_PO.
- Executes the function module BBP_PROCDOC_SAVE
- Executes the commit work and update changes to database.
- Executes the method FIRE_EVENT_REFRESH of the ABAP class /SAPSRM/CL_CH_BO_MAPPER.
- Executes the method /SAPSRM/IF_BBP_PO~GET_HEADER and /SAPSRM/IF_BBP_PO~GET_ITEM of /SAPSRM/CL_PDO_BO_PO.

3.5 Summary

In this chapter, you have learned the technical layers of SRM7 and what are ABAP objects are available with respect to the technical layers. Also, you have learned the basic of floor plan manager concepts and how it has been used in SRM7. The UI layer and usage of Channel Layer Logic provides very clear understanding of SRM7 complexity. The data flow topic provides basic technical flow of the technical objects used in SRM.

Enhancement provides flexibility of the system tailoring the system suit Customer requirements. SRM enhancements are highly based on BADIs and Web Dynpro applications.

4 SRM Enhancements

SRM is a flexible system with a range of configurations. You can implement these configurations using SAP IMG. SRM provides also a number of enhancements outside of IMG configuration. The enhancements can be UI or process related. Before making enhancements, you need to understand the processes involved and customer requirements. The GAP analysis and understanding of SRM technology helps the developer to provide optimal solutions. This chapter explains some IMG configurations related to UI enhancements and technical development related to enhancements.

The custom fields' enhancement is one of common extensions in the SRM projects. The standard SAP fields may not cover all customer requirements. New custom fields are required to manage customer requirements. You can handle the custom fields at header, item or any set type (like Partner, Organization data, etc.). In SRM7, Meta Data Framework configuration provides technical framework for custom fields' setup. You can access MDF in IMG configuration. You can also use dynamic configuration using ABAP classes in the MDF. Also, there are UI enhancements required to add these custom fields. You can do UI enhancements by Web Dynpro enhancement.

SRM provides a wide range of BADIs to control the SRM processes. You can provide a better solution by understanding these BADIs. In SRM, the common used BADIs are at the SRM Document level. These BADIs cover all SRM documents processing enhancements. You can see high traffic at these BADIs.

In this chapter, we are discussing enhancement framework, MDF, document BADIs, and UI enhancements. Also, a number of technical challenges and its solutions are discussed.

4.1 Enhancement Framework

Enhancement framework brings all enhancement techniques under one roof and improves the way SAP is enhanced. This can be also switched using the Switch Framework. There are four enhancement technologies available under this framework. All these enhancements are considering enhancement and not modifying the system.

- **Source code enhancement** - Enhancement needs to be incorporated directly into ABAP source code. This implementation technology is known as Source Plug-In. There are two types of source code enhancements possible.
  - Implicit enhancement option
  - Explicit enhancement option
- Explicit enhancement options are provided at specific source code places explicitly by SAP. There are two ABAP statements ENHANCEMENT-POINT and ENHANCEMENT-SECTION. When the enhancement section is implemented, only the implementation gets executed and the original code does not get executed. Implicit enhancement options are automatically available at pre-defined places such as:
  - At end of all the programs, after the last statement
  - At the beginning and end of FORM subroutines
  - At the end of all function modules
  - At the end of all visibility areas (public, protected and private) of local class
- **Function group enhancement** - You can enhance the function module by adding parameters. These parameters must be optional. You can use source plug-in to enhance source code logic for the new parameters.
- **Class enhancement** - You can enhance the global classes and interfaces for the following.
  - Adding new parameters to the existing methods. Parameters must be optional.
  - Adding new methods
  - Adding Pre-exit, Post-exit or Overwrite-exit to an existing method.
- **Kernel-BADI enhancement** - is improvement of old classic BADI and integrated into enhancement framework. Kernel BADI is much faster than classic BADI.

In this section, you can basic concept on enhancements using BADI and Web Dynpro enhancements.

4.1.1 BADI

Business Add-In (BADI) is an enhancement technique based on ABAP objects. BADI is an anticipated point of extension or well-defined interface in the source code to do enhancements. There are two types of BADI supported by SAP viz., classic and kernel-based BADIs. Kernel BADIs are highly integrated directly in ABAP runtime environment. Kernel BADIs are highly flexible and faster than classic BADI. The navigation screens are different between classic and kernel BADIs. You can list the BADIs using the transaction code SE94. Note that SRM BADIs are prefixed with BBP, /SAPSRM/ or /SAPPSSRM.

SRM has two components BADI Definition and BADI Implementation. SAP provides the definition and you can implement the code for standard SAP BADI. You can define your own custom BADI also. You can access BADI definition using the transaction code SE18 and implementation using the transaction code SE19.

The important attributes of BADIs are *multiple-use* and *BADI filter*. The BADI filter is implementation will be executed based on the filter value at runtime environment. So, you can implement a separate implementation for each filter value combination. You can implement more than one implementation when the BADI has set to multi-use flag. When you do multiple implementations, make sure that each implement is not dependent on each other. The sequence of implementation is based on compilation. So, there is possible that you can have different sequence of implementations between development and Test or Product landscapes.

4.1.2 Web Dynpro Enhancement

An implicit enhancement can be implemented in ABAP Web Dynpro application. You can see Enhance (Swirl) button at icon tool bar of the Web Dynpro. You can implement more than one enhancement implementations on the Web Dynpro Application. Make sure that enhancement implementations should follow some namespace standards. It will help you to maintain the changes easier. You can implement the enhancements in View, Controller and/or Window components.

View Component	New UI elements Suppress UI elements Add Inbound plug-ins Add Outbound plug-ins Actions Methods

Controller	Context Node and Attributes Methods

In enhancement of existing methods or actions, you can use pre-exit, post-exit or overwrite method. The pre-exit enhancement will execute code before method is executed. The post-exit enhancement will execute the code after the method is executed. The overwrite option will execute the new code instead of existing standard code. The method enhancement is similar to class implicit enhancements and the only difference is rewrite option. If you have more than implementation on the method, the execution will be arbitrary. Make sure that code changes are independent and not conflicting each other.

4.2 Database Changes

One of common requirements is extending SRM procurement documents with new custom fields. The custom fields can be added at Header or Item level. In SRM5.0, there is a step-by-step procedure how to extend each SRM procurement document. The custom fields should be added to a particular include structures related to the procurement document. In SRM7.0, SAP made it easier so custom fields can be added in one step using the IMG configuration. The IMG path is SRM Server->Cross-Application Basic Settings->Extensions and Field Control->Configure Customer Fields. You require necessary authorization to add new custom fields like developer access and activate the changes.

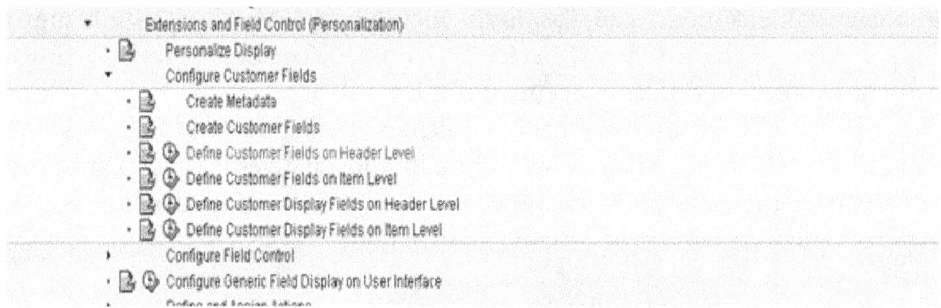

The customer fields can be configured at Auction, AVL, Bid Invitation, Confirmation, Contract, Invoice, PO, Response and Shopping cart on Header and Item level.

Associated include structures are listed in the following table at Header level.

Object	Include Structure
Generic Header	INCL_EEW_PD_HEADER_CSF

Auction Header	INCL_EEW_PD_HEADER_CSF_AUC
Supplier List	INCL_EEW_PD_HEADER_CSF_AVL
Bid Invitation	INCL_EEW_PD_HEADER_CSF_BID
Confirmation	INCL_EEW_PD_HEADER_CSF_CONF
Invoice	INCL_EEW_PD_HEADER_CSF_INV
Quote	INCL_EEW_PD_HEADER_CSF_QUOT
Shopping Cart	INCL_EEW_PD_HEADER_CSF_SC

The Item level include structures associated are listed as below.

Object	Include Structure
Generic Header	INCL_EEW_PD_ITEM_CSF
Auction Header	INCL_EEW_PD_ITEM_CSF_AUC
Supplier List	INCL_EEW_PD_ITEM_CSF_AVL
Bid Invitation	INCL_EEW_PD_ITEM_CSF_BID
Confirmation	INCL_EEW_PD_ITEM_CSF_CONF
Invoice	INCL_EEW_PD_ITEM_CSF_INV
Quote	INCL_EEW_PD_ITEM_CSF_QUOT
Shopping Cart	INCL_EEW_PD_ITEM_CSF_SC

The customer fields can be extended in the UI application layer. The later section will discuss how to add these customer fields in the UI screen. There is display fields that can be description and information read from other documents or from ECC back-end systems. Like customer field configuration, there is IMG configuration for display only fields.

Object	**Include Structure**
Auction Header	INCL_EEW_PD_HEADER_CSD_AUC
Supplier List	INCL_EEW_PD_HEADER_CSD_AVL
Bid Invitation	INCL_EEW_PD_HEADER_CSD_BID
Confirmation	INCL_EEW_PD_HEADER_CSD_CONF
Invoice	INCL_EEW_PD_HEADER_CSD_INV
Quote	INCL_EEW_PD_HEADER_CSD_QUOT

Shopping Cart	INCL_EEW_PD_HEADER_CSD_SC
Auction Header	INCL_EEW_PD_ITEM_CSD_AUC
Supplier List	INCL_EEW_PD_ITEM_CSD_AVL
Bid Invitation	INCL_EEW_PD_ITEM_CSD_BID
Confirmation	INCL_EEW_PD_ITEM_CSD_CONF
Invoice	INCL_EEW_PD_ITEM_CSD_INV
Quote	INCL_EEW_PD_ITEM_CSD_QUOT
Shopping Cart	INCL_EEW_PD_ITEM_CSD_SC

There are two BADIs to fill display-only customer fields at Header and Item level. The BADIs are:

- /SAPSRM/BD_PDO_FE_FILL_HEADER
- /SAPSRM/BD_PDO_FE_FILL_ITEM.

Note that these BADIs are multi-use and filter is based on Business Object Type and Field Name.

Name: /SAPSRM/BD_PDO_FE_FILL_HEADER		Multiple Use: Yes	Filter: Yes
Description: BADI to fill Header display only customer fields			
Method: FILL_EXTENSION_FIELDS ***Description***: Fill display-only extension fields. Parameters:			
Name	Type	Data Type	Description
IV_FLT_BUS_OBJ_TYPE	Import	BBP_SEARCH_OBJTYP	Object Type
IV_FLT_FIELD_NAME	Import	FIELDNAME	Field Name
IV_HEADER_GUID	Import	CRMT_OBJECT_GUID	Object GUID
CS_HEADER_DATA	Change	DATA	Data structure based on the object type
Sample code: The sample code is for technical solution. cs_header_data-zzdsplfld1 = 'VALUE1'.			

Name: /SAPSRM/BD_PDO_FE_FILL_ITEM			Multiple Use:Yes	Filter: Yes
Description: BADI to fill Item display only customer fields				
Method: FILL_EXTENSION_FIELDS *Description*: Fill display-only extension fields. Parameters:				
Name	Type	Data Type		Description
IV_FLT_BUS_OBJ_TYPE	Import	BBP_SEARCH_OBJTYP		Object Type
IV_FLT_FIELD_NAME	Import	FIELDNAME		Field Name
IV_HEADER_GUID	Import	CRMT_OBJECT_GUID		Object GUID
CT_ITEM_DATA	Change	TABLE		Table Data structure based on the object type

Sample code: The sample code is for technical solution.

```
Loop at ct_item_data INTO ls_item_data.
 IF cond1 is not initial.
  ls_item_data-ZZDSPFLG = 'True'.
 ELSE.
  ls_item_data-ZZDSPFLG = 'False'.
 ENDIF.
 MODIFY ct_item_data FROM ls_item_data.
ENDIF.
```

Technical Tips: You can use iv_header_guid to fetch the procurement document detail. This BADI is defined at field name level. So, it may hit multiple times for same procurement document. You can use static value in the BADI so you reduce performance bottlenecks.

Custom Table-Like structure Extension

SRM provides option to table like-extension i.e. for each object type, you can extend table like extension at Header and Item level. All these database fields must be added to append for business object-independent fields. The custom table extension can be accessed by IMG path SRM Server->Cross-Application Basic Settings->Extensions and Field Control->Create Table Extensions and Supply with Data.

Object	**Include Structure**
Auction Header	INCL_EEW_PD_HEADER_CST_AUC
Supplier List	INCL_EEW_PD_HEADER_CST_AVL
Bid Invitation	INCL_EEW_PD_HEADER_CST_BID
Confirmation	INCL_EEW_PD_HEADER_CST_CONF
Invoice	INCL_EEW_PD_HEADER_CST_INV
Quote	INCL_EEW_PD_HEADER_CST_QUOT
Shopping Cart	INCL_EEW_PD_HEADER_CST_SC
Auction Header	INCL_EEW_PD_ITEM_CST_AUC
Supplier List	INCL_EEW_PD_ITEM_CST_AVL
Bid Invitation	INCL_EEW_PD_ITEM_CST_BID
Confirmation	INCL_EEW_PD_ITEM_CST_CONF
Invoice	INCL_EEW_PD_ITEM_CST_INV
Quote	INCL_EEW_PD_ITEM_CST_QUOT
Shopping Cart	INCL_EEW_PD_ITEM_CST_SC

4.3 Meta Data Framework

Meta data is data about the data. SRM Meta Data framework provides option to define and control the behavior of the UI layer. SAP provides basic configuration for Meta data determines whether the fields are visible or hidden on the user interface. Meta Data Framework is applicable for Field Attributes, Sets and Actions using both static and dynamic methods.

Meta data is highly restricted by the following hierarchy:

- Dependent Object Manager provides least restrictive metadata.
- Business Objects restrict metadata according to BO context. At this level, you can restrict metadata even deeper if required.
- CLL and GUI can further limit metadata properties for specific channel requirements.

All Web Dynpro Applications are designed to handle corresponding Meta data configuration at initial stage. In earlier version of SRM5.x, the BADI BBP_CUF_BADI_2 is used to control screen attributes. It requires ABAP coding. From SRM6.0, this BADI is obsolete. Using Meta Data configuration, you can configure the basic custom field control. For complex scenarios, configuration provides Dynamic configuration option by adding the associate ABAP Object and Class. The dynamic configuration is discussed later in this chapter.

4.3.1 Field Control

Field Control is one of powerful configuration to control SRM field attributes. It requires minimum or no code to configure field control. The field control includes most of SRM standard fields and can be extended to any custom fields. Meta data configuration allows configuring the business object fields with one of the following attributes:

- Visible – Determines whether a field is visible on UI
- Enabled – Determines whether a field can be changed on UI. Note that when display mode, the field is not editable.
- Required – Determines whether the field is marked as required on the UI. Note that this is only applicable for mandatory mark on UI only not at data validation. The data validation should be done through BBP_DOC_CHECK_BADI or BBP_ITEM_CHECK_BADI based on the requirements.

The following attribute value is allowed for control field attributes.

Value	Description
Space	No
X	Yes
0	No (default value)
1	Yes (default value)

The field control configuration can be categorized as the following level:

- Header Level field configuration
- Item Level field configuration
- Set Type (Substructure) field configuration.

The good example of set type is Account Assignments or Partner, etc. The list of the Set Types is as follows:

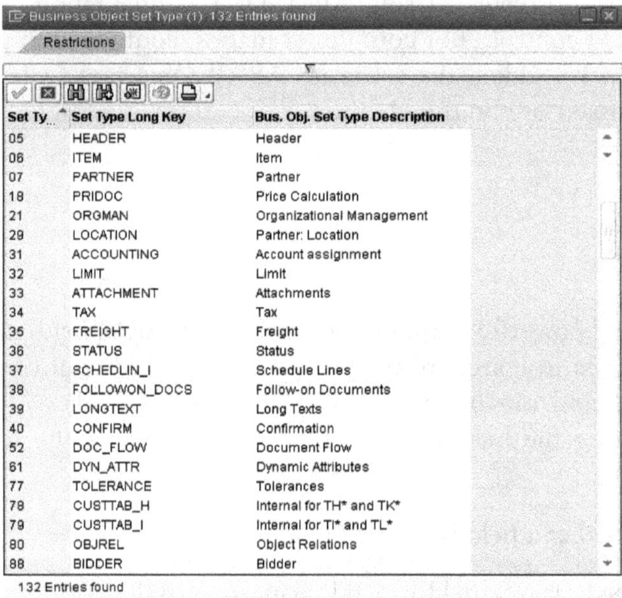
Business Object Set Type (1) 132 Entries found

Restrictions

Set Ty...	Set Type Long Key	Bus. Obj. Set Type Description
05	HEADER	Header
06	ITEM	Item
07	PARTNER	Partner
18	PRIDOC	Price Calculation
21	ORGMAN	Organizational Management
29	LOCATION	Partner: Location
31	ACCOUNTING	Account assignment
32	LIMIT	Limit
33	ATTACHMENT	Attachments
34	TAX	Tax
35	FREIGHT	Freight
36	STATUS	Status
37	SCHEDLIN_I	Schedule Lines
38	FOLLOWON_DOCS	Follow-on Documents
39	LONGTEXT	Long Texts
40	CONFIRM	Confirmation
52	DOC_FLOW	Document Flow
61	DYN_ATTR	Dynamic Attributes
77	TOLERANCE	Tolerances
78	CUSTTAB_H	Internal for TH* and TK*
79	CUSTTAB_I	Internal for TI* and TL*
80	OBJREL	Object Relations
88	BIDDER	Bidder

132 Entries found

Basic Configuration

You can control simple field control like what fields required to be displayed, required or enabled. The configuration includes both standard SRM fields and custom fields. The configuration can be accessed in the following IMG Menu Path: SRM Server->Cross-Application Basic Settings->Extensions and Field Control-> Configure Field Control.

Configure Field Control for Document Header fields: The custom fields can be added for each object type with Visible, Enabled and Required fields.

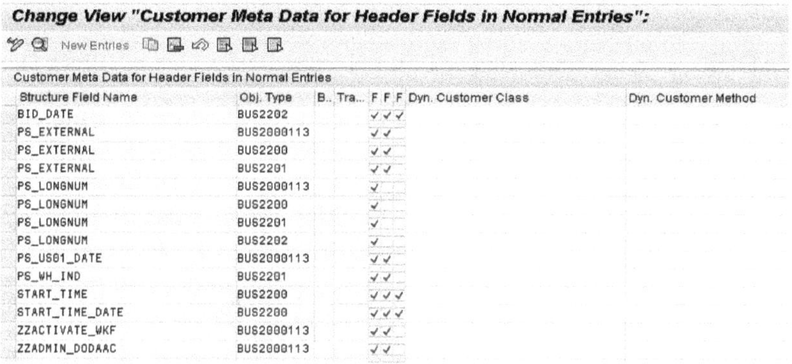

Change View "Customer Meta Data for Header Fields in Normal Entries":

New Entries

Customer Meta Data for Header Fields in Normal Entries

Structure Field Name	Obj. Type	B..	Tra...	F	F	F	Dyn. Customer Class	Dyn. Customer Method
BID_DATE	BUS2202			✓	✓	✓		
PS_EXTERNAL	BUS2000113			✓	✓			
PS_EXTERNAL	BUS2200			✓	✓			
PS_EXTERNAL	BUS2201			✓	✓			
PS_LONGNUM	BUS2000113			✓				
PS_LONGNUM	BUS2200			✓				
PS_LONGNUM	BUS2201			✓				
PS_LONGNUM	BUS2202			✓				
PS_US01_DATE	BUS2000113			✓	✓			
PS_WH_IND	BUS2201			✓	✓			
START_TIME	BUS2200			✓	✓	✓		
START_TIME_DATE	BUS2200			✓	✓	✓		
ZZACTIVATE_WKF	BUS2000113			✓	✓			
ZZADMIN_DODAAC	BUS2000113			✓	✓			

Like custom field control configuration, there is configuration to visibility control of table-like structure. The only difference is the fields visible, enabled or required which are replaced by SET_EXITS.

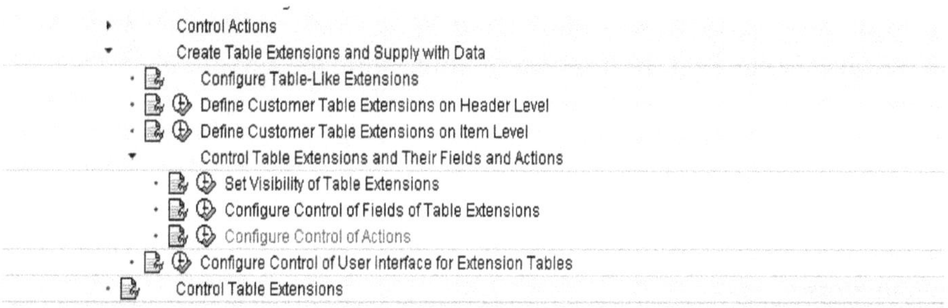

- Control Actions
- Create Table Extensions and Supply with Data
  - Configure Table-Like Extensions
  - Define Customer Table Extensions on Header Level
  - Define Customer Table Extensions on Item Level
  - Control Table Extensions and Their Fields and Actions
    - Set Visibility of Table Extensions
    - Configure Control of Fields of Table Extensions
    - Configure Control of Actions
  - Configure Control of User Interface for Extension Tables
- Control Table Extensions

Dynamic Configuration

The basic configuration may not cover a complicated process. For example, a field value at header/Item data determines the control of fields (like required or not editable). You cannot implement this kind of control in the base IMG configuration. You can resolve this requirement by dynamic configuration. The dynamic configuration uses a custom (or standard) ABAP Class and method. Using ABAP code, the attributes can be set dynamically based on the data information. In this section, you can see how to define the ABAP Object and its methods.

There are some restrictions in defining the method. The method used in dynamic configuration must be public static method. Based on the header, item and set level, you must define a specific set of the parameters for the method. Note that any non-adherence parameters may cause a short dump.

The following signature parameters are required for the Header level.

Parameter	Type	Data Type	Description
IV_OBJECT_TYPE	Importing	BBP_BUS_OBJECT_TYPE	Object Type
IV_FIELD_NAME	Importing	/SAPSRM/PDO_META	Field Name

		_FIELD_NAME	
IS_HEADER	Importing	PDO Header	PDO Header structure e.g., BBP_PDS_QUOT_HEADER_D for Quote Object
IS_ADD_DATA	Importing	/SAPSRM/S_PDO_META_FLD_ADD_DAT	Additional data
CS_METADATA	Changing	/SAPSRM/S_PDO_FIELD_METADATA	Field Properties

The item level field configuration requires one more parameter.

IS_ITEM	Importing	PDO Item	PDO Item structure e.g., /SAPSRM/S_PDO_QTE_ITEM for Quote Object

The set types (like Long Text, Partner, etc.) require one more parameter.

IS_SET	Importing	ANY	Based on set, you can define data type. For example Long Text - /SAPSRM/S_LONGTEXT

You can write the field properties in the parameter CS_METADATA using the import parameters.

Technical Challenges: There is a custom long text (ZTXT) configured for shopping cart and long text is populated using Change BADI. The requirement is that long text should not be edited. The text must be in display mode while editing.

Solution: Create ABAP Object ZCL_TEXT_CONTROL and public static method text_display. Make sure that the variable IS_SET has data type /SAPSRM/S_LONGTEXT. For a wrong data type, you will get a dump.

The following is sample code control make particular long text is always visible but not editable.

```
IF is_set-text_id = 'ZTXT'.
  cs_metadata-visible = abap_true.
  cs_metadata-requied = '0'.
ENDIF.
```

Configure the field control with the ABAP object and class in dynamic configuration. You can access IMG configuration using path SRM Server->Cross Application Settings->Extensions and Field Control-> Configure Field Control->Configure Control for Fields for substructure.

Change View "Customer Meta Data for Substructure Fields in Normal Entr

New Entries

Customer Meta Data for Substructure Fields in Normal Entries

Set ...	Structure Field Na...	Obj. Type	Set L...	Set Subtype	F	F	F	Dyn. Customer Class	Dyn. Customer Method
39	LONGTEXT	BUS2201	HEADER					ZCL_PDO_long_text	textcontrol
TSCUS	ZZADP_DODAAC	BBP000	HEADER		✓	✓			
TSCUS	ZZALT_MAIL_CITY	BBP000	HEADER		✓	✓			

Technical Tips: You can combine common logic on field controls into few methods (or one method) for ease of maintenance. Also, you can use static attributes to increase performance on issue.

4.3.2 Action Control

SRM provides a number of actions for each SRM business object. The actions are used to retrieve metadata for buttons and hyperlinks added to the user interface from PDO layer. Actions can be defined and assigned to PDO object types in the IMG configuration. SRM provides a set of actions and assigned to the object types. The configuration allows either enabling or disabling actions using the IMG configuration.

Basic Configuration

In an action control procedure, you can enable or disable the buttons or hyperlinks using dynamic configuration. For example, you can disable the RFX publish button for a set of people who has no authority to order the PO. You can access basic configuration using the following IMG path: SRM Server -> Cross-Application Basic Settings ->Extensions and Field Control->Control Actions. You can configure actions at the Header, Item and Substructure Level. The action can be controlled in the display and edit mode.

- Document Archiving
- Extensions and Field Control (Personalization)
  - Personalize Display
  - Configure Customer Fields
  - Configure Field Control
  - Configure Generic Field Display on User Interface
  - Define and Assign Actions
  - Control Actions
    - Control Actions
    - Display Standard Metadata Tables for Actions on Header Level
    - Configure Control of Actions on Header Level
    - Display Standard Metadata Tables for Actions on Item Level
    - Configure Control of Actions on Item Level
    - Display Standard Metadata for Actions on Substructure Level
    - Configure Control of Actions on Substructure Level

You can control header level actions at business object type, subtype (optional) and transaction Type (optional). Using this activity you can enable/disable action. The dynamic configuration is also supported. You can assign a dynamic class and method for the dynamic configuration. You can deactivate using the dynamic configuration. To deactivate using dynamic configuration, you must set PDO action as active. You cannot activate any action in dynamic configuration when PDO action is set as inactive.

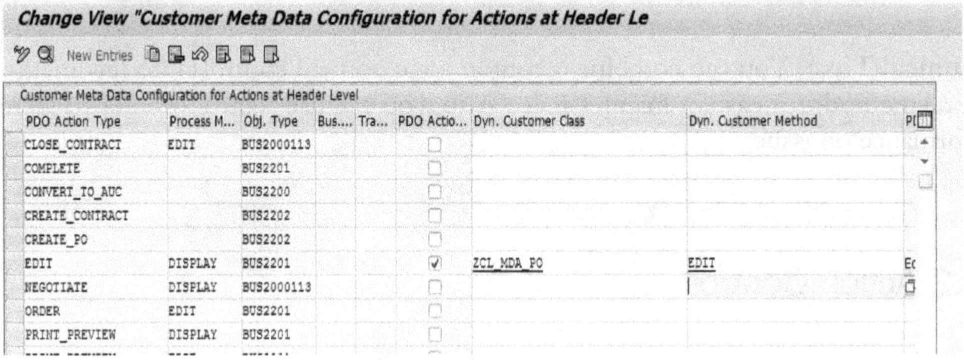

Change View "Customer Meta Data Configuration for Actions at Header Le

New Entries

Customer Meta Data Configuration for Actions at Header Level

PDO Action Type	Process M...	Obj. Type	Bus....	Tra...	PDO Actio...	Dyn. Customer Class	Dyn. Customer Method	P(
CLOSE_CONTRACT	EDIT	BUS2000113			☐			
COMPLETE		BUS2201			☐			
CONVERT_TO_AUC		BUS2200			☐			
CREATE_CONTRACT		BUS2202			☐			
CREATE_PO		BUS2202			☐			
EDIT	DISPLAY	BUS2201			☑	ZCL_MDA_PO	EDIT	Ec
NEGOTIATE	DISPLAY	BUS2000113			☐			
ORDER	EDIT	BUS2201			☐			
PRINT_PREVIEW	DISPLAY	BUS2201			☐			

Item level configuration can include Item Type and Item process Type along with Header level information. The substructure (subtype) level configuration includes Object Type, Set Level and Set subtype.

Dynamic Configuration

The basic dynamic configuration of action is similar to field control dynamic configuration. You can add your ABAP class and method to control the enable/disable metadata actions. You can configure dynamic customer method of ABAP object that can override configured PDO enable action. Note that method must be public static class with the following parameters:

Parameter	Type	Data Type	Description
IV_ACTION	Importing	/SAPSRM/PDO_ACTION_TYPE	Action
IS_HEADER	Importing	Any	PDO Header structure e.g., BBP_PDS_QUOT_HEADER_D for Quote Object
IV_OBJECT_TYPE	Importing	BBP_BUS_OBJECT_TYPE	Object Type
IV_MODE	Importing	/SAPSRM/PDO_INST_MODE	Display or Edit mode
IS_ADD_DATA	Importing	/SAPSRM/S_PDO_META_ACT_ADD_DAT	Additional data

CS_METADATA	Changing	/SAPSRM/S_PDO_ACTION_METADATA	Action enabled or Disabled

Item Level requires one more parameter.

IS_ITEM	Importing	Any	PDO Item structure based on Object Type

The set types (like Long Text, Partner, etc) require one more parameter.

IS_SET	Importing	Any	Set Type.

Technical Challenges: The requirement is providing Generate Report (It generates the custom report and requires GUID of the SRM document) and requires feedback about report generation. The button should be added in toolbar button of the Purchase Order.

Solution: You need to identify the configuration ID for the SRM PO object from your PO UI screen. Note that you need to F1 help at toolbar button screen. The main Web Dynpro application is FPM_OIF_COMPONENT. You can enhance the configuration by editing configuration. Add your new button in the configuration. You can add button using Add Toolbar Element.

You need to configure new button action using the IMG action control. Make sure that action name should match with new button element name.

Now you need to write code on how to handle the new button. It can be achieved by enhancing the FPM_OIF_COMPONENT->CNR_VIEW-> ONACTIONBUTTON_PRESSED. The enhancement is post-exit on the button action pressed. Note that the same can be achieved in the PO PDO Identification mapper object.

Sample code is for ONACTIONBUTTON_PRESSED post exit.

```
DATA:
  lv_id           TYPE string,
  lv_event_id        TYPE fpm_event_id,
```

```
    lv_bo_guid            TYPE bbp_guid,
    lo_task_factory       TYPE REF TO /sapsrm/if_cll_taskcon_factory,
    lo_task_container     TYPE REF TO /sapsrm/if_cll_task_container.
    lv_id = wdevent->get_string( 'ID' ).
    check lv_id cs 'OTHER_FUNCTIONS'.
    lv_event_id = get_event_id( lv_id ).
* Get the Business Object GUID
    lo_task_factory = /sapsrm/cl_ch_wd_taskcont_fact=>get_instance( ).
* Get the task container from factory class
    CALL METHOD lo_task_factory->get_task_container
      RECEIVING
        ro_task_container = lo_task_container.
* Get the BO object
    CALL METHOD lo_task_container->get_bo_guid
      RECEIVING
        rv_bo_guid = lv_bo_guid.
    CALL METHOD zcl_myclass=>mymethod
     EXPORTING
        i_event_id = lv_event_id
        i_guid     = lv_bo_guid.
```

Technical Tips: Make sure that event ID contains OTHER_FUNCTIONS. Otherwise, short dump may occur for non-other function button actions.

The MDF IMG configuration is stored in the following list of views. You can use these views for direct database access.

View	Description
/SAPSRM/V_MDA_HC	Customer Meta Data Configuration for Actions at Header Level
/SAPSRM/V_MDA_IC	Customer Metadata Configuration for Actions on Item Level
/SAPSRM/V_MDASBC	Customer Action Meta Data Configuration at Set Level
/SAPSRM/V_MDF_HY	Customer Meta Data Configuration for Header Fields
/SAPSRM/V_MDF_IY	Customer Metadata Configuration of Item Fields

/SAPSRM/V_MDFSBY	Customer Configuration Table for Metadata of Set Fields
/SAPSRM/V_MDS_HC	Customer Meta Data Configuration for Header Set Types
/SAPSRM/V_MDS_IC	Customer Meta Data Configuration of Set Types at Item Level

SAP provided a set of ABAP objects for the dynamic control methods in hierarchical classes. Below table provides few BO classes only. Other ABAP objects can be found in the same name pattern. The object classes are listed by fields and actions.

Hierarchical Class	Description
/SAPSRM/CL_PDO_DYN_META_BASE	Top level class for all metadata
* /SAPSRM/CL_PDO_DYN_META_FIELD	Dynamic control classes for field metadata
* /SAPSRM/CL_PDO_DYN_MDF_HD	Dynamic control classes for header fields
* /SAPSRM/CL_PDO_DYN_MDF_HD_GEN	Dynamic control for generic header fields
* /SAPSRM/CL_PDO_DYN_MDF_HD_PO	Dynamic control for PO header fields
* /SAPSRM/CL_PDO_DYN_MDF_HD_QTE	Dynamic control for Quote header fields
* /SAPSRM/CL_PDO_DYN_MDF_HD_RFX	Dynamic control for Bid Invitation header fields
* /SAPSRM/CL_PDO_DYN_MDF_HD_SC	Dynamic control for shopping cart header fields
* /SAPSRM/CL_PDO_DYN_MDF_IT	Dynamic control classes for Item fields
* /SAPSRM/CL_PDO_DYN_MDF_IT_GEN	Dynamic control for generic Item fields
* /SAPSRM/CL_PDO_DYN_MDF_IT_PO	Dynamic control for PO Item fields
* /SAPSRM/CL_PDO_DYN_MDF_IT_QTE	Dynamic control for Quote Item fields
* /SAPSRM/CL_PDO_DYN_MDF_IT_RFX	Dynamic control for Bid Invitation Item fields
* /SAPSRM/CL_PDO_DYN_MDF_IT_SC	Dynamic control for shopping

			cart Item fields
*	/SAPSRM/CL_PDO_DYN_MDA_HD		Dynamic control classes for header fields
	*	/SAPSRM/CL_PDO_DYN_MDA_HD_GEN	Dynamic control for generic header fields
	*	/SAPSRM/CL_PDO_DYN_MDA_HD_PO	Dynamic control for PO header fields
	*	/SAPSRM/CL_PDO_DYN_MDA_HD_QTE	Dynamic control for Quote header fields
	*	/SAPSRM/CL_PDO_DYN_MDA_HD_RFX	Dynamic control for Bid Invitation header fields
	*	/SAPSRM/CL_PDO_DYN_MDA_HD_SC	Dynamic control for shopping cart header fields
*	/SAPSRM/CL_PDO_DYN_MDA_IT		Dynamic control classes for Item fields
	*	/SAPSRM/CL_PDO_DYN_MDA_IT_GEN	Dynamic control for generic Item fields
	*	/SAPSRM/CL_PDO_DYN_MDA_IT_PO	Dynamic control for PO Item fields
	*	/SAPSRM/CL_PDO_DYN_MDA_IT_QTE	Dynamic control for Quote Item fields
	*	/SAPSRM/CL_PDO_DYN_MDA_IT_RFX	Dynamic control for Bid Invitation Item fields
	*	/SAPSRM/CL_PDO_DYN_MDA_IT_SC	Dynamic control for shopping cart Item fields

4.4 Document BADI

Business Add-In (BADI) is enhancement technique based on ABAP Objects. SRM provides a big set of BADIs to enhance SRM system for a big extent. The document BADI can be applicable to all SRM object types. It covers import processes of SRM documents viz., check, change and save BADI. There are a separate BADI for check, change and change. These three BADIs are playing a vital role in SRM basic enhancements.

4.4.1 Check BADI

One of important enhancement is validation of the data entered by customer. The standard validations are provided by SAP and which cannot cover all of the customer's business requirements on the validation. The custom fields may need new validations to validate the custom process. You can cover most of your data validations in the check BADI. The check BADI will return error messages and warning messages. You can validate the data and populate the error or warning messages. These messages are shown in the SRM document UI. The hard error(s) will not allow you to process further.

The SRM documents can be checked into three categories.

- Document header level check
- Single line item level check
- Entire document level check

The SRM document update calls the single line item level check, which should be carried out only when a new item is created or changed, or there is a consistency check for performance reasons. The first and third categories can be done using the BADI BBP_DOC_CHECK_BADI. The second category check can be done using the BADI BBP_ITEM_CHECK_BADI.

For example, the validation on the item level details when there is a change at Header level but there is no change at the Item level. Then you cannot use the Item BADI to validate the item level. The item BADI will execute only when there is change or update at item level.

The BADI BBP_DOC_CHECK_BADI is an exit function to validate the cross-checks on the SRM document. The BADI supports filter value based on the SRM object type. BADI interfaces only one method BBP_DOC_CHECK. Check BADI will stop further action when hard error message is populated in ET_MESSAGE. The messages in ET_MESSAGE will be displayed at UI message screen.

The sample code:

```
* get data of an object using the field IV_DOC_GUID
* If your validation fails then create the error message
  MESSAGE e100(zbbp_iv) INTO lf_dummy.    "dummy for where used
  CLEAR ls_message.
  ls_message-msgty    = sy-msgty.  "Error or Warning
  ls_message-msgid    = sy-msgid.
  ls_message-msgno    = sy-msgno.
  SELECT SINGLE text FROM t100 INTO ls_message-message
```

```
                WHERE sprsl = sy-langu
                and arbgb = sy-msgid
                and msgnr = sy-msgno.
    APPEND ls_message TO et_messages.
```

You can implement DOC_CHECK_BADI at SRM Object type level like Shopping Cart, PO, etc. Note that this BADI is not 'multiple use'. So, you can implement BADI only one once. Cross check on the Object type must be defined in a single implementation of SRM Object type. You can do your validations and populate the messages onto the parameter ET_MESSAGES. These messages will be displayed in the UI screen. When one of error message is error-typed then the SRM document cannot processed further. But you can save the document for future process.

Using GUID, you can get the SRM document data using the PDO Function Module or the PDO wrapper classes. While implementing the BADI, the user action is useful information to design validation process. The check BADI is executed while at Check, Save or Order level. The action is based on the UI screen like Check, Save or Order. The SYST variable SY-UCOMM will have user action. The following code is way to get user action and it is supported by SRM FPM framework.

```
* Getting the user actions
  lo_transaction_context =
/sapsrm/cl_transaction_context=>/sapsrm/if_transaction_context~get_instance().
  lv_user_action = lo_transaction_context->get_current_action( ).
```

BBP_ITEM_CHECK_BADI – The Item Check BADI is called when a new item is created or changed or a check button is clicked. Implement the Item Check BADI when the validations are applicable to Item level only.

4.4.2 Change BADI

The Change BADI is the exit point to make changes to the document after user entry and before the save the document. The Change BADI provides the filter on the SRM object types. In the Change BADI, there is no generic method as in the BADI BBP_DOC_CHECK_BADI. There are multiple methods defined and each method is applicable for the SRM Object type. Even though the BADI supports the Filter Value on the document type, the specific method will be executed in the Document Update process. The following methods are defined in the BADI interface.

Method	Description
BBP_BID_CHANGE	Bid Invitation Change
BBP_AUC_CHANGE	Auction Change
BBP_QUOT_CHANGE	Quote Change
BBP_CONF_CHANGE	Confirmation Change
BBP_SC_CHANGE	Shopping Cart Change
BBP_PO_CHANGE	PO Change
BBP_IV_CHANGE	Invoice Change
BBP_CTR_CHANGE	Contract Change
BBP_SUSPCO_CHANGE	SUS Purchase Confirmation Change
BBP_SUSPO_CHANGE	SUS PO Change
BBP_SUSASN_CHANGE	SUS ASN Change
BBP_SUSINV_CHANGE	SUS Invoice Change
BBP_PCO_CHANGE	Purchase Confirmation change
BBP_SUSCF_CHANGE	SUS Confirmation Change

Each method has its own parameter interfaces with respect the PDO structure definition at Header and Item parameters. The interface parameters include the following (It has both Import and Export parameters):

- Account
- Organization Data
- Header Custom Fields
- Item Custom Fields

The change parameters are Long Text and Value Limit. It is not applicable for all items. The Change BADI change parameters use a different structure (BBPS_<BO>_HEADER_BADI) than the standard PDO update structure. The BADI structure does not considering of all fields. So, you cannot update all fields using the Change BADI. For example, you cannot update posting date using this BADI.

Implementation of this BADI requires the exporting parameters should be populated. You can populate exporting parameters using importing parameters. Make sure that any changes should adapt standard SAP validations and custom validations. This is part of procurement update object layer.

```
MOVE-CORRESPONDING is_header TO es_header.
LOOP AT it_item INTO ls_it_item_temp.
 MOVE-CORRESPONDING ls_it_item_temp TO ls_et_item_temp.
 APPEND ls_et_item_temp TO et_item.
ENDLOOP.
et_partner[]    = it_partner[].
et_orgdata[]    = it_orgdata[].
et_dyn_attr[]   = it_dyn_attr[].
et_hcf[]        = it_hcf[].
et_icf[]        = it_icf[].
et_sdln[]       = it_sdln[].
* You can overwrite exporting parameters with your logic
```

4.4.3 SAVE BADI

The Save BADI (BBP_DOC_SAVE_BADI) is used to update custom data and table in the same Logical Unit of Work (LUW) when saving a document to the database. The purpose of SAVE BADI is to update additional update like a custom tables update or external update. This BADI will execute using BBP_PD_<BO>_SAVE function module. It can be implemented based on the FLT_VAL SRM Object Type. There is only one method BBP_DOC_SAVE and it has only one importing parameter IV_DOC_GUID. You can use this BADI to initiate a new interface or custom table update.

All other BADIs are discussed in the later chapters. The BADIs are discussed based on context and usage.

Custom Switch

Most of SRM enhancements are based on BADI enhancement. There are multiple real time scenarios where you need to deactivate the BADI changes to test the application. One situation, when you are applying OSS notes or supporting OSS custom message resolution, there is a possibility to deactivate the BADI to support the scenario. When you deactivate BADI, it may stop all other development, testing and business activities. You need to wait until the task is completed.

To handle this situation, we are suggesting a custom switch solution. The basic idea is from the SAP switch framework concept. But SAP uses switch framework which activates and deactivates of the solutions at global level. This custom switch solution will allow you to continue all activities and switch off the BADI or part of BADI execution for a particular user or a set of users. Note that this you can use this switch on your custom code too. This section explains how to implement custom switch on our custom coding.

To create a custom switch mechanism, you need to create two custom tables which must have provisions to maintain entries in SM30. First one is header table which controls switch at header level. The second one is the user-level table which controls switch at user level. The technical structure is as follows.

Write an ABAP class or a function module to read the switch flag for given business scenario and user name. The logic is that when switch is set at header level then you can return with flag (that means the flag is set at global level) and if it is not set then check the user level table with scenario and user name. If the user level table has entry with a flag then return as business scenario is valid. Note that the scenario should be meant that whether the program required skipping the BADI or not.

You can execute your custom code to get switch flag in your BADI code. If the flag is set then skip the BADI code or part of logic. To deactivate a particular BADI, maintain custom table for business scenario and user. You can implement the custom switch mechanism at high level. You can define what are possible switches needed and define it. Note that you can implement these switches to any code logic, not only at BADI level.

4.5 UI Enhancements

SRM7 uses Web Dynpro applications for their UI interface. The ABAP flexibility and Web Dynpro flexibility provides option to you enhance Web Dynpro Application good extent of changes. The section 4.1 explains you what are enhancements can be done at Web Dynpro components. More than SRM7 provides more Meta data configuration to control flow data and UI changes. You need not to use all Web Dynpro flexibility to achieve those results. Based on your requirements, you can determine how much of Meta Data Configuration can be used and core Web Dynpro application flexibility. This section explains how to add Custom fields, table-like Extensions and other Web Dynpro Applications.

4.5.1 Web Dynpro Enhancement

The implicit enhancement options are pre-defined in the ABAP programs. In SRM, you can enhance your UI by FPM configuration. SRM7 uses this configuration for each SRM object. You can enhance this FPM configuration or creating new configuration to change your layout. You can use it add new actions or changes in the screen. SRM7.0 bounds all Web Dynpro applications in FPM with a complex programming logic. If you make any changes then make sure that you are not breaking any. Standard functions

Technical Challenges: The Header area of the PO document has standard document information. There are few important custom fields are required to display at Header Level.

Solution: In this solution, you need to know that how to add custom fields in the Header Area of PO document? Each SRM object does have an Identification Mapper ABAP object. For instance, PO header area uses the ABAP object /SAPSRM/CL_CH_WD_IDEN_MAP_PO. You need to enhance the method /SAPSRM/IF_CLL_MAPPER~REFRESH to add your required fields. The sample code is as follows:

```
DATA: lo_idr     TYPE REF TO if_fpm_idr,
      lo_fpm     TYPE REF TO if_fpm,
      lv_remove_item_key        TYPE i,
      lv_ev_key                 TYPE i,
     lt_myitems      TYPE TABLE OF IF_FPM_IDR=>T_ITEMS_REF,
      lv_myitems  LIKE LINE OF lt_myitems,
     lt_item_group_keys   TYPE IF_FPM_IDR=>T_ITEM_GROUP_KEYS.

* Get the FPM(Floor Plan Manager) instance
  lo_fpm = cl_fpm_factory=>get_instance( ).
  lo_idr ?= lo_fpm->get_service( cl_fpm_service_manager=>gc_key_idr ).
  CALL METHOD me->core_object->get_mo_idr(
   RECEIVING
    mo_idr1 = lo_mo_idr ).
  CALL METHOD lo_idr->get_item_group_keys
    RECEIVING
     rt_keys = lt_item_group_keys.
```

```
* Delete the window each time and start over
  LOOP AT lt_item_group_keys INTO lv_remove_item_key.
    TRY
      CALL METHOD lo_idr->remove_item_group
        EXPORTING
          iv_key = lv_remove_item_key.
     CATCH cx_fpm_idr.
    ENDTRY.
  ENDLOOP.
* Get the RFx GUID
  CALL METHOD core_object->get_task_container
   RECEIVING       ro_task_container = lo_task_container.
  CALL METHOD lo_task_container->get_bom_rfq
   RECEIVING
    ro_bom_rfq = lo_bom_rfq.
  CHECK lo_bom_rfq IS NOT INITIAL.
  CALL METHOD lo_bom_rfq->/sapsrm/if_cll_bo_mapper~get_bo_guid
   RECEIVING
    rv_bo_guid = lv_object_guid.
*  Populate lt_myitems which will be added to IDR Header Area
*  lv_myitems-label_name = ‘Label’.
*  lv_myitems-value      = ‘Value’.
*  append lv_myitems TO lt_myitems
* You can add all items to displayed at Header Area based on GUID
  CALL METHOD lo_idr->add_item_group_by_val
   EXPORTING
    it_items = lt_myitems
   IMPORTING
    ev_key   = lv_ev_key.
```

Note that if you want to create blank field then create lt_myitems with value field as initial.

4.5.2 Custom Fields

The custom fields must be configured using the IMG as defined in the previous section. The custom fields should be extended in the Web Dynpro application so you can see it in UI screen. The steps of the adding customer fields are as follows:

To add the custom field to the SRM Web Dynpro screen:

1. Identify the Screen View to add the field to. Right click on screen and click More Field Help to identify the screen name. This is explained in Chapter 1 under UI Layer section.

2. Create/Change a Screen View Enhancement.

Identify whether you are creating new enhancement or using any existing enhancement based on your technical guidelines.

3. Add the custom field to the View Context.

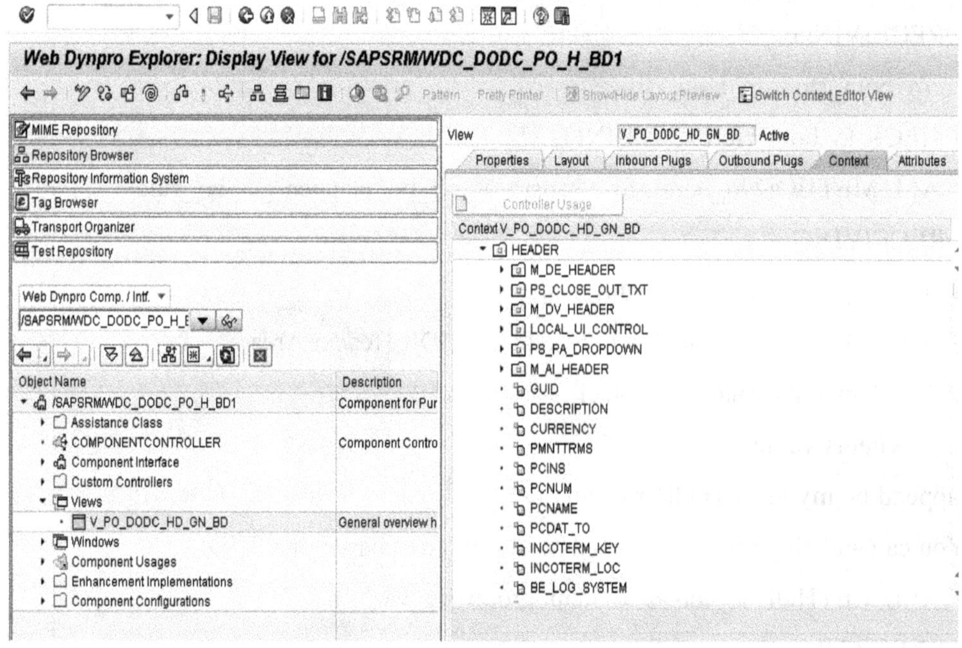

Extend the contextual by adding custom fields in the header contextual object.

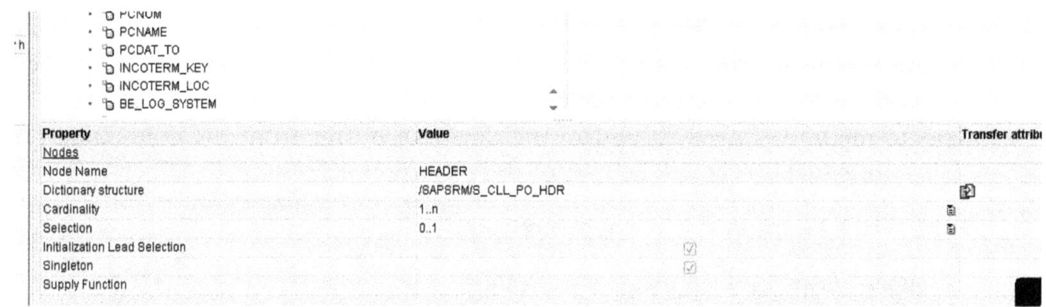

4. Add the custom field and a field label to the View Layout. You can add any tray or list of custom fields in the screen using your enhancement.

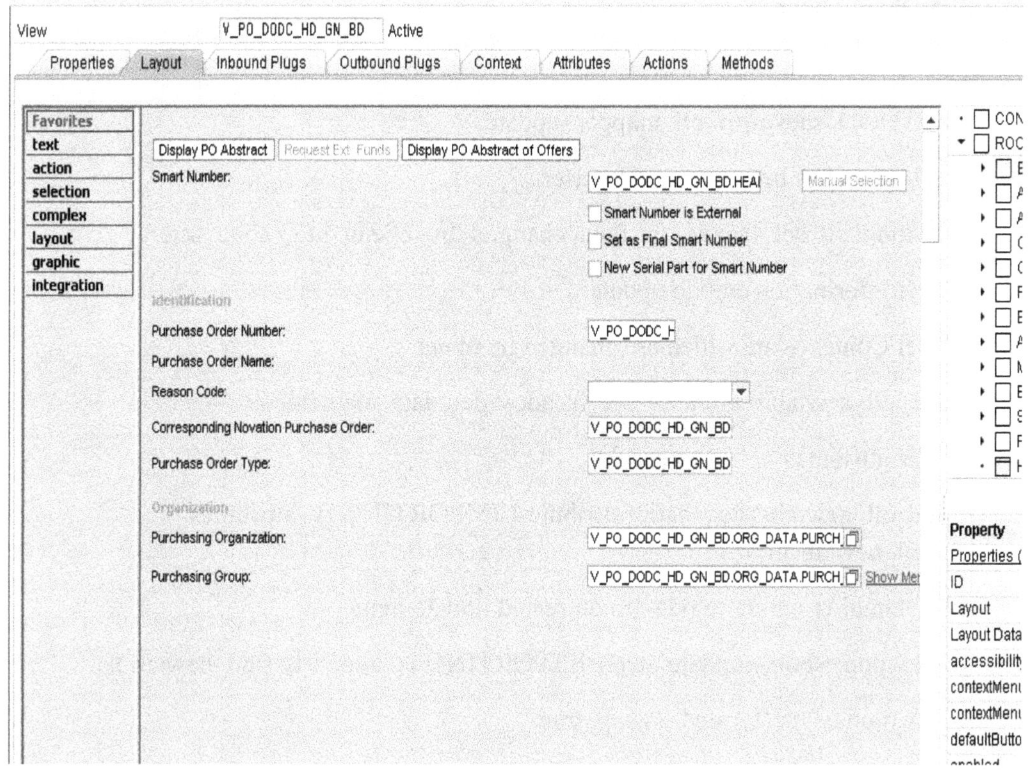

5. Link the custom fields in the screen and contextual object fields.

4.5.3 Custom Tab-strip

The table-like extension can be shown in the UI interface using a custom tab strip. The custom tab strip can be added at the header or line item level based on your table-like extension. Custom tab strip requires the following steps:

- Create your custom CLL mapper class with inheritance from /SAPSRM/CL_CH_WD_DO_MAPPER, /SAPSRM/IF_CLL_MAPPER,

/SAPSRM/IF_CLL_MAPPER_C and your own mapper interface if any. You can redefine refresh, update and add new methods to handle your data. The refresh method can be used to fetch your data and populate it into contextual object. The update method is used to update the database buffer from the contextual object. The contextual object will be part of the constructor method.

```
METHOD /sapsrm/if_cll_mapper~refresh.
  super->/sapsrm/if_cll_mapper~refresh( ).
  CALL METHOD GET_REFRESH_DETAILS( ). "Refresh Logic for your
object
ENDMETHOD.
```

```
METHOD /sapsrm/if_cll_mapper~update.
* The data has been changed by user
  IF mon_cll_set_facade->is_data_changed_by_client( ) EQ abap_true.
* Get information and do update
* Get Context-data which are changed by client
  loe_cll_newtab = mon_cll_set_facade->get_data_element( ).
* Get attributes
  loe_cll_newtab->get_static_attributes( IMPORTING rv_attributes =
ls_cll_newtab ).
*   Map ui-structure to pdo-structure and update item
    lo_pdo_<bo>->update_item( EXPORTING is_item = ls_pdo_newtab ).
   ev_update_performed = abap_true.
  ENDIF.
ENDMETHOD.
```

- Create a custom Mapper Factory interface and class to instantiate your UI context mapper. The interface class should have static GET_INSTANCE and your required methods to instantiate your tab strip CLL mapper class.

```
method ZI_CH_WD_MAP_FACTORY~GET_INSTANCE.
  IF go_factory IS INITIAL.
    CREATE OBJECT go_factory.
  ENDIF.
```

```
  rr_factory = go_factory.
endmethod.
```

Use the following sample code to instantiate your custom class.

```
method ZIFRR_CH_WD_MAP_FACTORY~CREATE_DODM_CUSTOM.
  DATA:
    lo_cll_aom_bev         TYPE REF TO /sapsrm/if_cll_aom_bev,
    lo_pdo_bid_act         TYPE REF TO /sapsrm/if_pdo_xo,
    lo_cll_dodm_bev_ca_awd  TYPE REF TO zifrr_cll_dodm_custom,
    lon_cll_set_facade      TYPE REF TO /sapsrm/if_ch_wd_set_facade.
  lo_cll_aom_bev ?= io_parent_ao_mapper.
  lo_pdo_bid_act     ?= lo_cll_aom_bev->get_pdo( ).
  CALL METHOD me-
>/sapsrm/if_ch_wd_map_factory~create_set_facade_by_pdo_xo
    EXPORTING
      ion_main_node  = ion_wd_set
      io_pdo_xo      = lo_pdo_bid_act
    RECEIVING
      ro_set_facade  = lon_cll_set_facade  .
  CREATE OBJECT lo_cll_dodm_custom  type zclrr_ch_wd_dodm_custom
    EXPORTING
      ion_cll_set_facade         = lon_cll_set_facade
      io_parent_ao_mapper        = io_parent_ao_mapper
      io_meta_init               = io_meta_init
      io_wd_view_controller      = io_wd_view_controller
      io_wd_component_controller = io_wd_component_controller .
  ro_dodm_custom = lo_cll_dodm_custom.
endmethod.
```

- Create a custom Web Dynpro application and with your business logic UI layout and logic. If your Web Dynpro application supports more than one SRM document object type like PO, Contract or Shopping Cart, then you may create a separate view for each SRM Object type. It will make coding simpler.

- Create window IV_I_FPC_CA_DETAILS and drag and drop your view on that. This window is required for extending SRM application. One more time is required to enhance Tabstrip is that implement interfaces /SAPSRM/WDI_I_FPC_CA_DTLS and /SAPSRM/WDI_L_FPC_GENERAL.
- Define the contextual object in your view based on your requirements. Try to cover all your requirements in one contextual object. We are going to pass your contextual object to a new custom CLL object. Note that your custom contextual object is passed to lon_comp_context and used in the constructor of custom CLL object. The following is the sample code for WDOINIT method.

```
* process Meta-Init
  CREATE OBJECT wd_this->mo_meta_init. "Meta_Init-Object must stored in wd_this,
because of usage in wdmodifyview
  lo_root_context_node_info = wd_context->get_node_info( ).
  wd_this->mo_meta_init->init_context(
    EXPORTING
      iv_root_context_node_info = lo_root_context_node_info ).
* collecting objects
  lon_comp_context = wd_context->get_child_node( name =
if_v_newview=>wdctx_newtab ).
  "lon_choose_awardee = lon_comp_context->get_child_node( name =
if_v_choose_awardee=>wdctx_awardee ).
  lo_wd_view_controller = wd_this->wd_get_api( ).
  lo_wd_component_controller ?= wd_comp_controller.
    lo_map_factory = zclrr_ch_wd_map_factory=>
zifrr_ch_wd_map_factory~get_instance( ).
wd_this->mo_dodm_newtab  = lo_map_factory->create_dodm_newtab(
        ion_wd_set                 = lon_comp_context
        io_wd_view_controller      = lo_wd_view_controller
        io_wd_component_controller = lo_wd_component_controller
        io_parent_ao_mapper        = wd_comp_controller->mo_aom_newtab
        io_meta_init               = wd_this->mo_meta_init    ).
* register the mapper to the component
  READ TABLE wd_comp_controller->mt_mapper
```

```
  WITH TABLE KEY mapper = wd_this->mo_dodm_newtab
  TRANSPORTING NO FIELDS.
IF sy-subrc <> 0. "add the mapper only one time (if several views use the same mapper)
  ls_mapper-mapper ?= wd_this->mo_dodm_newtab.
  INSERT ls_mapper INTO TABLE wd_comp_controller->mt_mapper.
ENDIF.
wd_this->mo_dodm_newtab->/sapsrm/if_cll_mapper~refresh( ).
```

- Identify your Web Dynpro application where you want to add the tabs-trip. Enhance or Copy Web Dynpro to add a tab-strip on Header or Item level based on your requirements.

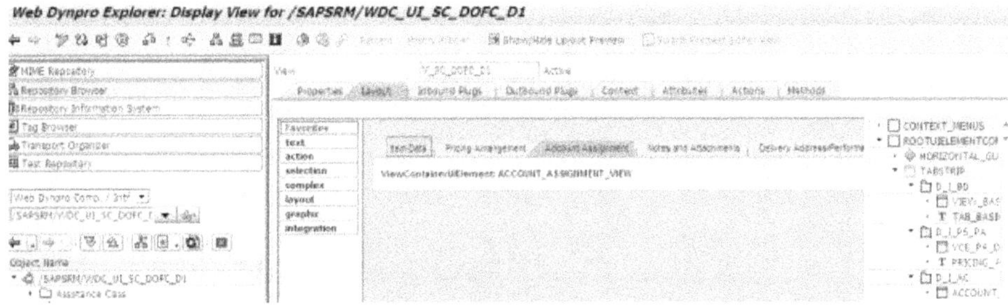

- Configure tab-strip information at view /SAPSRM/V_TS_EXT. The view maintenance can be accessed by IMG path SRM Server->Cross-Application Basic Settings->Extensions and Field Control parameters->Extensions and Field Control->Create Table Extensions and Supply with data->Configure Control of User Interface for Extension Tables. This view is used to link between the base Web Dynpro application, Tab strips and its corresponding Web Dynpro application components. The Tab Strip ID of the entry must be same as tab-strip ID of Configuration. If you are not configured this entry and tab-strip is defined in Web Dynpro configuration then you will get a navigation popup message.

Display View "Additional Tabs on Web Dynpro UI": Overview

Additional Tabs on Web Dynpro UI

Web Dynpro Component	Web Dynpro View	Tab Strip ID	Used Component	Component Usag
/SAPSRM/WDC_DOFC_CTR_H_D1	V_CTR_DOFC_HD_D1	D_H_PS_ENH_DOC_TOT	/SAPPSSRM/WDC_DO_DOC_TOT	USAGE_ENH_DOC_
/SAPSRM/WDC_DOFC_CTR_H_D1	V_CTR_DOFC_HD_D1	D_H_PS_ENH_SYNP	/SAPPSSRM/WDC_DO_SYNOPSIS	/SAPPSSRM/USE_[
/SAPSRM/WDC_DOFC_CTR_H_D1	V_CTR_DOFC_HD_D1	D_H_PS_GM_ACC	/SAPPSSRM/WDC_GM_ACC	/SAPPSSRM/USEA(
/SAPSRM/WDC_DOFC_CTR_H_D1	V_CTR_DOFC_HD_D1	D_H_PS_PAYMENT_ENH	/SAPPSSRM/WDC_DO_HD_PAYMT	USAGE_ENH_PS_P/
/SAPSRM/WDC_DOFC_CTR_H_D1	V_CTR_DOFC_HD_D1	D_H_PS_USR_STAT	/SAPPSSRM/WDC_DO_USR_STAT	USAGE_USER_STA
/SAPSRM/WDC_DOFC_CTR_I_D1	V_CTR_DOFC_ITM_D1	D_I_CPSRM_CFBP_ENH	/CPSRM/WDC_DO_IT_CFBP	USAGE_ENH_CFBP_

The static class /SAPSRM/CL_WD_TS_EXT_HELPER are used handle tab strip initialization and generating. This is part of standard SRM code. The method GET_TAB_INFO can be used to get possible Web Dynpro application and view name. Note that adding a new tab-strip can be used to add a new functionality in SRM UI document too. It will follow all steps above defined and redefining update method may not be required.

4.6 Summary

In this chapter, you have learned basics of enhancement framework, database level changes, MDF concepts, document BADI and UI enhancements. The chapter will help you to enhance SRM7 system.

All master data is available locally in SRM. This data includes Product Master Records, Business Partner Master Records and Product Categories.

5 Master Data

Master data is information that is key information to operation of the business. Master data is data that can be reused in the transaction processing. Most of business transactions can be automated if proper master data is pre-maintained. SRM Master Data includes Product master data, Business partner Master data, Product Category and Locations. Business Partner master Correspond to Vendor Master Records in R/3 System. In SRM, the business partners refer more than the vendor. Business partner has multiple partner roles. Both materials and services are considered as products. Materials can be distinguished from Services by product type. Product categories correspond to the material group in the back-end system.

This chapter explains details of Business partner and its technical orientation, material mater replication process, Vendor Synchronization, Product Categories and plant locations.

5.1 Business Partner

SRM uses the SAP Business Partner component. The BP component enables you to create and manage business partners centrally. The BP can be categorized into business partner category individual, group or organization. You can maintain or view the business partner using the transaction BP. An internal or external Business Partner is created in SRM for every person, organization or group of people that could be involved in a business transaction.

Within the context of a SRM transaction (a PO or BID Invitation) Business Partners can adopt various partner function. Business Partners aggregate the master data of a person, organization or a group of people. Table BUT000 is the base table for a Business partner. The table represents the business partner's general data. You can list out all business partner tables by prefix BUT0*.

The business partner is highly flexible and complex designed technical component. Note that change document techniques are used in the business partner. You can view all changes made on a business partner.

SRM uses business partners in multiple partner roles like Bidder, Vendor, Contact, etc. The following table lists the possible partner function used in the SRM system.

Function	Description	Abbrev	Created By
00000016	Requester	RQ	SAP
00000017	Contact Person	CP	SAP
00000018	Bidder	BI	SAP
00000019	Vendor	VD	SAP
00000020	Goods Recipient	GR	SAP
00000025	Portal Provider	PP	SAP
00000026	Responsible Employee	RE	SAP
00000027	Ship-To Address	DP	SAP
00000029	Invoice Recipient	IR	SAP
00000030	Invoicing Party	IP	SAP
00000034	Ship-From Address	SP	SAP
00000038	Plant	PLNT	SAP
00000039	Sold-to Party	ORDR	SAP
00000901	Load Port Terminal	ZLPT	Customer
00000902	Offshore Port	ZOP	Customer
00000903	Discharge Port	ZDP	Customer

Business partners are categorized into Internal and External business partners. The following functions require external partner integration with SRM system.

- Enter Bids
- Enter Invoices
- Confirm goods delivery

The following tables having SRM related tables associated with BP.

Table Name	Description

BBPM_BUT_FRG0010	General BBP Admin data
BBPM_BUT_FRG0011	General BBP data
BBPM_BUT_FRG0020	Bidder BBP Admin data
BBPM_BUT_FRG0021	Bidder BBP data
BBPM_BUT_FRG0030	Quality standard BBP Admin data
BBPM_BUT_FRG0031	Quality standard BBP data
BBPM_BUT_FRG0040	Accepted payment card Admin data
BBPM_BUT_FRG0041	Accepted payment card data
BBPM_BUT_FRG0060	BBP Purchasing Admin data
BBPM_BUT_FRG0061	BBP Purchasing data

5.1.1 External Business Partner

Business Partners with vendor or Bidder Roles are created in the Organizational structure underneath the central organizational unit for a Vendor or Bidder. For every external employee of a Vendor or Bidder, a contact person is created in addition to the Business Partner for that company.

Technical Challenge: When a Business Partner is converted to Bidder, SRM creates a vendor in the back-end (ECC). The challenge is that extend the Vendor to a Purchase Organization and Company Code.

Solution: When a Self Service Supplier is approved as Bidder, standard SAP creates the Supplier as a Business Partner back-end ECC and creates the Vendor at the Client Level. The challenge is to extend this Business Partner to a Company Code and Purchasing Organization as well as creating additional roles for this Business Partner (Custom roles to extend Business Partner as Central Vendor and Freight Vendor).

The solution can be implemented using the following BADIs.

- BADI BUPA_ROLES_UPDATE
- BADI BUPA_INBOUND

Using BUPA_INBOUND BADI, create the additional roles FLVN00 and FLVN01.

Name: BUPA_INBOUND	Multiple Use: Yes	Filter:No
Description: This BADI will add the tow custom Roles to the Business Partner, when it is created in ECC from SRM. Technical name of the Role and Role category will be required during the conversion		

Method: CHECK_BEFORE_INBOUND

Description: Add the custom roles in this method

Parameters:

Name	**Type**	**Data Type**	**Description**
IV_PARTNER	Import	BU_PARTNER	Business Partner
IV_PARTNERGUID	Import	BU_PARTNER_GUID	BP Guid
IV_OBJECTTASK	Import	BUS_EI_OBJECT_TASK	External Interface: Change Indicator Object
C_BP_CENTRAL_DATA	Change	BUS_EI_CENTRAL_DATA	External central data

Sample code:

```
DATA: WA_DATA TYPE BUS_EI_CENTRAL_DATA.
DATA: EA_ROLE TYPE BUS_EI_ROLES.
DATA: IT_ROLES TYPE TABLE OF BUS_EI_BUPA_ROLES.
DATA: WA_ROLES TYPE BUS_EI_BUPA_ROLES.
IT_ROLES = C_BP_CENTRAL_DATA-ROLE-ROLES.
LOOP AT IT_ROLES INTO WA_ROLES WHERE DATA_KEY =
'BBP000'.
  WA_ROLES-DATA_KEY = 'FLVN00'.
  WA_ROLES-DATA-ROLECATEGORY = 'FLVN00'.
  APPEND WA_ROLES TO IT_ROLES.
  WA_ROLES-DATA_KEY = 'FLVN01'.
  WA_ROLES-DATA-ROLECATEGORY = 'FLVN01'.
  APPEND WA_ROLES TO IT_ROLES.
ENDLOOP.
C_BP_CENTRAL_DATA-ROLE-ROLES = IT_ROLES.
```

Name: BUPA_ROLES_UPDATE	Multiple Use: Yes	Filter: No
Description: This BADI will create the Vendor by reading the roles parameter from FM memory. The actual Vendor creation was implemented using Idocs, since there is no BAPI is available to create Vendors in ECC. Note that BADI will be called on commit subroutine.		

Method: CHANGE_BEFORE_UPDATE ***Description***: Add the custom roles in this method. The program will only pass the GUID and need use the callback routine to retrieve the information. Parameters:

Name	**Type**	**Data Type**	**Description**
IT_CHANGED_INSTANCES	Import	BU_PARTNER_GUID_T	

Sample code:

```
data: l_bp       type BAPIBUS1006_HEAD-BPARTNER,
      lt_return  type table of bapiret2,
      l_return   type bapiret2,
      lt_bproles type table of BAPIBUS1006_BPROLES,
       l_bproles type BAPIBUS1006_BPROLES.
  data: lv_bp_guid type guid,
      lv_fm_guid type BU_PARTNER_GUID_BAPI.
  data: p_bpguid  type BU_PARTNER_GUID_T.
  data: l_bprolecategory type BAPIBUS1006_BPROLES-
PARTNERROLECATEGORY,
      lall_businesspartnerroles type BAPIBUS1006_X-MARK,
      l_DIFFTYPEVALUE type BAPIBUS1006_BPROLES-
DIFFTYPEVALUE,
      l_validfromdate type BAPIBUS1006_BPROLE_VALIDITY-
BPROLEVALIDFROM,
      l_validuntildate type BAPIBUS1006_BPROLE_VALIDITY-
BPROLEVALIDTO value '99991231',
      l_iv_x_save      type BAPI4001_1-SAVE_ADDR VALUE ' '.


  data: lt_vbut100 type table of vbut100,
      lt_oldbut100 type table of vbut100,
       L_VBUT100 TYPE VBUT100.
****************************************************************
  p_bpguid = it_changed_instances.
  loop at p_bpguid into lv_bp_guid.
```

```
  exit.
 endloop.
*Get BP Number from GUID
 check not p_bpguid is initial.
 lv_fm_guid = lv_bp_guid.

 CALL FUNCTION 'BAPI_BUPA_GET_NUMBERS'
  EXPORTING
   BUSINESSPARTNERGUID          = lv_fm_guid
  IMPORTING
   BUSINESSPARTNEROUT           = l_bp
  TABLES
   RETURN                       = lt_return.
 check lt_return[] is initial.
* Use callback program to retrieve the information
 CALL FUNCTION 'BUP_MEMORY_BUT100_GET'
   EXPORTING
    IV_PARTNER          = l_bp
*    IV_DATE            =
   TABLES
    ET_BUT100           = lt_vbut100
    ET_BUT100_OLD       = lt_oldbut100
  EXCEPTIONS
   NOT_FOUND            = 1
   PARAMETER_ERROR      = 2
   OTHERS               = 3.
 IF SY-SUBRC <> 0.
* MESSAGE ID SY-MSGID TYPE SY-MSGTY NUMBER SY-MSGNO
*        WITH SY-MSGV1 SY-MSGV2 SY-MSGV3 SY-MSGV4.
 ENDIF.
 check lt_return[] is initial.
```

```
*Cannot add any role without BP0000 Being in there
 loop at lt_vbut100 into l_vbut100 where rltyp = 'BBP000'.
 endloop.
 IF SY-SUBRC NE 0.
   EXIT.
 ENDIF.
*l_bproles-partnerrole = 'ZCNTVX'.  "Add logic here to select appropriate role
clear L_vbut100-rltyp.
*Create BP on Company code/Purch. org at this point
* This is a custom function module to create the Business partners.
 CALL FUNCTION 'ZF_BP_CREATE_VENDOR_ORG'
   EXPORTING
     P_BP                   = l_bp
   EXCEPTIONS
     VENDOR_NOT_FOUND          = 1
     VENDOR_EXISTS_COMPANY_CODE = 2
     VENDOR_EXISTS_PURCH_ORG    = 3
     VENDOR_NOT_EXTENDED        = 4
     OTHERS                    = 5.
 IF SY-SUBRC <> 0.
* MESSAGE ID SY-MSGID TYPE SY-MSGTY NUMBER SY-MSGNO
*         WITH SY-MSGV1 SY-MSGV2 SY-MSGV3 SY-MSGV4.
 ENDIF.
```

5.1.2 Internal Business Partner

The internal business partners are created for the Organizational Unit or employee of the organizational structure (with the exception of location). When a Business Partner is created for an employee, this Business Partner is assigned to the relevant organizational unit within the organizational structure.

The following Partner functions exist for an Internal Business Partner

- Requester - Employee in a company that requests a requirement. A requirement coverage request can also be created on behalf of another employee

- Purchasing company - Company that uses *Enterprise Buyer* for procurement
- Goods recipient - Employee in a company that confirms goods receipt or performance of service
- Location - Business partner that represents a delivery address or an R/3 plant
- Ship-to address - Delivery address of a company to where the goods are delivered
- Invoice recipient - Business partner to whom the invoice is sent
- Employee responsible - Employee in the company who is responsible for the contract

5.1.3 Replication

You can replicate the supplier master from back-end system to the SRM system. This is mandatory when you want to use existing supplier master in the system. Before replicate supplier master, make sure that supplier is assigned to a purchasing organization at back-end system and same purchase organization is configured in SRM organizational plan. The business partner grouping must be defined and configured in number range interval.

You can replicate the supplier master data by executing the transaction BBPGETVD (or report BBP_VENDOR_GET_DATA) at SRM system. Note that you can update the supplier data after it is transferred. You must exercise the data integrity between systems.

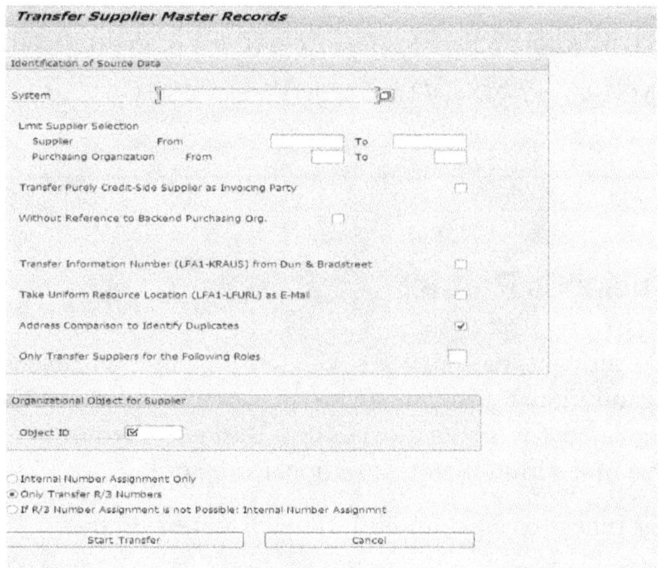

You can use the report BBP_NONR3_PARTNER_UPLOAD to upload the data from Non-SAP system. You must implement BBP_NONR3_PARTNER to get partner data.

You can compare vendor master records using the transaction BBPUDDVD. You can synchronize the back-end system suppliers with SRM by executing the program BBP_VENDOR_SYNC. You can schedule this program at background jobs. The synchronization program uses the function modules BBP_VENDOR_GET_UPDATE and BBP_VENDOR_GET_NON_BAPI to update the vendor master.

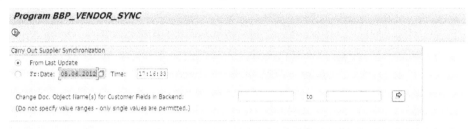

Program BBP_VENDOR_SYNC

Carry Out Supplier Synchronization

From Last Update

Fr:Date: 05.06.2012 Time: 17:16:33

Change Doc. Object Name(s) for Customer Fields in Backend: to

(Do not specify value ranges - only single values are permitted.)

Enhancements

The following enhancements are at BP level.

- BBP_TRANSDATA_PREP - The BADI is used to change vendor data before it saves in
- BBP_GET_VMDATA_CF - The BADI is used to replicate Customer fields
- BBP_SEND_MEDIUM_MODE - The BADI can change the default medium.
- BBP_NONR3_PARTNER

You can use the report BBP_UPDATE_PARTNER_PROT to modify standard communication type of external business partners.

5.1.4 Editing Addresses

A number of addresses can be created and managed for a business partner. The following address types are available:

- Ordering address - address where purchase goes
- Ship-from address - address where goods are sent from
- Ship-to address - address where the goods are delivered
- Invoicing party address - address where the invoice is sent
- Invoicing recipient address -address where the invoicing party sends the invoice.

- Goods recipient address - address of the receiving party.

Enhancements

- BUPA_ADDR_CHECK - Additional Checks for Business Partner addresses
- BUPA_ADDR_EXPORT - SAP BP: Exports Address references (BUT020)
- BUPA_ADDR_IMPORT- SAP BP: Imports Address references (BUT020)
- BUPA_ADDR_UPDATE - Business Partner Addresses
- BUPA_ADDRDUPL_ADDFIELDS - BADI for additional fields on Address

5.2 Product Master

The product master is stored locally in the SRM system. The product master is in SRM system is a subset of the ECC system. SRM supports only purchasing view compare to ECC has a lot of extended views of the material master. You can maintain the data integrity between SRM and ECC system by replicate the material data from ECC to SRM. The replication process will move only purchasing view from ECC system. You can maintain the product master using the transactions COMMPR01 and the COMM_HIERARCHY.

5.2.1 Product Master Extension

When you enhance the material master's purchasing view in ECC system then you must to enhance the product master in SRM. So, the replication process will fetch the additional fields from ECC to SRM. In this section, we are discussing how to enhance the product master at SRM system.

Attributes and Set Types

The additional custom fields are referred to attributes. The attributes can be assigned to a set type. The set type is used to grouping the attributes. You can create set types for material and/or service. You can use the transaction COMM_ATTRSET to create attributes and set types. You can create a transport request for the set types you crated. Make sure that *Create API Append* flag is set. For each set type, there is a corresponding DB table created automatically. Make sure that they do not associate more than 20 attributes.

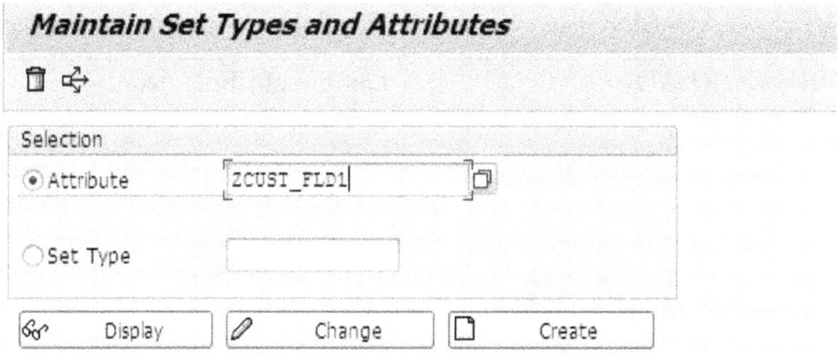

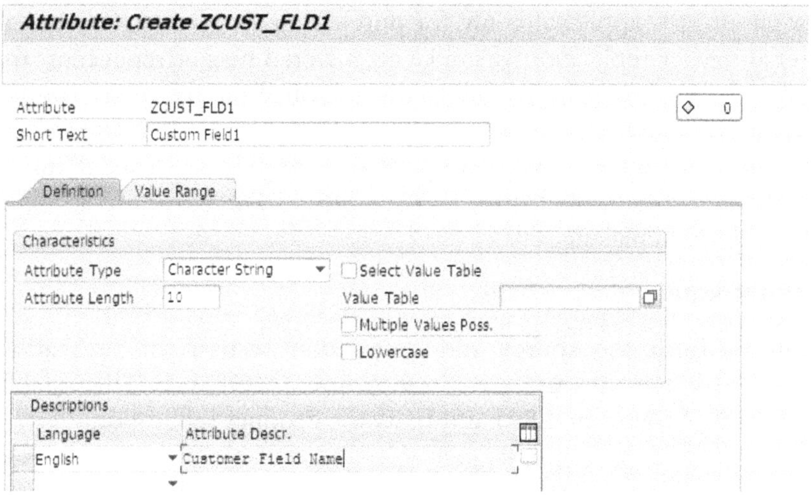

You must assign the set types to the categories in hierarchy and category maintenance. You can use the transaction code COMM_HIERARCHY to do this. SRM provides hierarchy R3MATCLASS for the purchasing application and R3PRODSTYP for the product application. Make sure that the set type table structure is in the structure COMT_PROD_MAT_MAINTAIN_API. The COMMPR01 transaction will display assigned new set types automatically.

You can assign the hierarchy ID to an application in IMG configuration. IMG path is Cross-Application Components->SAP Product->Product Category->Assign Category Hierarchies to Applications.

The important function modules related to product, categories and set types.

Function Module	Description
COM_PROD_CAT_REL_READ_WITH_PR	Get all categories for given product GUID
COM_CAT_FRAG_REL_READ	Get all related set types defined for a given category GUID

COM_SETTYPE_READ_SINGLE	Get Set type information
COM_ATTRIBUTE_READ	Get the attribute detail

5.2.2 Material Master Replication

Material master replication is to replicate the material master from ECC to SRM system. The replication is applicable only for purchasing view of ECC material master. Note that material master replication is similar to material master replication from ECC to CRM. A single initial download is used to download all the required materials. Delta replication is triggered automatically when you change any changes and new materials created in SAP ERP. You can configure IMG TO replicate material master. The custom fields can be also replicated from ECC to SRM. The custom field replication is discussed in the technical challenges.

Define Sites (SRM side)

You can establish the source and destination system for replication in site definition. You can define sites using the transaction SMOEAC. This establishes the communication channels between SRM and ECC for Product replication.

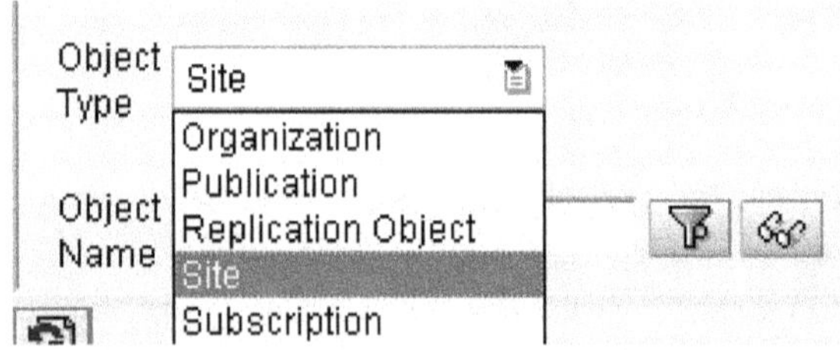

SRM Adapter Setup

In this step, you can establish the material master data and filter setup related to the replication. If certain materials need to be skipped, filters are setup in this transaction to ensure that only procurement specific materials are replicated. This can be done using the transaction R3AC1.

Adapter Object Overview

Tables In-/Active

Business Adapter Objects

Name	Description	Inactive	Filter Settings	Assign Object Class
MATERIAL	R/3 Material Master			

The only customer specific activity needed is the setup of filters for material replication. Ensure that the object data contains Material related information as shown below. Switch to tab 'Filter Settings' for setup any filters for the material replication process.

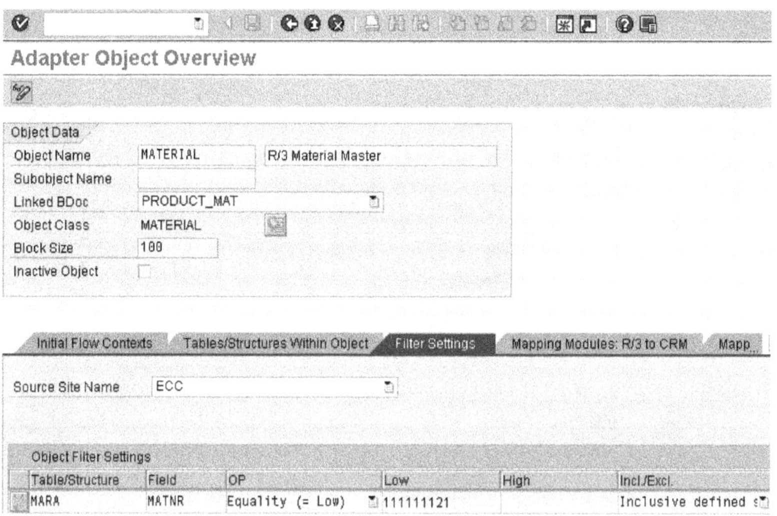

Middleware Setup

The material master data is transferred using the middleware. The SRM uses middleware object BBP_MATERIAL.

- Using transaction SM30, check and maintain table CRMCONSUM in ECC if necessary. The consumer must match SMOEAC entry made in preivous step for SRM.

User	Active	Description	Q Prefix
CRM	X	SRM Connection	R3A

- Add following entries to table CRMSUBTAB using the transaction SM30 (Subscription table for up and download object)

User	Object Name	U/D	Obj. Class	Function	Obj Type	Func.Name
CRM	Empty	Download	Material	Empty	Empty	CRS_MATERIAL_EXTRACT
CRM	Empty	Download	Material	Empty	Empty	CRS_CUSTOMIZING_EXTRACT
CRM	Empty	Download	Material	Empty	Empty	CRS_SERVICE_EXTRACT

- Add the following entries to table CRMRFCPAR for definitions of RFC Connections and add following values

User	Object Name	Destination	Load Type	INFO	InQueue Flag	Send XML
CRM	*	SR1CLNT300	Initial Download	SR1CLNT300	X	SEND xml
CRM	*	SR1CLNT300	Request	SR1CLNT300	X	SEND xml
CRM	MATERIAL	SR1CLNT300	Delta Download	SR1CLNT300	X	SEND xml

- Configure filter for the material master

Parameter Name	Parameter Name2	Param Name3	User	Param Value	Param Value2
CRM_FILTER_ACTIVE	MATERIAL	Empty	CRM	X	

- Edit the table for application indicator. Transaction SE16N on R/3 and select table TBE11. Add application component BC-MID and edit activity settings (field active = 'X')

- Generate Repository objects

- With this procedure, generate middle ware function modules (BDoc Object type) for the material master. Transaction SMOGGEN and chose object PRODUCT_MAT and PRODUCT_SRV. Generate services for all object categories

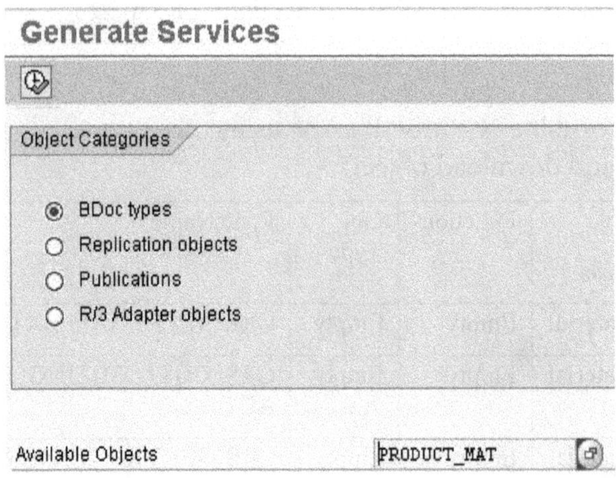

- Run the transaction R3AS to initial download. You can monitor load objects using the transaction R3AM1.

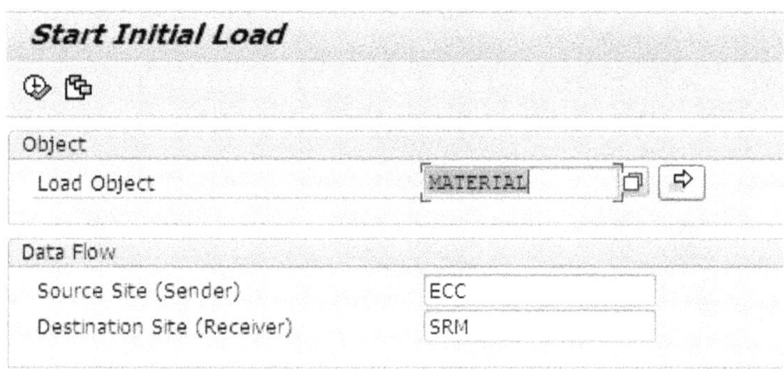

Utilities

SRM provides a number of utilities to monitor the status of the material master replication process.

Monitor Load Objects - You can execute the transaction R3AM1 to view the utility.

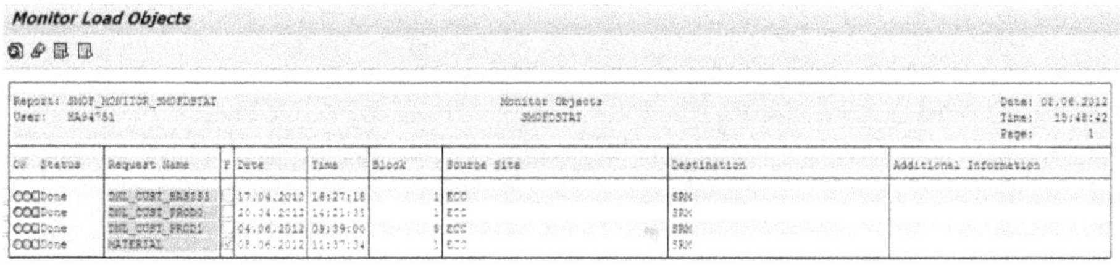

Middleware settings - The transaction BBP_PRODUCT_SETTINGS can be executed to view all middleware settings for SRM systems. This transaction is available at the SRM side.

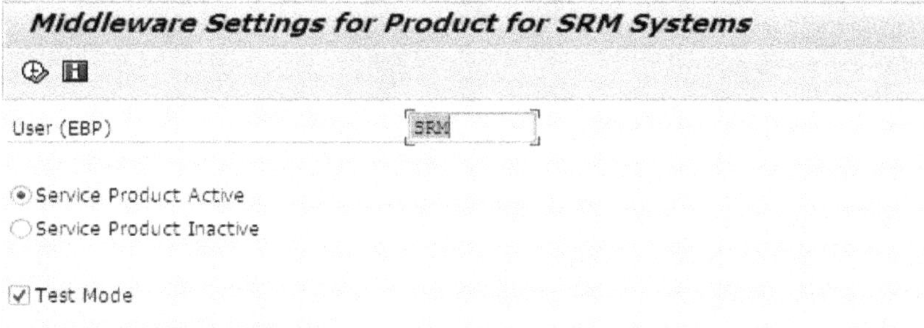

Middleware Settings for Product for SRM Systems

```
Middleware Settings for Product for SRM Systems

Settings Log:                         EBP Without CRM
             ***** Test Mode *****

Set Middleware Objects to Active/Inactive
All Business Objects Except MATERIAL and DNL_PLANT Will Be Set to Inactive
All Customizing Objects Except DNL_CUST_PROD0/_PROD1 Will Be Set to Inactive
All Condition Objects Will Be Set to Inactive
Objects SERVICE_MASTER and DNL_CUST_SRVMAS Will Also Be Activated

User of Download Objects Will Be Adjusted (Table SMOFINICON)

Object:      MATERIAL
Following Tables Will Be Deactivated:
  MARC
  MLAN
  MVKE
  STXH
  STXL

Object:      DNL_CUST_PROD1
Following Tables Will Be Deactivated:
  T179
  T179T

Middleware Objects Will Be Regenerated


EBP Will Be Flagged As Active Application (Table SMOFAPPL)
CRM Will Be Flagged As Inactive Application (Table SMOFAPPL)


Customizing Indicator 'Multiple-Backends' Set (Table COMC_HIERARCHY)
```

Middleware Monitoring Cockpit - You can execute the transaction SMWP to view the CRM middleware monitoring cockpit. The monitor cockpit provides you the status information and access to important administration and monitoring activities. Traffic light indicates the status of individual entries. The main nodes are General information, Runtime information, System settings, Monitoring tools/statistics and Background jobs.

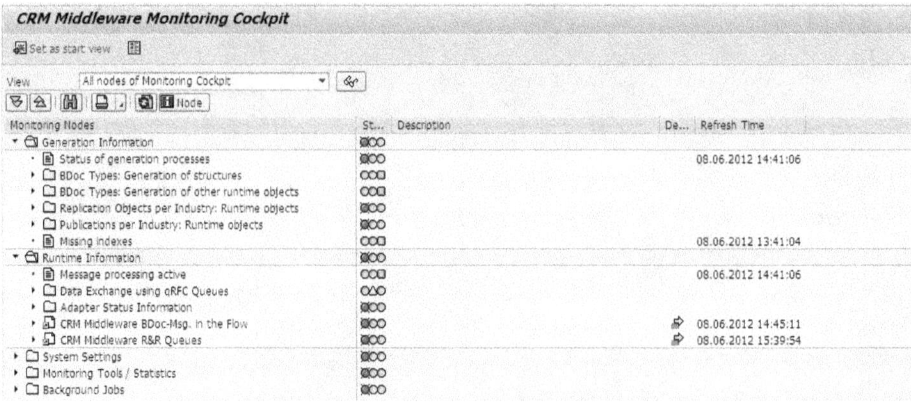

Technical Challenges: Replicate the material master with custom fields.

Solution: This is a multi-steps solution. You need to implement changes at both ECC and SRM sides. You need to extend the product master in SRM as defined in the previous section.

ECC Side Development

- Create the function module ZF_EXIT_MAT_OLTP with the following parameter interfaces:

```
• *"*"Local Interface:
• *"  TABLES
• *"     T_INT_TABLES STRUCTURE  BAPIMTCS
• *"     T_BAPISTRUCT STRUCTURE  BAPIMTCS
• *"     T_MESSAGES STRUCTURE  BAPICRMMSG
• *"     T_OTHER_INFO STRUCTURE  BAPIEXTC
```

- Sample Code: You have to populate T_OTHER_INFO table in this function module. The BAPIEXTC has four fields with 250 characters long. You need to use it wisely. The general practice is that use first field for key information and next three for data. This table has been interpreted in the SRM system.

```
FIELD-SYMBOLS:
 <source_x> TYPE x,
 <target_x> TYPE x.
DATA:
  ls_mara TYPE mara,
  ls_marm TYPE marm,
  ls_mvke TYPE mvke,
  ls_marc TYPE marc.
** Begin of Mapping
LOOP AT t_int_tables WHERE tabname = 'MARA'.
  ASSIGN ls_mara TO <target_x> CASTING.
  ASSIGN t_int_tables-data TO <source_x> CASTING.
  IF <source_x> IS ASSIGNED AND
     <target_x> IS ASSIGNED.
    <target_x> = <source_x>.
  ENDIF.
```

```
    ls_mara_key-struc_name = 'MARA'.
    ls_mara_key-matnr = ls_mara-matnr.
    ls_mara_data-zzfld1 = ls_mara-zzfld1.
    ls_mara_data-zzfld2 = ls_mara-zzfld2.
    t_other_info-field1 = ls_mara_key.
    t_other_info-field2 = ls_mara_data.
    APPEND t_other_info.
  ENDLOOP.
```

- Create function module which establish the connection between ECC R3 adapter and the function module created in the previous step. You can copy the function module SAMPLE_PROCESS_CRM0_200.

```
*"*"Local Interface:
*"  IMPORTING
*"     VALUE(I_OBJ_CLASS) LIKE  BAPICRMOBJ-OBJCLASS
*"     VALUE(I_OBJ_NAME) LIKE  BAPICRMOBJ-OBJ_NAME
*"     VALUE(I_BAPICRMDH2) LIKE  BAPICRMDH2 STRUCTURE  BAPI
CRMDH2
*"     REFERENCE(I_KEYWORD_IN) LIKE  CRM_PARA-KEYWORD_IN
*"     REFERENCE(I_CRMRFCPAR) LIKE  CRMRFCPAR STRUCTURE  C
RMRFCPAR
*"  EXPORTING
*"     REFERENCE(E_DO_NOT_SEND) LIKE  CRM_PARA-XFELD
*"  TABLES
*"      T_INT_TABLES STRUCTURE  BAPIMTCS
*"      T_BAPISTRUCT STRUCTURE  BAPIMTCS
*"      T_MESSAGES STRUCTURE  BAPICRMMSG
*"      T_KEY_INFO STRUCTURE  BAPICRMKEY
*"      T_BAPIIDLIST STRUCTURE  BAPIIDLIST
*"      T_OTHER_INFO STRUCTURE  BAPIEXTC
*"  CHANGING
*"     REFERENCE(C_BAPICRMDH2) LIKE  BAPICRMDH2 STRUCTURE
BAPICRMDH2
*"     REFERENCE(C_RFCDEST) LIKE  CRMRFCPAR STRUCTURE  CRM
```

```
RFCPAR
*"    REFERENCE(C_OBJNAME) LIKE  BAPICRMOBJ-OBJ_NAME
```

Sample Code:

```
CASE i_obj_name.
  WHEN 'MATERIAL'.
    CALL FUNCTION 'ZF_EXIT_MAT_OLTP'
      TABLES
        t_int_tables = t_int_tables
        t_bapistruct = t_bapistruct
        t_messages   = t_messages
        t_other_info = t_other_info.
ENDCASE.
```

- Create an entry in the table TPS34 using the transaction SM30.

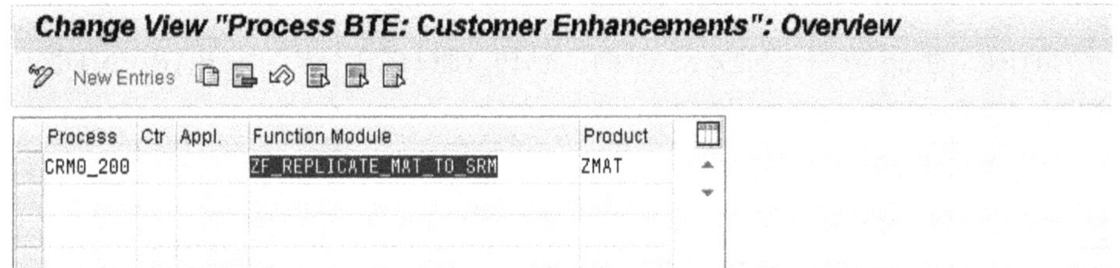

- Create an entry in the table TBE24 using the transaction SM30.

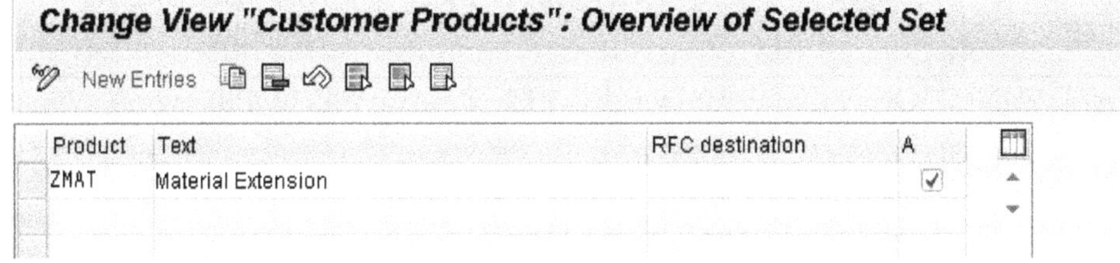

SRM Side Development

- Implement the BADI PRODUCT_CUSTOMER2.

Name: *PRODUCT_CUSTOMER2*	Multiple Use: No	Filter:No
Description: *The BADI PRODUCT_CUSTOMER2 is executed when the R/3 data is unpacked and mapped to CRM structures in R/3 adapters of the SRM system.*		
Method: ***MAP_R3_TO_CRM_MATERIAL*** Description: Mapping of Material Master Data to Generic Set Types		

Parameters:			
Name	**Type**	**Data Type**	**Description**
IS_MARA	Import	BBPS_BAPIMATMRA	MARA structure
IT_MAKT	Import	BBPT_BAPIMATMKT_TAB	Mat. Text
IT_MARM	Import	BBPT_BAPIMATMRM_TAB	MARM structure
IT_MARC	Import	BBPT_BAPIMATMRC_TAB	MARC structure
IT_MARD	Import	BBPT_BAPIMATMRD_TAB	MARD structure
IT_MVKE	Import	BBPT_BAPIMATMVK_TAB	MVKE structure
IT_MLAN	Import	BBPT_BAPIMATMLN_TAB	MLAN structure
IT_MEAN	Import	BBPT_BAPIMATMEN_TAB	MEAN structure
IT_MBEW	Import	BBPT_BAPIMATMBW_TAB	MBEW structure
IT_LONGT EXT	Import	COMT_PRLGTEXT_MAINT AIN_TAB	Long text
IT_OTHER _INFO	Import	CND_MAPTT_BAPI_OTHER _INFO	TT for BAPIEXTC
EV_ERRO R	Export	COMT_BOOLEAN	Error Flag
ET_BAPIR ETURN	Export	BAPIRET2_TAB	Error Message
CS_PRODU CT_BDOC	Change	COMT_PROD_MATERIAL_ BDOC	API Material Data Structure

```
CALL FUNCTION 'COM_PROD_CAT_REL_READ_WITH_PR'
  EXPORTING
    iv_product_guid  = cs_product_bdoc-header-com_product-product_guid
    iv_update_buffer = space
  IMPORTING
    et_set           = lt_categories.
LOOP AT cs_product_bdoc-header-categories INTO ls_category_bdoc.
  MOVE-CORRESPONDING ls_category_bdoc-data TO ls_category.
  READ TABLE lt_categories WITH KEY hierarchy_guid = ls_category-
hierarchy_guid TRANSPORTING NO FIELDS.
  IF sy-subrc = 0.
    MODIFY lt_categories FROM ls_category INDEX sy-tabix.
```

```
    ELSE.
      APPEND ls_category TO lt_categories.
    ENDIF.
  ENDLOOP.
  LOOP AT lt_categories INTO ls_category.
    CALL FUNCTION 'COM_CAT_FRAG_REL_READ'
      EXPORTING
        iv_category_guid = ls_category-category_guid
      IMPORTING
        et_cat_frag_rel  = lt_cat_settype_rel
      EXCEPTIONS
        wrong_call       = 1
        OTHERS           = 2.
    IF sy-subrc = 0.
      APPEND LINES OF lt_cat_settype_rel TO i_cat_settype_rel_all.
    ENDIF.
  ENDLOOP.
DELETE ADJACENT DUPLICATES FROM lt_cat_settype_rel.
***** Custom Fields from R/3 MM
  LOOP AT it_other_info INTO ls_other_info
    WHERE   field1+20(40) = is_mara-material.
***** Key fields are in field1 column
    ASSIGN ls_other_info-field1 TO <fssource_x> CASTING.
    ASSIGN ls_mat_info TO <fstarget_x> CASTING.
    IF <fssource_x> IS ASSIGNED
   AND <fstarget_x> IS ASSIGNED.
      <fstarget_x> = <fssource_x>.
    ELSE.
      CONTINUE.
    ENDIF.
    CASE ls_mat_info-struc_name.
```

```
  WHEN 'MARA'.
   LOOP AT lt_cat_settype_rel_all
     INTO ls_cat_settype_rel.
    CALL FUNCTION 'COM_SETTYPE_READ_SINGLE'
     EXPORTING
      iv_settype_guid  = ls_cat_settype_rel-frgtype_guid
     IMPORTING
      es_settype       = ls_settype
     EXCEPTIONS
      not_found        = 1
      no_import_values = 2
      no_text_found    = 3.
    CASE ls_settype-frgtype_id.
     WHEN 'ZR_SETTYPE1'.
*Populate all values of settype.  Update settype and data
      APPEND ls_settype-frgtype_id TO cs_product_bdoc-data-mnt_settype.
    APPEND ls_zr_settype1 TO cs_product_bdoc-data-zr_settype1.
    ENDCASE.
   ENDLOOP.
  WHEN 'MVKE'.
 ENDCASE.
ENDLOOP.
```

5.3 Organization Management

Organization management is one of the core components of SRM. SRM relies on organizational structure hierarchy for SRM users for their day to day activities. The organizational plan is a representation of the task-related, functional structure of your enterprise. You can access the organization management IMG using the path SRM Server->Cross-Application Basic Settings->Organization management. The transactions are PPOCA_BBP (create organizational plan), PPOMA_BBP (change organizational plan) and PPOSA_BBP (display organizational plan).

The organization structure is a representation of the reporting structure and the distribution tasks using organizational units. The root organization unit is the highest organizational structure. SRM maintains three types of organization structure.

- SRM Organization structure - is structure used by the employee and HR organizational plan. This can be maintained manually or replicated from ECC HR organization structure. SRM workflow uses organization structure to determine which agents are responsible for approving procurement documents.
- Vendor Organization structure - is org structure for vendor groups and vendors. The vendor org structure can be accessed by the transaction code PPOMV_BBP. You can maintain vendor organization as a part of business partner replication from ECC to SRM.
- Purchasing Organization structure - is the hierarchy of various purchasing departments and groups in the enterprise. Two major organization units are purchasing organization and purchasing group. The purchasing organization is highest organizational unit for purchasing organization structure. The purchasing group organizational units are created when we have purchase organization in back-end system.

Object Types

Object type is a grouping of the object in the org structure. The object type and object ID form unique identification of org structure. SRM supports the following object types:

- Org Unit - represents various unit of the enterprise. This is represented by object type 'O'.
- Position - are organization specific. A number of positions can be based on the same job. As a general rule, each position represents only one employee. This is represented by 'S'.
- Central Person - are objects which hold the position. This is represented by 'CP'.

Attributes

Each object can have a number of attributes. These attributes are inherited based on the relationships. You can define attributes at position or organization unit level. The attributes are stored in the table T77OMATTR and you maintain attributes using transaction SM30.

SRM supports only one scenario BBP. You can associate attributes to scenario and object types. These attributes will be displayed in the organization structure.

Display View "Attributes": Overview

Dialog Structure
- Attributes
- Scenarios
  - Attributes/Scenario
  - Object Types

Attributes

Attribute	Description	Area	Multi-val	Default vals a...	Table	Field
ACC_CMITEM	Commitment Item	☐	☑	☑	BBP_ATTR_F1	ACC_CMITEM
ACC_FCAREA	Funct. Area	☐	☑	☑	BBP_ATTR_F1	ACC_FCAREA
ACC_FCENTR	Funds Center	☐	☑	☑	BBP_ATTR_F1	ACC_FCENTR
ACC_FUND	Fund	☐	☑	☑	BBP_ATTR_F1	ACC_FUND
ACC_GRANT	Grant	☐	☑	☑	BBP_ATTR_F1	ACC_GRANT
ACS	System Alias for Account...	☐	☐	☐	BBP_ATTR_F1	ACS
ADDR_BILLT	Invoice Recipient Address	☐	☑	☑	BBP_ATTR_F1	ADDR_BILLT
ADDR_SHIPT	Delivery address	☐	☑	☑	BBP_ATTR_F1	ADDR_SHIPT
AN1	Attachment	☐	☑	☑	BBP_ATTR_F1	AN1
AN2	Asset Subnumber	☐	☑	☑	BBP_ATTR_F1	AN2
ANK	Asset Class	☐	☑	☑	BBP_ATTR_F1	ANK
ANR	Request	☐	☑	☑	BBP_ATTR_F1	ANR
APO	Sales Order Item	☐	☑	☑	BBP_ATTR_F1	APO
APPRV_LIM	Approval Limit	☐	☐	☐	BBP_ATTR_F1_STRUCT	APPRV_LIM

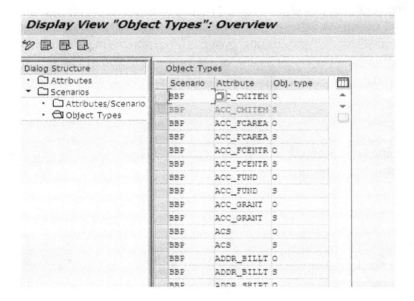

Display View "Object Types": Overview

Dialog Structure
- Attributes
- Scenarios
  - Attributes/Scenario
  - Object Types

Object Types

Scenario	Attribute	Obj. type
BBP	C_CMITEM	O
BBP	ACC_CMITEM	S
BBP	ACC_FCAREA	O
BBP	ACC_FCAREA	S
BBP	ACC_FCENTR	O
BBP	ACC_FCENTR	S
BBP	ACC_FUND	O
BBP	ACC_FUND	S
BBP	ACC_GRANT	O
BBP	ACC_GRANT	S
BBP	ACS	O
BBP	ACS	S
BBP	ADDR_BILLT	O
BBP	ADDR_BILLT	S

The utility report RHOMATTRIBUTES_REPLACE can change attribute values in SRM organization structure. The program is very useful when a non-production system is copied from the production system. The attributes of the production system may not match with the non-production system. You can use this utility report to change the attribute values to your local system value.

Useful function modules in attributes are:

- BBP_READ_ATTRIBUTES - You can get attribute values for a given org unit.
- BBP_UPDATE_ATTRIBUTES - You can update attribute values for a given org unit.

Extended Attributes

SRM extended attributes is attributes related to product categories, PO value limit, locations and storage locations.

- Product categories - You can maintain the product categories that can be used while shopping. If there is no product categories defined, then the user will not select any product category.
- PO vale limits - This is used in PO approval workflow.
- Locations - User can use these locations (plants) while shopping.
- Storage locations - User can use these storage locations while creating shopping cart.

The extended attributes are stored in the following database tables.

- HRP5500/HRT5500 - Company code, purchase org and purchase group
- HRP5501/HRT5501 - Product category
- HRP5502/HRT5502 - Location, plant and storage location
- HRP5503 - PO value limit

Function Module	**Description**
BBP_OM_FIND_PURCH_ORGS_EXT	Get purchase organization info
BBP_PARTNER_GET_PURCH_DATA	Get purchase data for a given partner and purchase org.
BBP_PARTNER_GET_PURCH_DATA_NEW	Get purchase data and PCard for a given partner and purchase org.
BBP_OM_FIND_PURCH_GRPS_BEI	Get purchase groups

Manage Users and Employee data

SRM provides a utility program to manage the SRM users and employee data. You can access this utility program using the transaction code USERS_GEN.

Manage User and Employee Data

General Task List

Select Action

Create

Copy User and Employee Data from Template

Generate User and Employee Data

Consistency check

Check User and Employee Data

Export

Export User and Employee Data

Correction

Delete User Accounts and Employees

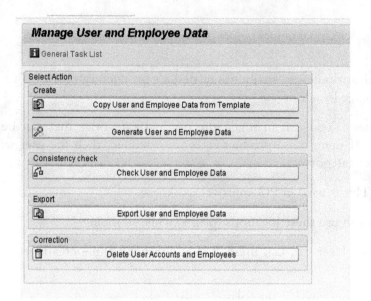

You can create SRM users using multiple options like uploading from a file, importing users from other systems via RFC, using existing SU01 users and importing from LDAP directory.

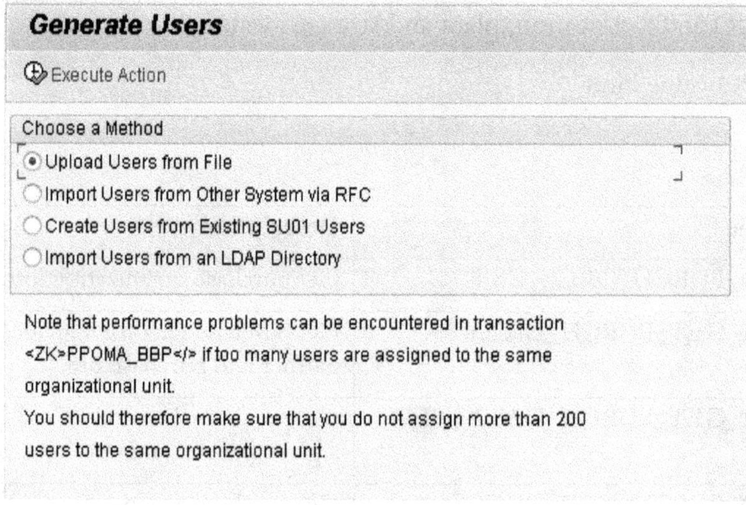

The users must be assigned under the purchase organization and purchase group. Once the user is created, you need to assign the attributes like company code, cost center, catalog id, account assignment category, local currency and back-end system. Also, you need to define extended attributes location and product categories.

BBP_CHECK_CONSISTENCY - You can use the report to check consistency of objects in the organization structure. The report offers you the functionality to remove the inconsistencies. It is recommended that you can schedule this report in the background at least once a week.

You can use the report BBP_XPA_ORGEH_TO_VENDOR_GROUP that migrate vendors from old org structure to new SRM7 org structure.

5.4 Summary

In this chapter, you have learned the basics of business partner, product master, organization management and product category. Vendor synchronization and material replication are discussed in detail with good sample code.

Application Objects explain SRM object types with respect to technical perspective and business scenarios. Portal Integration and Alert Management, Shopping Cart, Bid Invitation, Bid Responses, PO and Invoices are technically discussed

6 Application Objects

This chapter discusses the overall framework of mySAP SRM, it various application objects and how it fits into different system environments. The SRM framework includes Portal Integration and Post processing framework. In this chapter, the application objects refer to the actual SRM application objects and also the processes. The application objects include external requirements sourcing, shopping cart transfer, bid invitation and responses, purchase order, and contract. Portal Integration describes how SAP provides portal users with role-based access to services of SRM Components with the help of SAP Enterprise Portal. Object-based navigation allows unification and connectivity, which in short is a runtime portal capable of navigating and passing business data between applications using user roles dynamically at run time. Alert management discusses predefined technical events for the business object that trigger alerts and messages in SRM and how event schemas are used to control the effect of events.

Post processing framework is a basis technology that is used in SAP SRM to schedule and process actions and outputs with an application document. PPF provides basic functions with default settings by the relevant application. This could be for Output of Forms, PDF, email or EDI messages. SRM event discusses predefined technical events supplied by SRM for business objects that are triggered by certain business changes made in the system. This is discussed in detail in the section Alert Management.

The External requirements topic describes the process of procurement of requirements for direct and indirect materials as well as for services originating in outside systems like ECC. Sourcing is the main application component which acts as an entry point for purchasers to identify sources of supply while creating POs, Auctions, Contracts, RFX which will be converted to shopping cart for back-end transfer. Enhancement discusses different BADIs available during the shopping cart creation process. Bid Invitation and response is an important topic which discusses the creation of Bid Invitation from PR and its processing of Bid responses. The chapter discusses the PO replication and Contract replication process in detail.

6.1 Portal Navigation

SAP NetWeaver portal unifies key information and applications to give users a single view that spans organizational boundaries. Portal offers intuitive web interface, Collaboration and knowledge management. The structure of SAP Enterprise portal is based on roles. Portal allows you to navigate to a specific iView or Page either relative or absolute navigation. You can access a web page by absolute the portal navigation using the method navigate_absolute of the interface if_wd_portal_integration. The relative navigation is same as absolute, the only difference being that you can use BASE URL (optional, if it is not defined then use current URL), level and path. Object navigation method is explained in the next section.

Object Based Navigation (OBN)

OBN allows you to navigate steps at higher level. OBN offers portal users an additional method of navigation that is role dependent and based on business objects from productive back-end systems instead of defining absolute or concrete target URL for a particular operation of a particular business object. In SRM, the business objects can be Shopping Cart, Contract, PO, etc. OBN is based on the structure of business objects having one or more operations associated with it.

In other words, OBN is a loosely coupled indirect communication, where the caller does not know what will be final transaction executed. Using OBN configuration, you can control what roles can access the object and method navigation. You can use OBN to access any procurement document access from your custom code. The OBN can be done by the method navigate_to_object of interface if_wd_portal_integration. The following is sample code to Navigate PO portal with display mode (note that navigate_to_obejct can be generated using Web Dynpro Code wizard).

```
CONSTANTS: c_object_type_po    TYPE string VALUE 'po',
        c_object_type_ctr   TYPE string VALUE 'cont',
      c_boid_sap_srm      TYPE string VALUE 'sapsrm_boid',
      c_operation         TYPE string VALUE 'display'.
DATA: v_obn_system   TYPE /sapsrm/obn_system.
DATA: it_parameters    TYPE wdy_key_value_table.
DATA: lo_api_component  TYPE REF TO if_wd_component,
      lo_portal_manager TYPE REF TO if_wd_portal_integration.
  wa_parameters-key   = c_boid_sap_srm.
  wa_parameters-value = iv_guid.
  APPEND wa_parameters TO it_parameters.
```

```
CALL METHOD /sapsrm/cl_url_service=>get_srm_system_alias
  RECEIVING
    rv_system_alias = v_obn_system.
lo_api_component = wd_comp_controller->wd_get_api( ).
lo_portal_manager = lo_api_component->get_portal_manager( ).
  CALL METHOD lo_portal_manager->navigate_to_object
    EXPORTING
      system              = v_obn_system
      object_type         = c_object_type_po
      operation           = c_operation
      business_parameters = it_parameters.
```

SRM OBN types are as follows:

```
constants C_OBN_OP_ACCEPT type STRING value 'accept'.
constants C_OBN_OP_CANCEL type STRING value 'cancel'.
constants C_OBN_OP_CHANGE type STRING value 'change'.
constants C_OBN_OP_CHECKCOMP type STRING value 'checkcomp'.
constants C_OBN_OP_CHNG type STRING value 'chng'.
constants C_OBN_OP_COMPARE type STRING value 'compare'.
constants C_OBN_OP_COPY type STRING value 'copy'.
constants C_OBN_OP_CREATE type STRING value 'create'.
constants C_OBN_OP_CREATEREF type STRING value 'createref'.
constants C_OBN_OP_CREATEREQ type STRING value 'createreq'.
constants C_OBN_OP_CREDITMEMO type STRING value 'creditmemo'.
constants C_OBN_OP_DELETE type STRING value 'delete'.
constants C_OBN_OP_DELIVERY type STRING value 'delivery'.
constants C_OBN_OP_DISPLAY type STRING value 'display'.
constants C_OBN_OP_DOWNLOAD type STRING value 'download'.
constants C_OBN_OP_EXPORT type STRING value 'export'.
constants C_OBN_OP_GOODSRECEIPT type STRING value 'goodsreceipt'.
```

```
constants C_OBN_OP_IMPORT type STRING value 'import'.
constants C_OBN_OP_INVOICE type STRING value 'invoice'.
constants C_OBN_OP_LIVEAUC type STRING value 'liveauc'.
constants C_OBN_OP_MASSCHANGES type STRING value 'masschanges'.
constants C_OBN_OP_MASSCHNG type STRING value 'masschng'.
constants C_OBN_OP_POST type STRING value 'post'.
constants C_OBN_OP_PUBLISH type STRING value 'publish'.
constants C_OBN_OP_REQUOT type STRING value 'requot'.
constants C_OBN_OP_RESPONSENAWARDS type STRING value 'responsenawards'.
constants C_OBN_OP_RETURN type STRING value 'return'.
constants C_OBN_OP_SHOP type STRING value 'shop'.
constants C_OBN_OP_SOURCE type STRING value 'source'.
constants C_OBN_OP_UPLOAD type STRING value 'upload'.
```

6.2 Alert Management

Alert Management is a component of SAP Web Application Server. Alert management identifies predefined business situations and communicates information to interested parties by sending an alert. An alert is a notification informing the recipients that a critical or important business situation has arisen. The alert is different from Workflow. Workflow is a business process to approve business objects, but Alert Management raises alert and processed immediately.

The alert is a business situation that needs action in order to be resolved. For example, alerts can be used to prevent delays in the processing of the critical situation by notifying appropriate recipients earlier. The alert can be defined in the alert category. The alert category defines the conditions when a specific alert is sent to defined recipients.

SRM Alert Management extends SAP Alert management to more specific SRM functionality. The SRM Alert Management function monitors pre-defined business processes in SRM. The event is a message about the change of status or attributes in the SRM document. SRM Alert management analyzes the events, triggers the alerts, messages or tasks to communicate users. The alert messages can be viewed in Universal Work List (UWL). The UWL is a web interface that enables portal users to manage their work like the SAP GUI Inbox.

6.2.1 Post Processing Framework

Alert Management is based on Post Processing Framework (PPF) technology. PPF provides a uniform interface for the condition-based actions like printing delivery notes, faxing order confirmations, etc. The actions will be generated based on the conditions, and can be processed directly or later as a scheduled report. PPF is a successor technique to Message Control and offers more functional scope and flexibility. PPF automatically generates action from document data. PPF provides uniform action administration and status management and processing log for every action. SRM Alert Management provides a PPF application BBP_PD. The package of the PPF application BBP_PD provides all action profiles, actions definition and processing types.

6.2.2 PPF Structure

PPF considers a set of information to definition and processing the action. The following is basic information about the PPF.

- Action Profile - Action profile is a collected area of actions. The action profiles are defined in a specific application.
- Action Definition – The action definition is configuring the action like Processing Time, flag to Scheduling immediately, partner function determination, Action determination and Action merging.
- Processing Types – Permitted processing types like Mail, Fax, Print and XML actions and its technical settings.

6.2.3 SRM PPF Definition

SRM provides a set of PPF actions and its processing types. You can access the PPF definition using the transaction code BBP_PO_ACTION_DEF. The PPF actions The action profile incudes base SRM document types. For each assignment type, you can define the corresponding form (smart form), Processing class, and Processing Method. Note that the ABAP class must be inherited from the super class CL_SF_PROCESSING_PPF.

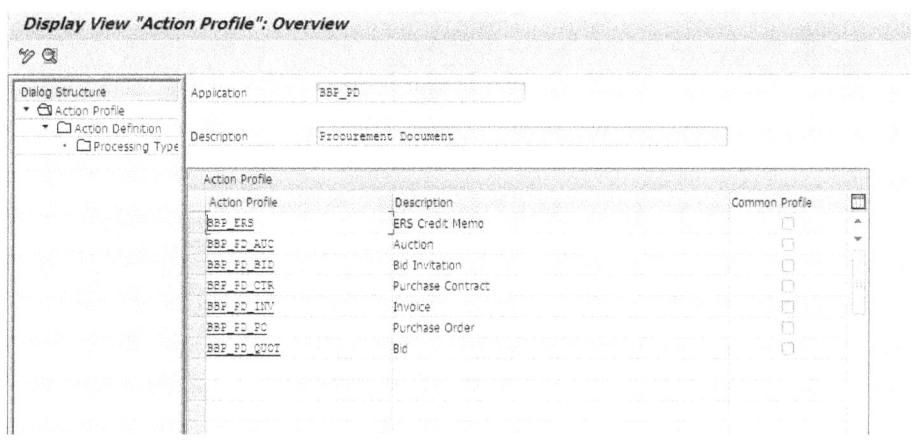

The following table explains PPF supported actions based on the SRM object type.

SRM Document	Print	Email	Fax	XML
Purchase Order	X	X	X	X
Contract	X	X	X	
Invoice (including ERS)				X
ERS Credit memo	X	X	X	
Bid Invitation	X	X	X	X
Bid	X	X	X	X
Auction (Live Auction)	X	X	X	

6.2.4 Output Forms

Output forms are ways of printing the objects into a specific layout. SRM uses smart forms for its output processing. There are a number of standard SRM smartforms and are listed below.

Form Name	Description
BBP_AUCTION	Output Form for Auction
BBP_BIDINV_BID	Mail Text Bid Invitat. Obsol.
BBP_BID_BGR_PROCESSING	Background Processing Bid Inv.
BBP_BID_INVITATION	Output form for Bid Invitation
BBP_BID_NOTIFICATION	Notif. on Submission of Bid
BBP_COMPANY	New Text

BBP_CONF	Invoice Output
BBP_CONTRACT	Output Form for Contract
BBP_CTR_BGR_PROCESSING	Output Form for Contract background
BBP_CTR_MASS_END	Mass Change to Contracts
BBP_ERS	Goods Receipt Settlement
BBP_ERS_CRETAX	Goods Receipt Settlement
BBP_INV	Invoice Output
BBP_INV_IMS_EXCEPTION	INV Exceptions to Vendor
BBP_OUTPUT_COVER	Form for E-mail Output
BBP_OUT_EXCEPTION	Event Framework Messages
BBP_OUT_EXCEPTION_UNKNOWN	New Text
BBP_OUT_OFFAPP	Form for Offline Approval
BBP_PD_DIFF	PO Version Comparison
BBP_PO	Purchase Order Output
BBP_PO_DIFF	PO Version Comparison
BBP_QUOTATION	Bid Invitation Output
BBP_QUOT_BGR_PROCESSING	Background Processing Bid
BBP_SC	Output Smartform SC
BBP_SOCO_BGR_PROCESSING	New Form
BBP_SUSASN	SUS Shipping Notif. Output
BBP_SUSCFCA	SUS GR Reversal Output
BBP_SUSCFCF	SUS GR Notification Output
BBP_SUSCFRT	SUS Return Delivery Output
BBP_SUSCM	SUS Credit Memo Output
BBP_SUSCONF	SUS Confirmation Output
BBP_SUSINV	SUS Invoice Output
BBP_SUSPO	SUS Purchase Order Output
BBP_SUSSR	SUS Sched.Agreem.Release Outp.
BBP_UM	Mail Output in User Management

The smartform definition creates a function module in background. You can execute the the generated function module to get the smartform output. You can get the associated function module using the function module SSF_FUNCTION_MODULE_NAME Note that the function module name can be different between development, test and production systesms for the smartform.

Technical Challenges: The standard PO smart form does not cover all client requirements. A new custom smart form ZSF_BBP_PO is created. You need to use the custom smart form in the output for the PO output. You also need changes in comparing versions within the PO preview.

Solution: This solution is applicable for smart form output only. Follow the steps:

- Copy from the standard form BBP_PO into custom form ZF_BBP_PO based on the naming convention. Make sure that the smart form has been activated.

- Implement the BADI BBP_OUTPUT_CHANGE_SF to point out the new custom smart form.

- Implement BADI BBP_CHANGE_SF_VERS

```
IF iv_object_type = 'BUS2201' and cv_smartform = ‘BBP_PO’.
 cv_smartform = 'ZSF_BBP_PO'.
ENDIF.
```

Author Tips: Note that BADI is used in the PO output function module BBP_OUTPUT_PO_GETDETAIL_SMART should use only smartform, Mail Smart form and Mail Subject. Other change parameters will not be passed to the PO output.

Also, the import parameter GUID provides the option to read the corresponding SRM document and form name, and subject mail can be derived based on the document information. Using this form, you can change from smart form to Adobe form. To change to Adobe form, set the CV_SMARTFORM as initial and set the Adobe form with the required value.

SRM7 provides the standard ABAP object CL_BBP_DOC_SEND_BCS that has two static methods to send email and fax. You can use it in your custom program.

6.2.5 Alert Category

The alert category defines conditions that when a specific alert is sent to whom. The alert is always associated with an alert category. You can configure alert categories using the transaction ALRTCATDEF. The SRM events will be under SRM alerts classification. The alert category has following tab pages.

- Properties - are properties of the alert category including description, priority, and expiration time and escalation information.
- Container - is a container for exchange of application-specific data like Object ID or event. It interfaces between the triggering application and alert central framework.
- Long and Short text - You can modify the message title, and short and long text of the alert.
- Optional subsequent activities - You can enter URLs for subsequent activities

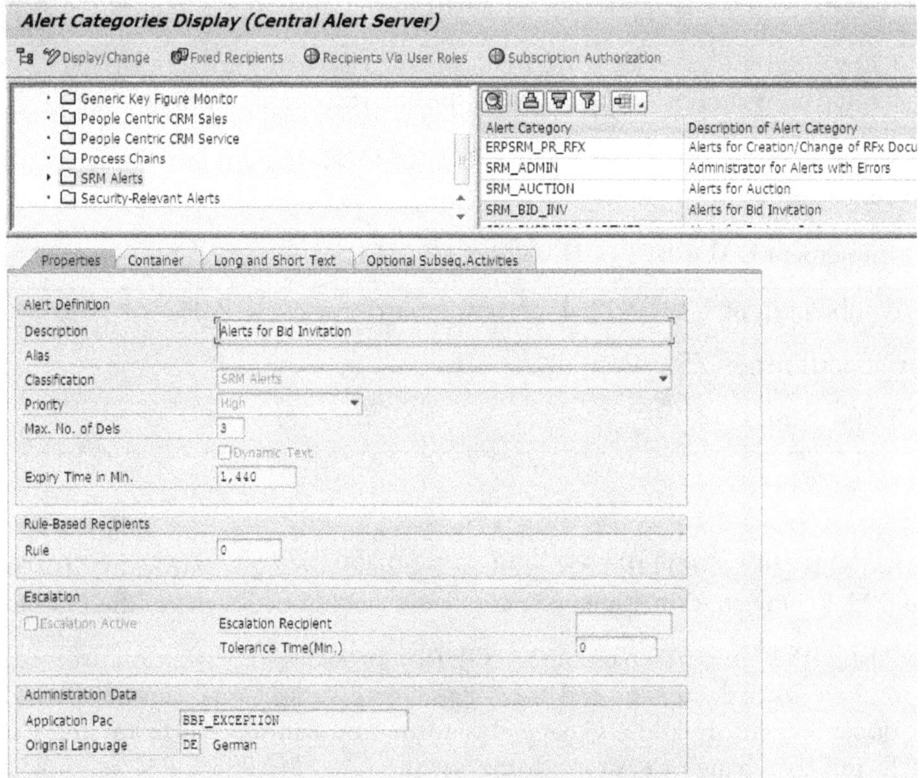

The BADI ALERT_TO_BE_ESCALATE is the exit function to populate the escalate recipients. The BADI will be executed only when no escalation recipient is stored in the alert category.

6.2.6 SRM Events

SRM delivered a set of technical events for each SRM object type. Events are triggered by particular business changes to SRM document like the release of a contract or passing of a deadline. If the events are assigned to an activated schema, they can trigger alerts or messages.

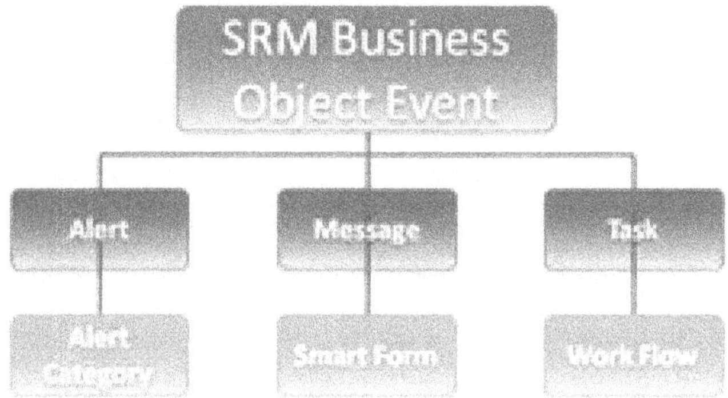

The pre-defined events are configured. The SRM provides options to customize the events in IMG. The new events can be configured in this IMG. IMG Path: SRM Server->Cross-Application->Event and Events Schema for Alert Management->Define Events.

Display View "Event Objects": Overview

Dialog Structure
- Event Objects
  - Event Definition

Event Objects

ObjectType	Description	Description (Long)
BUS1006003	Employee	Employee
BUS2000113	Purchase Contract	EBP Purchase Contract
BUS2121	Shopping Cart	EBP Shopping Cart
BUS2200	Bid Invitation	EBP Bid Invitation
BUS2201	Purchase Order	EBP Purchase Order
BUS2202	Vendor Quotation	Vendor Quotation EBP
BUS2203	Confirmation	EBP Confirmation of Goods/Service
BUS2205	Incoming Invoice	EBP Incoming Invoice
BUS2206	Vendor List	EBP Vendor List
BUS2208	Auction	EBP Auktion
BUS2209	Purch.Order Response	EBP Purchase Order Response
BUS2210	Invoice Default	EBP Invoice Default
BUS2230	SUS Purchase Order	SUS Purchase Order
BUS2231	Shipping Notif.	SUS Shipping Notification
BUS2232	SUS PO Confirmation	SUS Purchase Order Confirmation
BUS2233	SUS Confirmation	SUS Confirmation of Goods/Service
BUS2234	SUS Invoice	SUS Invoice

Each object type is delivered with the list of events. New event can be raised. How to raise a new event for the business requirement is explained in the following technical challenge. The event configuration in the IMG involves only with the event Name and its short text description. SRM-provided events are pre-defined in the code. Also, deletion of these events may cause issues.

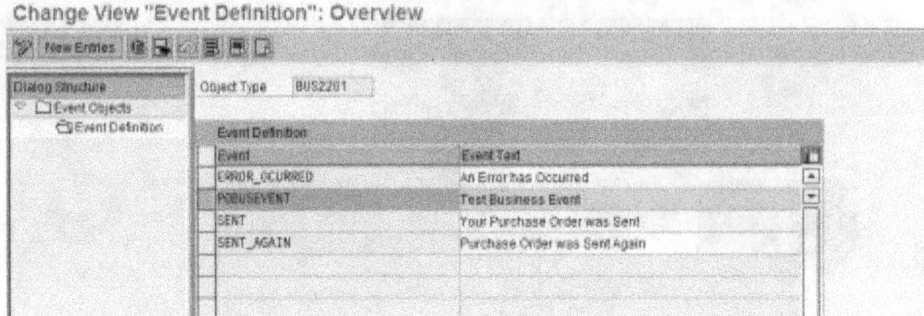

In this configuration, you can define all events associated with the business object. The Event schema can be configured to group the events. Each business object can have one or more event schemas. The event schema can be invoked by IMG path: SRM Server->Cross-Application->Event and Events Schema for Alert Management->Define Event Schema.

Choose the event objects and schema can be listed.

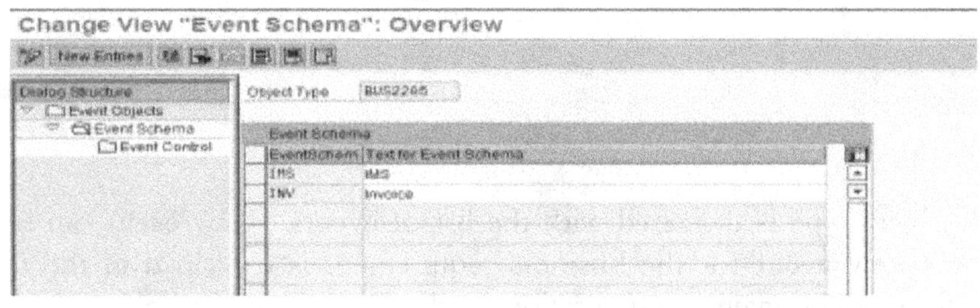

Events can be associated with the schema.

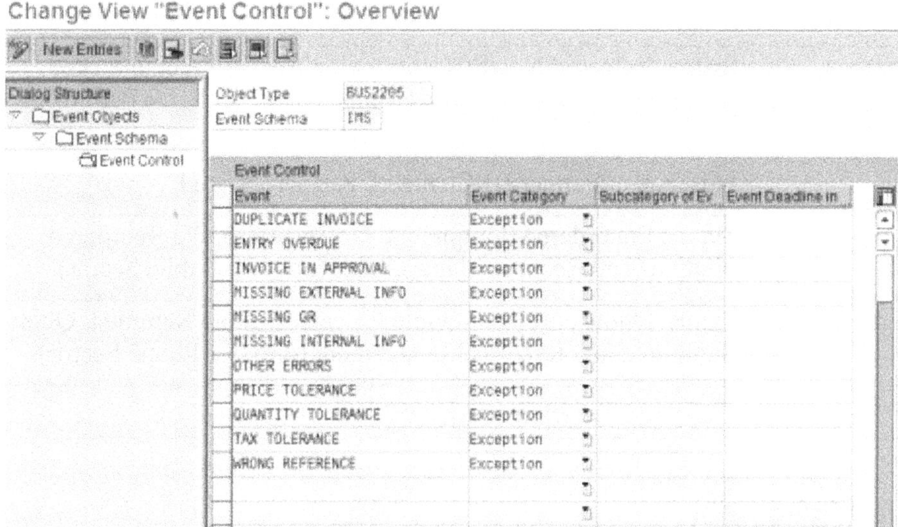

Make sure that event schema can be activated by the transaction types of the object type. When there is no event defined in the transaction type, the event function is deactivated for the transaction type. The transaction type can be configured at SRM Server->Cross-Application Basic Settings->Define Transaction type.

Custom Transaction Type

Event schema cannot be assigned to Custom Transaction Type automatically. Make sure your transaction type is configured with Event Schema.

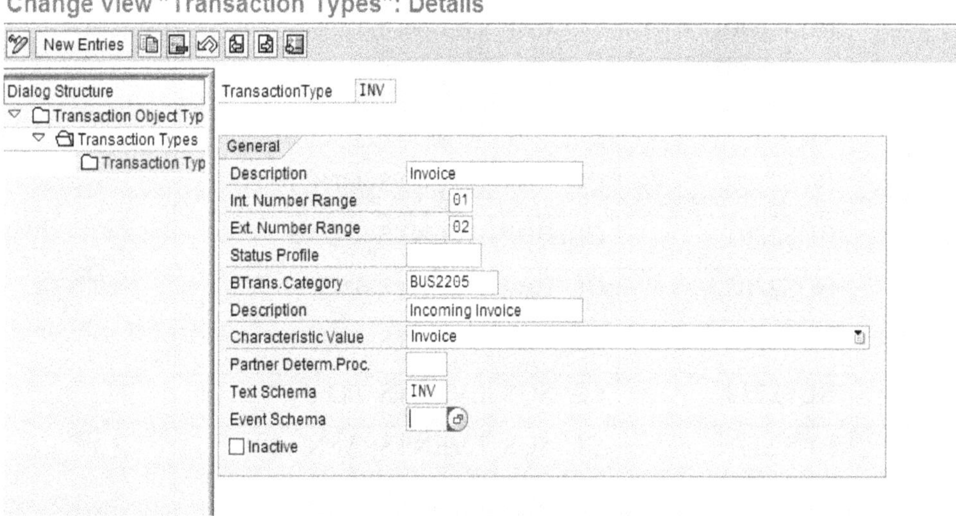

The following standard events are handled by SRM Objects.

Object Type	Events
Bid	Status: Published, Republished and Records Management (only for Public Sector).

	Deadline: No Quote submitted and Not all Bids Approved.
Contract	Status: Released Newly, Contract locked, Contract unlocked, Released Again and Records Management (only for Public Sector). Difference: Partner ID Changed, Partner Deleted,
PO	Status: PO ordered (Output and Notification), PO Reordered (Output) and Records Management (only for Public Sector).
Quote	Status: Quote accepted, Quote Rejected, Quote Returned, Quote Submitted and Records Management (only for Public Sector)
Invoice	In Processing, Rejected, Cancelled

Technical Information

Events processing for SRM documents are carried by the function module BBP_EV_API_EVENTS_SAVE. The function module has been called while executing the FM BBP_PROCDOC_SAVE. Each object type is associated with an ABAP Class to identify and process the events. The ABAP class information can be accessed by the FM BBPC_EVENT_CLASS_GET. The object type and its associated Event ABAP class are stored in the DB table BBPC_EVENTMAP.

Object Type	Event Class
BUS1006003	CL_BBP_EVENTS_BP
BUS2000113	CL_BBP_EVENTS_CTR
BUS2200	CL_BBP_EVENTS_BID
BUS2201	CL_BBP_EVENTS_PO
BUS2202	CL_BBP_EVENTS_QUOT
BUS2203	CL_BBP_EVENTS_CONF
BUS2205	CL_BBP_EVENTS_INV
BUS2208	CL_BBP_EVENTS_AUCT
BUS2230	CL_SUS_EVENTS_PO
BUS2231	CL_SUS_EVENTS_ASN
BUS2232	CL_SUS_EVENTS_PCO
BUS2233	CL_SUS_EVENTS_CONF
BUS2234	CL_SUS_EVENTS_INV

All these events' ABAP Object Classes are inherited from the super class CL_BBP_EVENTS. You can use the function module SALRT_CREATE_API to create an alert programmatically.

6.2.7 Event Type

SRM provides a wide range of SRM event types and each event type is associated with structured technical objects. SRM categorizes the events into the following categories:

- Status Events – Events are based on status changes: for example, releasing the contract.
- Difference Events – The events can be raised based on a change in a particular attribute.
- Message Events - Output type events.
- Deadline Events – Deadline related messages such as a week before the deadline.
- ICC Events – SAP Provided internal events
- Custom Events – Custom events using BADI exit.

Each event can be categorized into the following:

- Alert
- Notification
- Output
- Task
- Deadline
- External
- Exception

The alert category is used to handle the event actions. Also, Alert Category can be subcategorized further. For example, the deadline category can be subdivided into 7 days notice, 2 days notice and passed deadline. For each event category, subcategory and object type, the ABAP classes can be configured. When the event is raised, the corresponding event class will be executed. The event class can be configured using the transaction SM30 for the table BBPC_ACTIONMAP.

Object	Category	Event Class
Purchase Contract	ALERT	CL_BBP_ACTION_ALERT_CTR
Purchase	NOTIFIC	CL_BBP_ACTION_NOTIFIC_EXC_CTR

Contract		
Purchase Contract	TASK	CL_BBP_ACTION_WORKFLOW_CTR
Bid Invitation	ALERT	CL_BBP_ACTION_ALERT_BID
Bid Invitation	DEADLINE	CL_BBP_ACTION_DEADLINE_BID
Bid Invitation	OUTPUT	CL_BBP_ACTION_OUTPUT_BID
Purchase Order	NOTIFIC	CL_BBP_ACTION_NOTIFIC_EXC_PO
Purchase Order	OUTPUT	CL_BBP_ACTION_OUTPUT_PO
Bid Quote	NOTIFIC	CL_BBP_ACTION_NOTIFIC_EXC_QUO
Bid Quote	OUTPUT	CL_BBP_ACTION_OUTPUT_BID_NOTIF
Bid Quote	OUTPUT	CL_BBP_ACTION_OUTPUT_QUOT
Confirmation	OUTPUT	CL_BBP_ACTION_OUTPUT_CONF
Incoming Invoice	EXCEPTION	CL_BBP_ACTION_PERSIST_INV
Incoming Invoice	OUTPUT	CL_BBP_ACTION_OUTPUT_INV
Auction	OUTPUT	CL_BBP_ACTION_OUTPUT_AUCT
SUS PO	ALERT	CL_SUS_ACTION_ALERT
SUS PO	DEADLINE	CL_SUS_ACTION_DEADLINE
SUS PO	NOTIFIC	CL_SUS_ACTION_NOTIFICATION
SUS ASN	ALERT	CL_SUS_ACTION_ALERT
SUS ASN	DEADLINE	CL_SUS_ACTION_DEADLINE
SUS ASN	NOTIFIC	CL_SUS_ACTION_NOTIFICATION
SUS ASN	OUTPUT	CL_SUS_ACTION_OUTPUT_ASN
SUS POC	ALERT	CL_SUS_ACTION_ALERT
SUS POC	DEADLINE	CL_SUS_ACTION_DEADLINE
SUS POC	NOTIFIC	CL_SUS_ACTION_NOTIFICATION
SUS POC	OUTPUT	CL_SUS_ACTION_OUTPUT_PCO
SUS POC	ALERT	CL_SUS_ACTION_ALERT
SUS POC	DEADLINE	CL_SUS_ACTION_DEADLINE

SUS POC	NOTIFIC	CL_SUS_ACTION_NOTIFICATION
SUS POC	OUTPUT	CL_SUS_ACTION_OUTPUT_CONF
SUS Invoice	ALERT	CL_SUS_ACTION_ALERT
SUS Invoice	DEADLINE	CL_SUS_ACTION_DEADLINE
SUS Invoice	NOTIFIC	CL_SUS_ACTION_NOTIFICATION
SUS Invoice	OUTPUT	CL_SUS_ACTION_OUTPUT_INV

Most of these events are raised by the standard SRM function. SAP provided an exit BADI to change standard provided events. For each object, there are entries for event category, event subcategory and Action class. The action class is an ABAP object that handles the object/category specific events. The BADI ***BBP_ALERTING*** can be used to add events based on the business requirements that are not defined in the standard SRM event programming. BADI is used in the analyzing, categorizing, determining the recipients, determining the follow-up URL and class name. The BADI allows the developer to modify the recipients. The notification category sends a notification to the recipients.

Technical Challenge: You need to send a specific notification to set of recipients when a particular custom field is modified when PO is ordered. You also need to execute a specific custom report as a subsequent activity.

Solution: This is a multi-steps solution to implement. Follow the steps:

- Implement the BBP_ALERTING to raise a new custom event.

Name: **BPP_ALERTING**		Multiple Use: No	Filter:No
Description: Exit function for SRM Alert Management.			
Method: BBP_EVENTS_ANALYSE ***Description***: Creating custom events Parameters:			
Name	**Type**	**Data Type**	**Description**
IV_OBJECT_TYPE	Import	BBP_OBJECT_TYPE	Object Type
IV_OBJECT_GUID	Import	BBP_GUID	Object GUID
IT_OLD_STATUS	Import	BBPT_STATUS	Old status list
IT_NEW_STATUS	Import	BBPT_STATUS	New status list
CT_EVENTS	Change	BBPT_EVENTS	Events Table
CT_MESSAGES	Change	BBP_PDT_MESSAGES	Error Messages

Sample code: The sample code is for technical solution.

```
 CASE IV_OBJECT_TYPE.
   WHEN /SAPSRM/IF_PDO_OBJ_TYPES_C=>GC_PDO_PO.
    READ TABLE ct_events INTO ls_oevent WITH KEY object_type =
iv_object_type.
    READ TABLE it_new_status WITH KEY
             stat = bbppd_ordered
             inact = space        TRANSPORTING NO FIELDS .
    IF sy-subrc = 0.
* check whether custom field is changed with your own logic
* if custom field is changed then
      ls_event-event        = 'TESTEVENT'.
      ls_event-object_key  = iv_object_guid.
      ls_event-object_id   = ls_oevent-object_id.
      ls_event-object_type = iv_object_type.
      ls_event-event_categ = bbpex_c_ev_categ_external.
      ls_event-event_sub_categ = 'TESTCATEG'.
      APPEND ls_event TO ct_events.
* endif.
    ENDIF.
   WHEN OTHERS.
 ENDCASE.
```

- Create a new custom action ABAP class ZCL_CUSTOM_ACTION. Make sure it is inheritied from CL_BBP_ACTION_NOTIFICATION, because our class will do notification to recipients. Redefine the method EXECUTE.

```
** for each notification event ...
 LOOP AT mt_events INTO ls_event.
   CHECK ls_event-event = 'TESTEVENT'.
   IF gc_badi_active IS NOT INITIAL.
*  call BADI to redefine recipients
     CALL BADI gb_badi_alerting->bbp_events_det_recipients
```

```
    EXPORTING
      iv_object_type = ls_event-object_type
      iv_object_guid = ls_event-object_key
      is_event       = ls_event
    CHANGING
      ct_recipients  = lt_recipient[].
* transfer recipients into our PO specific recipient table
   LOOP AT lt_recipient INTO ls_recipient.
    MOVE-CORRESPONDING ls_recipient TO ls_recipient_id_map
ls_recipient.
    APPEND ls_recipient_id_map TO lt_recipient_id_map.
   ENDLOOP.
  ENDIF.
* ...determine follow-up actions
  CALL METHOD me->determine_follow_actions
   EXPORTING
    is_event         = ls_event
   IMPORTING
    et_follow_actions = lt_followup_action.
* Get PO detail and populate Message and Subject
*.....
* Send email to
* execute the custom program
```

- Configure the new event and ABAP class in the table BBPC_ACTIONMAP

ObjectType	Event ...	Subcategory of...	Class/Interface	+	+
BUS2201	Noti...	TESTEVENT	ZCL_CUSTOM_ACTION	☐	☐
BUS2201	Outp...		CL_BBP_ACTION_OUTPUT_PO	☐	☑

6.3 External Requirements

The External requirement is nothing but a shopping cart in SRM. When the shopping cart is transferred from back-end ECC Purchase Requisitions, then the shopping cart is called External Requirements. PR Transfers are applicable for Classic and Extended Classic scenarios. Most of SRM business scenarios use external requirements transfer. PR creation is based on your business scenarios. PRs can be created manually or by External Fulfillment Sales Orders or by MRP program. The PRs are transferred into SRM external requirements using a Transfer Utility.

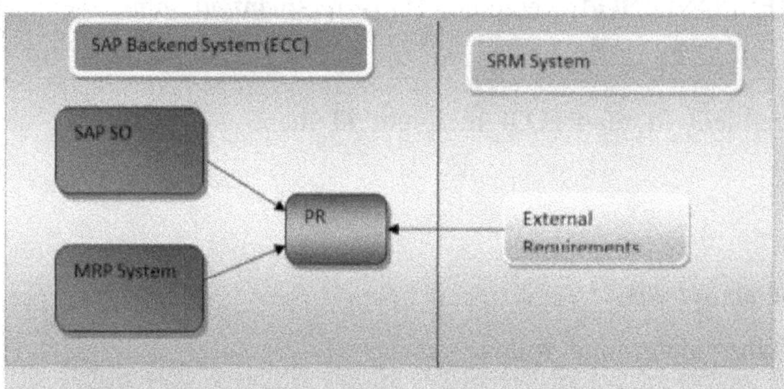

SRM provides a standard program BBP_EXTREQ_TRANSFER to transfer the PRs from ECC to the SRM. The tool is available at the ECC back-end system only. This program uses qRFC call to create the requirements using the function module BBP_BC_EXTREQ_INB in the SRM with queue name BBP_EXTREQ_TRANS. You can schedule this program as a background job that can be executed for a time interval.

The standard SRM program BBP_EXTREQ_TRANSFER provides very basic selection criteria and executes function module BBP_EXTREQ_TRANSFER. This is a base function module to transfer PRs into SRM external requirements. One common practice used in client places is copying the program BBP_EXTREQ_TRANSFER into a custom program. You can implement your custom requirements, like filtering PR document type or validating PR before transferring in the custom program.

From a technical perspective, the database table EPRTRANS plays an instrumental role in transfer programming. The PR creation/update creates the entry at EPTRANS table automatically. The FM BBP_EXTREQ_TRANSFER reads the PR information from EPTRANS table and validates the transfer date. The FM uses the queue RFC concept to transfer the data. That means it executes SRM RFC function module BBP_BC_EXTREQ_INB in the background.

You can avoid qRFC and execute direct RFC function module to create external requirements. You can achieve this only by debug mode (with change permission). You can change value of lv_qrfc as initial (in the include LBBP_EXTREQ18). Then it will execute RFC function module directly. In direct RFC, there are possible to debug SRM external requirement creation RFC function module. It allows you to change RFC destination and you can debug using destination logon information.

6.3.1 Enhancement

The custom fields defined in EBAN will not automatically transfer to External requirements. You need to extend BBPS_ER_SC_HEADER_CUST_C, BBPS_ER_SC_ITEM_CUST_C_PI and BBPS_ER_ACC_CUST_C structures for Header, Item and Account Assignment respectively. ITEM_CUST fields will be populated with Material Item or Service Item.

SRM provides BADI BBP_BADI_EXTREQ_OUT to update standard PR data, custom structures (Header, Item table and Account assignment table) and customer add-on fields. Add-On fields are supporting as in follow structures:

SCHEADER	BBPS_PDEXT_SC_HEADER_IC
SCITEM	BBPS_PDEXT_SC_ITEM_ICU
SCACCOUNT	BBPS_PDEXT_ACC.

Technical Challenges – There are new custom fields that available in ECC. The custom fields should be mapped to corresponding SRM document fields at the header and item level. Also, there is custom text information that needs to be transferred into the custom SRM fields. The text IDs between SRM and ECC are different. There is a cross reference table that maps between ECC and SRM Text IDs. All Text IDs are configured in both ECC and SRM. The transfer program should transfer text data into the appropriate text in SRM side.

Solution: ECC PR transfer program provides the option of group mapping BADI. The BADI is executed before PR data transfer to SRM side. The BADI BBP_BADI_EXTREQ_OUT and its method BBP_GROUPING_MAPPING can be used to populate text table parameters. You can also populate any fields that are not covered in standard structure and pass them as Add-On Fields. Add-On fields support SCHEADER (BBPS_PDEXT_SC_HEADER_IC), SCITEM (BBPS_PDEXT_SC_ITEM_ICU) and SCACCOUNT(BBPS_PDEXT_ACC).

```
TYPES: BEGIN OF ty_textmap,
      ecc_textid TYPE textid,
      srm_textid TYPE textid,
     END OF ty_textmap.
DATA lv_name       TYPE tdobname.
DATA lt_text_head   TYPE bbpt_er_thead.
DATA lt_textmap     TYPE TABLE OF ty_textmap.
DATA lv_textmap     TYPE t_textmap.
DATA ls_text       TYPE bbps_er_text_i.
DATA lt_tline      TYPE bbpt_er_tline.
DATA lv_tline      TYPE tline.


LOOP AT item_imp INTO lw_item .
  READ TABLE item_cust_imp INTO lw_item_cust
     WITH KEY parent_guid = lw_item-item_guid.
  IF sy-subrc = 0.
   lw_addon_fields-fieldname = 'ZCUSTOMFIELD'.
   lw_addon_fields-refobject = 'SCITEM'     .
   lw_addon_fields-reffield1 = 'PARENT_GUID'.
   lw_addon_fields-refval1   = lw_item_cust-parent_guid.
   lw_addon_fields-container = lw_item_cust-bsart.
   lw_addon_fields-type      = 'C'          .
   APPEND lw_addon_fields TO addon_fields.
  ENDIF.
ENDLOOP.
CONCATENATE
  transtab_imp-eban-banfn transtab_imp-eban-bnfpo INTO lv_name.
* Table maintenance all relation between ECC and
* SRM get all text ids that need to transfer to SRM
```

```
SELECT ecc_textid srm_textid
    FROM zt_text_map
    INTO TABLE lt_textmap.
 LOOP AT lt_textmap INTO lv_textmap.
   ls_text-text_id = lv_textmap-srm_textid.
   ls_text-langu_iso = sy-langu.
   REFRESH lt_tline.
   CALL FUNCTION 'READ_TEXT'
     EXPORTING
       ID       = lv_textmap-ecc_textid
       language = sy-langu
       name     = lv_name
       object   = c_eban
     TABLES
       lines    = lt_tline.
     LOOP AT lt_tline INTO lv_tline.
       MOVE lv_tline-tdline TO ls_text-text_line.
       APPEND ls_text TO text_imp.
     ENDLOOP.
 ENDLOOP.
```

For SCHEADER Add-On, you need not pass PARENT_GUID. The PARENT_GUID should pass with item GUID for SCITEM Add-On.

SRM Enhancement

In SRM side, you can modify Purchase group and Organization using the BADI BBP_PGRP_ASSIGN_BADI. This is a common BADI used to derive Purchase group and organization for Shopping Cart, External Requirement, Contract, PO and Bid Invitation. You must implement this BADI with filter value EXTREQ_INB and method BBP_SC_PGRP_ASSIGN.

Troubleshooting

While transferring PR from ECC to SRM, there are a number of possibilities that can fail the transfer. All RFC Queue information (based on SRM transfer program's Queue name) can be viewed in the transaction SMQ1. Note that once PR data is passed to RFC queue, the EPRTRANS entries will be deleted, so, you cannot reprocess using the transfer program. You can process RFC queue using the transaction SMQ1. Any failure in RFC queue may have the application log (with Object name BBP_EXTREQ or as in Queue name parameter) in the SRM side.

The SRM function module creates/updates External Requirements and maintains the application log under object name BBP_EXTREQ. These application log messages can be viewed using the transaction SLG1.

Analyse Application Log

Object	BBP_EXTREQ	External Requirement
Subobject	*	
External ID	*	

Time Restriction

From (Date/Time)	03/12/2009	00:00:00
To (Date/Time)	03/23/2009	23:59:59

Log Triggered By

User	*
Transaction code	*
Program	*

Log Class
- ○ Only very important logs
- ○ Only important logs
- ○ Also less important logs
- ◉ All logs

Log Creation
- ◉ Any
- ○ Dialog
- ○ In batch mode
- ○ Batch input

Log Source and Formatting
- ◉ Format Completely from Database
- ○ Format Only Header Data from Database
- ○ Format Completely from Archive

Most customers prefer the External Requirement Transfer Alert Programming. When the Queue is failed or hanging, an E-mail must be sent to Administrator. So, they can fix External Requirement Transfer Queue. This is a very useful program on External Requirement Transfer. There are a number of Queue related FMs are available. The following code is basic code to get all hanging queue information.

```
* Get Blocked Queues
 LOOP AT S_QUEUES.
  CLEAR   GS_ERR_QUEUE.
* CHECK IF QUEUE IS BLOCKED
  CALL FUNCTION 'TRFC_QOUT_GET_HANGING_QUEUES'
   EXPORTING
    QNAME     = S_QUEUES-LOW
    DEST      = '*'
    CLIENT    = SY-MANDT
   TABLES
```

```
    ERR_QUEUE = IT_ERR_QUEUE.
  READ TABLE IT_ERR_QUEUE INDEX 1 INTO WA_ERR_QUEUE.
* IF THE QUEUE IS BLOCKED, APPEND THE RECORD
  CHECK SY-SUBRC = 0.
 ENDLOOP.
```

Retrieve PR Information from Queue Information. You can assign all values from ARFCSDATA01 onwards to a string. Therefore, you can find the occurrence of I_HEADER in the string.

```
 SELECT *
  FROM ARFCSDATA
  INTO TABLE LT_ARFCSDATA
  FOR ALL ENTRIES IN IT_ERR_QUEUE
  WHERE ARFCIPID  = IT_ERR_QUEUE-ARFCIPID
   AND  ARFCPID   = IT_ERR_QUEUE-ARFCPID
   AND  ARFCTIME  = IT_ERR_QUEUE-ARFCTIME
   AND  ARFCTIDCNT = IT_ERR_QUEUE-ARFCTIDCNT.
* You can get PR number from ARFCSDATA-ARFCSDATA01 to 07
* You can see after string I_HEADER the PR number will be
* some offset. From PR number, you can access EBAN to
* other information to form Mail subject and Email Body
```

6.4 Sourcing

Sourcing is one of the vital SRM functions that finds, evaluates and provides procurement strategy. The shopping carts and external requirements (back-end purchase requisitions) are basis for the sourcing strategy. This section provides basic functional information and technical background and tips for sourcing. Sourcing can be configured in IMG based on the product categories. The IMG path is SRM Server->Sourcing. There are two IMG activities: define sourcing for product categories and define sourcing via Supplier List only. When you do activate the sourcing via supplier list, all the sourcing is carried out exclusively via the vendor list. Otherwise, the system considers all the source of supply. You can define sourcing option for the product category and source logical system. You can use the wildcard * for all product categories.

The possible values for source determination are listed as follows:

Value	Description
1	Sourcing Never Carried Out - SRM does not transfer any items to the sorucing application.
2	Sourcing Always Carried Out. SRM transfers all the items to the sourcing application.
3	Sourcing Carried Out for Items Without Assigned Source of Supply - SRM creates a PO for all items that do not have a source of supply.
4	Automatic creation of RFx w/o source of supply - SRM creates a bid invitation for all items that do not have a source of supply.
5	Automatic grouping for items w/o assigned source - If a source of supply is assigned, the report Automatic Grouping atemmpts to create a PO automatically. If it is unable to create then you can do it manually.
6	Automatic grouping, Sourcing is never carried out - If a source of supply is assigned, the report Automatic Grouping atemmpts to create a PO automatically.
7	Automatic grouping and creation of RFx item w/o source - If a source of supply is not assigned and the report Automatic Grouping attempts to create a bid invitation automatically.

SRM7 provides a PDO Layer ABAP object /SAPSRM/CL_PDO_AO_SOCO for Sourcing and ABAP object /SAPSRM/CL_PDO_DO_SOS for Source of Supply. The following picture gives the basic flow of Sourcing.

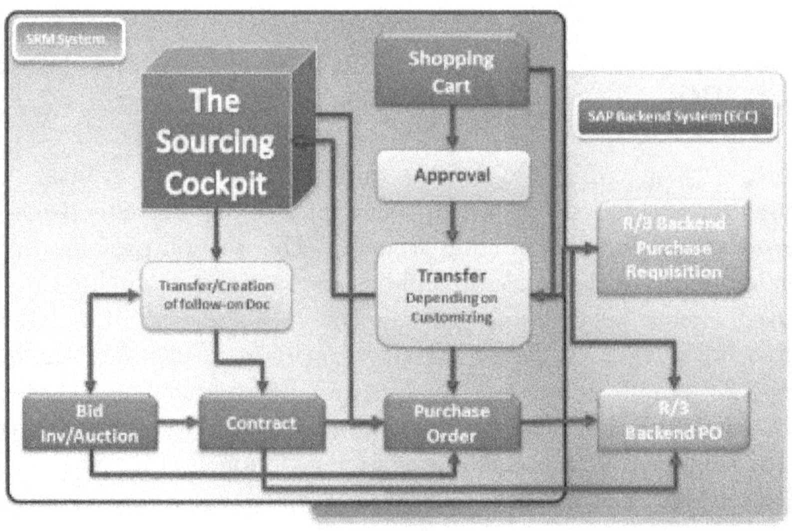

Source of Supply is a way to fulfill Shopping Carts and External requirements. You can create Purchase Orders, Auctions, Contracts or Bid Invitations (RFxs) as follow-on documents. The source of supply may be Contract, Supplier List and Inter-linkages. The function module BBP_PD_SOS_FIND is used to determine the source of supply. You can configure in IMG such that the source of supply is only via Supplier List. The source of supply can be determined automatically or by Sourcing Cockpit.

6.4.1 Automatic Sourcing

SRM sourcing determines sources of supply for a requirement automatically depending on the configuration settings defined for the product category. When a valid source of supply is assigned in a shopping cart, then a purchase order is created on approval of shopping cart. A bid invitation is created for all requirements without a source of supply.

6.4.2 Sourcing Cockpit

Based on your IMG configuration, if the shopping carts or external requirements are not automatically sourced or a multiple source of supply then external requirements can be sourced manually using the Sourcing cockpit. The sourcing cockpit is an UI framework to handle Purchaser's Work List. It will source the shopping carts and create the corresponding follow-on document. It uses Guided Activity Framework floor plan manager and it has the following four steps.

- Select Requisitions
- Assign Source of Supply
- Review Data
- Summary Screen

6.4.3 Enhancements

SRM provides a number of Enhancement BADIs in Sourcing Application.

- The BADI BBP_SRC_DETERMINE will override sourcing IMG implementation. This BADI is very useful when sourcing is not by product category. For instance, you can force particular process types of shopping cart to always go through Bid Invitation. The BADI has header GUID and item GUID. The BADI is explained in the following technical challenge.

- The BADI BBP_AVL_DETERMINE can be used to determine if sourcing for shopping carts or External requirements is to take place using the vendor list only.
- The BADI BBP_SOS_BADI can be implemented to define your custom logic for determining the Source of Supply. You can override the source of supply list. The BADI is executed in the function module BBP_PD_SOS_SEARCH.
- The BADI BBP_SOURCING_BADI has inactive CTRL_CTR_CREATION implementation. If you activate this BADI, it will keep the external requirements in the purchaser's work list if any contract is created at later date.
- The BADI BBP_CREAT_RFQ_IN_DPE can be used to change data in Bid Invitation as a follow-on document creation. The changing parameter is CT_RFQ_AI and it is in XML format.
- The BADI /SAPSRM/BD_DS_AS_CHNG_SELCRIT can be used to change selection criteria on Select Requisitions Step at SOCO. For example, if you want to filter external requirements belongs a particular set of associated Purchasing groups (by user level), you can implement filters on custom fields search at Header and/or Item level. Note that you need to implement this BADI with filter SOCO as Object Type.
- Search BADI BBP_WF_LIST can be implemented at object type SOCO and use method BBP_WF_LIST_SOCO.

6.4.4 Grouping

You can group the external requirements in Sourcing cockpit. You can process the sourcing group by the program BBP_SC_TRANSFER_GROUPED. The program creates the follow-on document based on your source of supply purchase order or bid invitation for the consolidated requirements. You can schedule this program as the background job. You can copy this program into a custom program to handle flexible grouping based on your business requirements. The standard program provides option to add alerts to EBP application monitor. The purchase order alerts are under Purchase Order -> Automated grouping and bid invitation alerts are under Bid Invitation -> Automated grouping.

The function module BBP_ALERT_<BO>_GROUPING adds an alert to EBP application monitor. It uses message BBP_ADMIN/048 for the alert.

Technical Information

The function module BBP_PD_INDEX_FIND can be used to search contracts and AVL. The selection criteria can be differentiated between hard and soft search criteria. Hard search criteria must match exact information. On the other hand, soft criteria may not match exact information, or the information may be blank.

Sourcing Relation Indicator is one of the important fields at item level which determines whether the shopping carts can be listed at sourcing cockpit. The source_rel_ind is at Shopping cart item level. Sourcing Indicator values are included in the include BBP_PD_CON. The following list provides sourcing relation indicator value and meanings.

```
* constants for the sourcing flag
CONSTANTS:
 gc_not_sourcing_relevant TYPE bbp_source_rel_ind VALUE space,
 gc_sourcing_relevant     TYPE bbp_source_rel_ind VALUE 'X',
 gc_grouping_relevant     TYPE bbp_source_rel_ind VALUE 'A',
 gc_sourcing_completed    TYPE bbp_source_rel_ind VALUE 'Y',
 gc_clear_sourcing_flag   TYPE bbp_source_rel_ind VALUE 'C',
 gc_grouping_bid_relevant TYPE bbp_source_rel_ind VALUE 'D',
 gc_rfq_from_sc           TYPE bbp_source_rel_ind VALUE 'N',
 gc_rfq_from_soco         TYPE bbp_source_rel_ind VALUE 'M',
 gc_rfq_from_sc_esoa      TYPE bbp_source_rel_ind VALUE 'E',
 gc_items_with_followon_doc  TYPE bbp_source_rel_ind VALUE 'T',
 gc_item_from_sc_esoa_back-end TYPE bbp_source_rel_ind VALUE 'P'.
* Constants for sourcing customizing
CONSTANTS:
    gc_no_sourcing TYPE bbp_sourcing_decision VALUE space,
    gc_sourcing    TYPE bbp_sourcing_decision VALUE 'X',
    gc_grouping    TYPE bbp_sourcing_decision VALUE 'A',
    gc_auto_bid    TYPE bbp_sourcing_decision VALUE 'B',
    gc_group_bid   TYPE bbp_sourcing_decision VALUE 'D'.
```

You can use the function module BBP_PDIGP_DB_DIRECT_UPDATE to update the sourcing relation indicator flag for a SC item. Or you can use FM BBP_PDH_DB_DIRECT_UPDATE to update the source relation indicator. The FM BBP_PD_SC_UPDATE will not update the sourcing relation indicator flag.

Technical Challenges: You need to set manual sourcing (using the sourcing cockpit) when the shopping cart process types are ZPR1, ZPR2and ZPR3. Also, when there is an associated contract item and the contract has an active change document, do not source automatically.

Solution: Implement BADI BBP_SRC_DETERMINE. Sourcing parameters defines the type of sourcing.

Name: BBP_SRC_DETERMINE		Multiple Use: No	Filter: Yes
Description: Determine execution of sourcing for an item			
Method: DETERMINE_SOURCING ***Description***: Determine sourcing for a shopping item. Parameters:			
Name	Type	Data Type	Description
HEADER_BBP_GUID	Import	BBP_GUID	Shopping Cart Header GUID
ITEM_BBP_GUID	Import	BBP_GUID	Shopping Cart Item GUID
SOURCING	Change	BBP_SOURCING _DECISION	Determine Sourcing

```
  DATA: lv_sc_header  TYPE bbp_pds_sc_header_d.
  DATA: lv_sc_item     TYPE bbp_pds_sc_item_d,
      lv_read_flags TYPE bbps_ctr_detail_requested,
      lv_version    TYPE bbp_pds_version_list_internal,
      et_version    TYPE TABLE OF bbp_pds_version_list_internal.
  CALL FUNCTION 'BBP_PD_SC_GETDETAIL'
   EXPORTING
    i_guid         = header_bbp_guid
    i_with_itemdata = ' '
   IMPORTING
    e_header       = lv_sc_header.
 IF lv_sc_header-process_type = c_zpr1 OR
   lv_sc_header-process_type = c_zpr2 OR
   lv_sc_header-process_type = c_zpr3.
  sourcing = 'A'.
 ENDIF.
```

```
CALL FUNCTION 'BBP_PD_SC_ITEM_GETDETAIL'
 EXPORTING
  i_guid = item_bbp_guid
 IMPORTING
  e_item = lv_sc_item.
CHECK lv_sc_item-ctr_hdr_number IS NOT INITIAL.
lv_ctr_objid = v_sc_item-ctr_hdr_number.
lv_read_flags-version_tab = 'X'.
CALL FUNCTION 'BBP_PD_CTR_GETDETAIL'
 EXPORTING
  i_object_id    = lv_ctr_objid
  i_with_itemdata = space
  i_read_flags   = lv_read_flags
 TABLES
  e_version      = et_version.
 LOOP AT et_version INTO lv_version.
              WHERE version_type = 'C' AND
                 inact = ' '.
 ENDLOOP.
 CHECK sy-subrc = 0.
 sourcing = 'A'.
```

You can create a follow-on document by the customer ABAP program instead of Sourcing Cockpit. The following function module can be sed to create any follow-on document by passing iv_object_type parameter. You can get application log message using the FM BBP_PD_LOG_GET_MESSAGES.

```
* iv_object_type determines the follow-on document type
* lv_transfer_action determines whether it is Simulation, park, commit
 CALL FUNCTION 'BBP_PD_SC_TRANSFER_MULTI'
  EXPORTING
   is_transfer_action = lv_transfer_action
   iv_object_type    = iv_object_type
   it_attach         = lt_attach[]
```

```
TABLES
  it_header        = it_header_sc
  it_item          = it_item_sc
  it_account       = it_account
  it_partner       = it_partner
  it_longtext      = it_longtext
  it_status        = it_status
  it_limit         = it_limit
  it_org           = it_org
  it_tax           = it_tax
  it_pridoc        = it_pridoc
  it_hcf           = it_hcf
  it_icf           = it_icf
  ct_reflist       = lt_local_ref
  et_header        = et_header_gen
  et_item          = et_item_gen
  et_messages      = lt_messages
  it_doc_descr     = it_doc_descr
  it_sdln          = it_sdln_sc.
```

6.5 Shopping Cart Transfer

Shopping cart transfer is the process during which the follow-on document is created in back-end ECC system. This process is applicable oly for the classic scenario. The Shopping Cart Transfer is started by the workflow when the shopping cart is released. The shopping cart transfer will be in background mode. The FM BBP_PD_SC_TRANSFER is used to transfer the shopping cart and create follow-on document. Note that the FM is used in both Classic and Extended Classic Scenario. Note also that you can use this FM to do manual transfer.

The Meta function module META_SC_BE_CRT is used to create follow-on document. The Meta function uses the ABAP object class adapter instead of the function module. These are the standard adapter classes used in the release 4.70.

Class Name	Description
CL_BBP_BS_ADAPTER_PO_CRT_470_1	PO Adapter
CL_BBP_BS_ADAPTER_RS_CRT_470	Reservation Adapter
CL_BBP_BS_ADAPTER_RQ_CRT_470	Requistion Adapter
CL_BBP_BS_ADAPTER_PO_CRT	Basic PO Adapter. Used when there is no adapter defined in mapping function.
CL_BBP_BS_ADAPTER_RS_CRT	Basic Reservation Adapter. Used when there is no adapter defined in mapping function.
CL_BBP_BS_ADAPTER_RQ_CRT	Basic Requisition Adapter. Used when there is no adapter defined in mapping function.

You can create a new custom adapter and adopt them with the BADI BBP_DRIVER_DETERMINE. The method CREATE_DOCUMENT defines what RFC function module to create the follow-on document.

6.5.1 Configuration

Target object determination will be based on the IMG configuration. The IMG can be accessed by the path SRM Server->Cross-Application Basic Settings->Define Objects in Back-end System. You can determine the follow-on document type based on Purchasing group, category and back-end system. The procurement type can be one of the following:

- Reservation if stock is available, otherwise external procurement – It will return the reservation follow-on type if the material is subject to Inventory management and enough stock quantity exists.
- Always Reservation for material subject to Inventory management – It will return the reservation follow-on type if the material is subject to IM irrespective of the stock level.
- Always external procurement – The system always procure the item externally.
- The external procurement can be configured as follows:
- Always Purchase requisition
- Purchase Order if item data complete, otherwise purchase requisition.

The follow-on document type will be determined by the back-end system only. The RFC function module BBP_INTERPRETE_DATA determines the follow-on document type based on your configuration.

6.5.2 Enhancements

A number of enhancements are available for the classic scenario shopping cart transfer process. These BADIs are explained briefly.

BBP_TARGET_OBJTYPE – Overriding the target object type determined by the IMG customization. The target object type is at ITEM_DATA-OBJ_TO_GEN field. Make sure that the field ITEM_DATA_PACK_OBJTYPE is also assigned properly along with obj_to_gen. The abbreviation of value on the field is as follows:

- 1 – Reservation (BUS2093)
- 2 – Purchase Requisition (BUS2105)
- 3 – Purchase Order (BUS2012)

BBP_CREATE_BE_PO_NEW – Changing all PO document data before it creates the PO. BADI provides two methods FILL_PO_INTERFACE and FILL_PO_INTERFACE1. Based on the adapter, one of these two methods will be executed. For 4.70 versions, FILL_PO_INTERFACE1 method will be executed. You can change PO document data in the structure BBPS_BADI_PO_CREATE1 which includes all document information. This BADI is replaces the old BADI BBP_CREATE_PO_BACK.

BBP_CREATE_BE_RQ_NEW – Changing all Requisition document data before it creates the PR. The PR data can be changed using the method FILL_RQ_INTERFACE. The changes are possible as it in the structure BBPS_BADI_RQ_CREATE. This BADI replaces the old BADI BBP_CREATE_REQ_BACK.

BBP_CREATE_BE_RS_NEW – Changing all Reservation/Confirmation document data before it creates the PO creation. BADI provides two methods FILL_RS_INTERFACE and FILL_RS_INTERFACE1. Based on the adapter, one of these two methods will be executed. For 4.70 versions, FILL_RS_INTERFACE1 method will be executed. You can change PO document data in the structure BBPS_BADI_RS_CREATE1 which includes all document information. This BADI is replacement of old BADI BBP_CREATE_RES_BACK.

BBP_BS_GROUP_BE – BADI is used create multiple follow-on documents based on the grouping of the shopping cart items. There are separate methods for Requisition (GROUP_RQ_BACKEND), Purchase Order (GROUP_PO_BACKEND) and Requirement (GROUP_RS_BACKEND). The system creates a separate purchase requisition for each document type. The purchase order grouping can be done by Vendor, Purchase organization, Purchasing Group, Contract, Document Type and Company Code. In the standard process, a separate reservation will be created for each shopping cart item. With this BADI, you can override and create a single reservation for all line items. There is one more method GET_NUMBER_OR_RANGE on this BADI. It can override the default number range or Number.

6.5.3 Administration Reports

There are a few reports to administrate the shopping cart transfer function.

- BBP_GET_STATUS_2 - The report update all requirement coverage requests for which the follow-on documents are created. You should schedule the job in background. SAP recommends that schedule this report daily.
- CLEAN_REQREQ_UP - Cleans REQREQ (BBP_DOCUMENT_TAB db table) entries. If the follow-on document is created then clear record from BBP_DOCUMENT_TAB.
- BBP_CLEANER - The program schedules a job to execute the report CLEAN_REQREQ_UP.

6.6 Bid Invitation & Bid Responses

A bid invitation is an invitation to potential Suppliers by the purchaser through the bidding process to submit a quotation for specific product or service. The lowest bidder is awarded the contract, provided they meet minimum criteria for the Bid. There are two types of Bid Invitation: Public and Private. Public bid invitations can be accessed by all the potential buyers on the web. The private bid invitation can be only accessed by known potential buyers only. Bidders can create a bid response for a RFx.

Bid Invitation can be created from scratch or manually from requirements. User master records are created for bidders and portal providers. Bid invitations can be created automatically. Emails are generated using Smart Forms for Bid notification.

SAP delivers Bidder history, Vendor evaluation, Price comparison list, and detailed bid comparison with attributes through BI reporting.

6.6.1 Enhancements

The following BADI enhancements are available at RFx Object. The BADIs are part of the sourcing and Bidding process.

- **BBP_TRANSFER_GROUP** - The Bid Invitation is follow-on document of PR(s) created automatically or by Sourcing Cockpit. One or more PRs can be grouped into a single Bid Invitation. The FM BP_PD_SC_TRANSFER_MULTI_RFQ creates the Bid Invitation document from External Requirements or Shopping Carts. Based on the customer requirements, there are situation that same requirements may need to span more than one Bid Invitation. The BADI BBP_TRANSFER_GROUP can be used to split PR requirements into multiple Bid Invitations.

- **BBP_SAVE_BID_ON_HOLD** - You can use this BADI to determine whether RFx can be published (if there is no edit check error) or put it hold. The BADI will pass RFx Header GUID and export rv_bid_on_hold flag. You can add the logic what kind of Bid Invitation requires a hold. This BADI is only applicable at Sourcing Bid Invitation creation.

- **BBP_BID_DET_PROCTYPE** - The BADI BBP_BID_DET_PROCTYPE can be used to determine the process type while transferring the shopping cart into a bid invitation. The BADI is executed in the FM BBP_RFQ_FROM_SOCO_CREATE.

- **BBP_DETERMINE_DYNATR** - The dynamic attributes are proposed by the product category as defined in IMG configuration. With this BADI, you can change the dynamic attribute and its value.

- **BBP_CFOLDER_BADI** – The BADI is to configure the system to perform customer-specific cFolder operations. It is relevant only when PLM cFolders and SRM integration. It is executed at the following events:

  - After a cFolder is created
  - After a cFolder is assigned to a bid
  - After the collaboration list is read
  - After a work area is generated for a vendor
  - Before authorizations are assigned
  - Before a cFolder assignment is deleted

Bid invitation provides you the option to add new bidder using the internal directory search of the bidder list. Web Dynpro component /SAPSRM/WDC_UI_DO_BIDDER supports the Bidder List internal search. The search can be done by Contact persons, Portal users, Suppliers and Vendor List. The search can use the standard search helps based on business partner type. The PDO object for Bidder is /SAPSRM/CL_PDO_DO_BIDDERS and search object is /SAPSRM/CL_PDO_DO_BIDDERS_SRCH. The DO object for Bidder is /SAPSRM/CL_CH_WD_DODM_BIDDER. You can extend these classes to make any changes in the search. For example, you can do your own search.

6.6.2 Awarding Bid Response

The Bid evaluation can be done by Live Cockpit. Few clients use their legacy Bid evaluation system. You need he interface between SAP and Legacy system when there is a legacy bid evaluation system. The follow-on document of Bid Response is Purchase Order or Contract. SRM provides the following function modules to create purchase order or Contract from the Bid.

Function Module	Comments
BBP_BID_TRANSFERRED_PO_CREATE	Award PO from Bid Response
BBP_CREATE_CONTRACT_FROM_BID	Create Contract from Bid Response
BBP_UPDATE_CONTRACT_FROM_BID	Update Contract from Bid Response

You can use these function modules to create follow-on document with partial quantity level. That means you can create multiple POs/Contracts for a Bid invitation and its Bid responses.

Some useful ABAP Objects:

- /SAPSRM/CL_RFQ_UTIL – Utility class for Bid Invitation. It has a number of static methods.
- /SAPSRM/CL_COND_UTILS_RFQ – Condition Utility class for Bid invitation.
- /SAPSRM/CL_BIDDER_UTILTIES – Utility class for Bidders functionality. The utility has methods to get Bidders, Adding Bidder, Notify Bidders and other Bidder related functions.
- /SAPSRM/CL_QTE_UTI – Utility class for Quote/Bid Response functionality. All methods are static methods. The method PREPARE_QUOTE will prepare quote data and other quote get methods can fetch standard quote data.
- /SAPSRM/CL_SUMMARY_UTILTIES – The utility object to get quote summary and attributes summary.

6.7 Purchase Order

Purchase Order in SRM comes into play in plan driven procurement scenarios. Purchase orders are used to procure direct materials integrating suppliers into the process. Purchase requisitions usually form the basis for the Purchase Order document. Purchase requisition is a demand that is provided to the purchasing department. It can be created manually or from a shopping cart.

Purchase order is part of the operational procurement of materials and services. The primary purpose of purchase orders is to convert demands, purchase requisitions, shopping carts into POs to monitor their fulfillment. To process a PO in BP, the following steps are necessary.

- Source of supply – Assign / check source of supply that will deliver the requested material or service
- Determine prices and conditions – Negotiate prices with a supplier if required
- Add further explanation by creating attachments, long texts..
- Account assignment data for financial purposes
- Define Incoterms and delivery instructions
- Define release process for purchase orders
- Version Management of purchase orders
- Message output to trigger EDI/Print/Fax communication to supplier

6.7.1 Parallel Check

The SRM7.0 UI does provide option to validate budget check before replicate PO into ECC. In SRM5.X, there is no back-end error check function module to validate PO replication. When the approval is successful and it will fail in PO replication error. It causes PO data integration issue. In SRM7.0, this issue has been resolved.

SRM7 provides the function module BBP_PD_PO_PARALLEL_CHECK to do back-end ECC PO creation/update validation. This check will execute META_DPO_TRANSFER with test run in a background task. This FM is accessed from check method of the PDO layer /SAPSRM/CL_PDO_PO. This check will be executed only when there is no SRM hard check error failure.

6.7.2 PO Replication

PO replication is applicable for the extended classic scenario. SRM Purchase Order is leading PO and all changes must be done at SRM level only. You cannot make any change on ECC side directly. On approval of SRM PO, the PO is replicated to ECC back-end system using RFC function module. The replication is done by function module META_DPO_TRANSFER and it uses The ECC function module BBP_PO_INBOUND. ECC function module can be used to transfer or simulate the PO replication. The PO replication log is stored under Object BBP/REPLICATION and the external number is stored as PO object id.

Custom Fields

The standard SRM/ECC integration provides an option to mapping between custom fields of SRM system to ECC system without any code changes. The custom mapping information is stored in the ECC table BBP_CUFMAP. The table can be maintained by transaction code SM30. This table has Document Type (either PO or INV), Key Type (S- Customer and Z – custom field), SRM field and ECC field name. For PO replication, you need to define BBP_CUFMAP with document type PO. This table is used to map between different SRM and ECC field names. If the map is not defined, the program tries to map the same custom field name in the ECC system.

The custom fields should be passed in the variable customer_fields. The customer fields will be populated based on the structures INCL_EEW_PD_HEADAER_CSF_PO and INCL_EEW_PD_HEADAER_CSF_PO for Header and Item respectively.

BBP_PO_INBOUND has BAPI_EXTENSIONIN to add extension information. The customer fields of SRM will be passed in BBP_PO_INBOUND and it is mapped into the parameter BAPI_EXTENSIONIN into PO Create or Change API. The ECC custom fields must be in ECC structures based on type of customer fields.

Type	Structure
Header	BAPI_TE_MEPOHEADER
Item	BAPI_TE_MEPOITEM
Accounting	BAPI_TE_MEPOACCONTING
Schedule	BAPI_TE_MEPOSCHEDULE
X Header	BAPI_TE_MEPOHEADERX
X Item	BAPI_TE_MEPOITEMX
X Accounting	BAPI_TE_MEPOACCONTINGX
X Schedule	BAPI_TE_MEPOSCHEDULEX

The standard SAP function will ignore mapping when any data type of MEPO structure has data type P. SAP ignores data type P due to mapping issue and possible short dumps. It is one of important thing to check at standard mapping. If the data structure has data type P then you can implement the CUFMAP at BADI BBP_PO_INBOUND_BADI. The sample code is defined in the BADI sample code (in previous section). You must set value 'X' to corresponding X type structures for value passed. The information is passed to BAPI_EXTENSIONINX. BAPI_EXTENSIONIN allows only 940 characters so any structure has more than 940 characters then the value of fields after 940 characters will not be passed to the PO create/update.

6.7.3 Enhancement

PO replication provides BADIs at SRM and ECC side. The BADI BBP_ECS_PO_OUT_BADI is used modify back-end system data. The method bbp_b46b_po_outbound should be implemented to make custom changes. In standard SRM, it includes all customer fields from Header and Item customer fields defined. You can modify or delete or add new customer fields and values.

ECC provides the BADI BBP_PO_INBOUND_BADI to handle changes in back-end system. The BADI has two methods BBP_MAP_BEFORE_BAPI (is executed before PO Create or Update) and BBP_MAP_AFTER_BAPI (after PO processing). The BBP_MAP_AFTER_BAPI can change basic data which can be used in APO interface.

6.8 Contract

Central contract management manages and distributes central contracts across SRM and associated ERP systems. A central contract is a legal binding agreement between a purchaser and a supplier. The purchase order quantity and value, limit confirmations, and invoices are released against the central contract.

The program BBP_CONTRACT_INITIAL_UPLOAD is used to upload the ECC (back-end systems) contracts into SRM system. The BADIs BBP_CTR_INIT_UP (SRM side) and BBP_CTR_INIT_UP_PI (ECC side) can be used to influence the contract data upload.

6.8.1 Contract Replication

Contract Replication is done through the Meta function module META_CTR_TRANSFER. The RFC FM BBPV_CONTRACT_TRANSFER program creates BLAORD03 IDOC. You can modify the contract data in SRM BADI before it executes the RFC function module.

Enhancements

There are enhancements for both contract replication methods. The following BADIs are for RFC contract transfer.

BBP_CTR_BE_CREATE – This is an SRM side BADI to change contract data before executing RFC function module. The BADI has following two methods:

- CONTRACT_PROCESS_TYPE_FILL – You can overwrite the transaction type of back-end system contract. Make sure that transaction type is configured in IMG.
- CONTRACT_INTERFACE_FILL – You can change contract interface data before it transfers to back-end function module.

BBP_CTR – This is an ECC side BADI and you can change the IDOC data, contract data structure and related conditions. This is only applicable when appropriate IDOCs have been setup completely. The IDOCs used are BLAORD03 and COND_A02. There are the following methods in this BADI:

- MODIFY_DATA_CTR – The method is executed before the mapping to the IDOC structure. You can modify this data before it is mapped to the IDOC structures.
- MODIFY_IDOC_DATA_CTR – The method is called after all the mappings to the Contract IDOC structures. You can change this result before the IDOC is updated to the database.
- MODIFY_IDOC_DATA_CND – The method is called after all the mappings to the Condition IDOC structures. You can change this result before the IDOC is updated to the database.

Procure-to-Pay Scenario Contract Management has been introduced in SRM 7.0. And it is designed as an integrated scenario between SRM 7.0 and ECC 6.04. The contract transfer does not using standard RFC function module to replicate the contract. Instead, it uses XI interfaces to replicate the contract. You must have user WF-BATCH under your SRM Organizational plan and should have the roles of /SAPSRM/ST_PURCHASER and /SAPSRM/EMPLOYEE. The following interfaces are used in the contract replication. You can view these interfaces in the SAP Integration Builder. The interface uses Service Oriented Architecture.

The following BADIs are for XI contract replication.

/SAPSRM/SE_CTRREPLICATION_ASYN – This SRM BADI is under the /SAPSRM/ES_SOA_MAPPING enhancement spot. Using this BADI, you can map your own data in the contract interface data. It has two methods viz., outbound processing and inbound processing. For our contract replication Outbound, the method /SAPSRM/IF_SE_CTRREPLICA_ASYN~OUTBOUND_PROCESSING is used to change contract data.

PUR_SE_PCSRMRPLCTNRQ_ASYN – This ECC side BADI for the Contract Replication Process. There are two methods for Inbound Processing and Outbound Processing. For Contract Replication, Inbound Processing helps update contract data.

6.8.2 Mass Contract Update

Mass contract update is a tool to update multiple contracts with same value. The mass contract update can be accessed from Advanced Search. The possible change on contract values is pre-defined and it is defined in the view BBPV_CTR_MASSOP. You can see a number of methods defined in this view and it is provided by the standard SAP package. You have the option to extend changing values. It can be done by implementing BADI /SAPSRM/CTR_MC_BADI. The BADI provides standard implementations for each change method defined in BBPV_CTR_MASSOP.

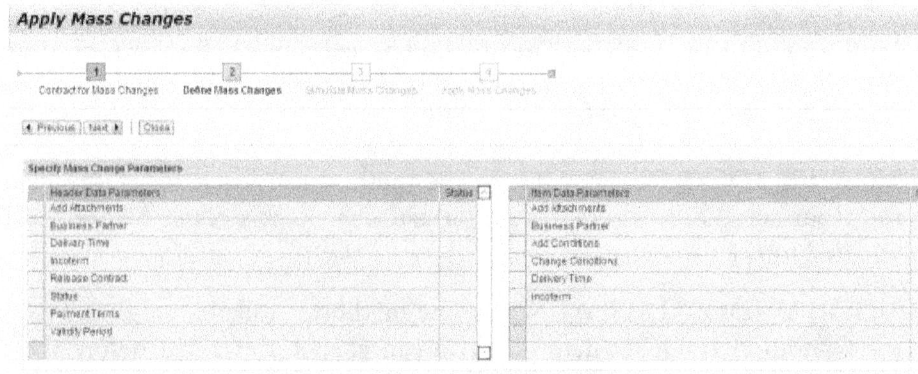

Technical Challenges: The standard Mass Contract Update provides the option to change few standard fields only. The customer requirement is that provision to add few standard fields and custom fields in the Mass Contract Update program.

Solution: Note you can add any fields in the Mass Contract Update are possible only if the field is in the structure BBP_PDS_CTR_HEDER_U. Adding standard fields and/or custom fields in the Mass Contract Update functionalities requires the following steps:

- Mass Contract Update shows the new fields only when the field name entry is in the views BBPV_CTR_MASSOP and BBPV_CTR_MASSOPT.

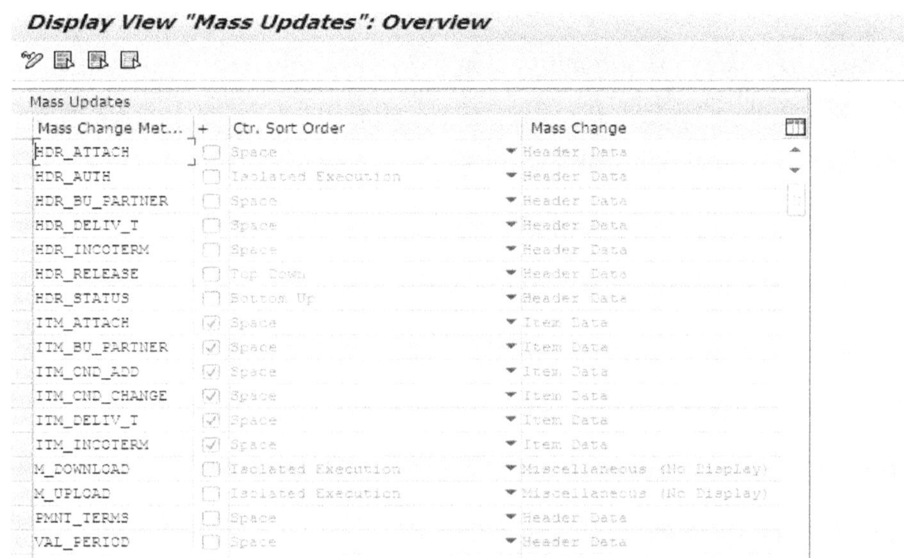

Display View "Mass Updates": Overview

Mass Updates

Mass Change Met...	+	Ctr. Sort Order	Mass Change
HDR_ATTACH	☐	Space	Header Data
HDR_AUTH	☐	Isolated Execution	Header Data
HDR_BU_PARTNER	☐	Space	Header Data
HDR_DELIV_T	☐	Space	Header Data
HDR_INCOTERM	☐	Space	Header Data
HDR_RELEASE	☐	Top Down	Header Data
HDR_STATUS	☐	Bottom Up	Header Data
ITM_ATTACH	☑	Space	Item Data
ITM_BU_PARTNER	☑	Space	Item Data
ITM_CND_ADD	☑	Space	Item Data
ITM_CND_CHANGE	☑	Space	Item Data
ITM_DELIV_T	☑	Space	Item Data
ITM_INCOTERM	☑	Space	Item Data
M_DOWNLOAD	☐	Isolated Execution	Miscellaneous (No Display)
M_UPLOAD	☐	Isolated Execution	Miscellaneous (No Display)
PMNT_TERMS	☐	Space	Header Data
VAL_PERIOD	☐	Space	Header Data

- Create a new customer structure for your new field. The structure should have the information about new, old and field from fields. Please refer /SAPSRM/S_PDO_CTR_MC_PMNT_TRMS structure for payment terms. You must create a separate structure for each field required in contract mass update functionality.

- Create table type for the new custom structure. This structure will be used in BADI implementation.

- Create a Custom Web Dynpro component. The standard Web Dynpro application is /SAPSRM/WDC_UI_AO_CT_MC_D.

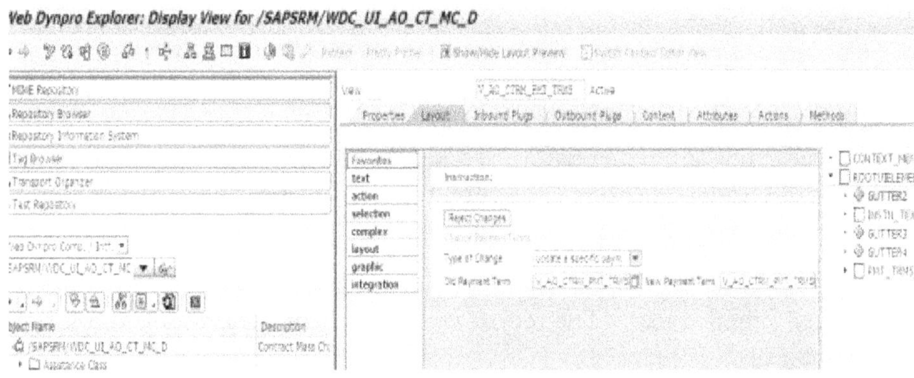

- Create a new Web Dynpro component in the Z or Y namespace and implement the interface /SAPSRM/WDI_CTR_MC.

- In method GET_VIEW_CONTEXT of the component controller, implement the following code, where <node_name> is the name of the context node:
- ron_context = wd_context->get_child_node (name = IF_COMPONENTCONTROLLER=>wdctx_<node_name>).
- Create a view and an inbound plug in the view. Embed the view to the window.
- Create a context node in the component controller with the required attributes from the structure that you created above, and link the node to the view controller context node.
- Create an action ACTIONREJ_CHNG in the view.
- Method ONACTIONACTIONREJ_CHNG is created automatically.
- Implement the following code in the method:

  wd_comp_controller->fire_reject_changes_evt ( ).
- For creating the view layout, refer payment term component /SAPSRM/WDC_UI_AO_CT_MC_D and view V_AO_CTRM_INCO_HEAD.

- Implement the BADI /SAPSRM/CTR_MASS_CHANGE for each field. The interface has the following methods:
  - CTR_DEFINE_UI – Provide screen information for the field. This is done through the new Web Dynpro component.
  - CTR_GET_READ_FLAGS – Distinguishes between header and item parameters.
  - CTR_CHANGE – Maps with new value with old and validate new value.
  - CTR_GET_STATUS_MESSAGE – Provides the status of mass change process.
  - CTR_VALIDATE – Validate the screen input values.

Refer the implementation /SAPSRM/CL_CTR_MC_HI_INCOTERM for handling both Header and Item level Inco term changes.

The ABAP object /SAPSRM/CL_PDO_AO_CTR_MC is SAP provided PDO object. There is an admin report BBP_CONTRACT_MASS_UPDATE for Contract Mass Change functionality. The report is used to achieve and delete mass change work pages periodically.

6.9 Summary

In this chapter, you have learned technical solutions related to application objects using SRM BADIs. You have learned portal integration and how to navigate the SRM objects from your custom programs. You have learned the Alert management with technical details and enhancements.

Advanced Search is an extension of Personalized Object Work List Framework. POWL is great option to Search the SRM documents and activities on the SRM document. The SRM Extension of POWL provides a greater flexibility to change selection criteria and results.

7 Advanced Search – POWL

The search utility is a required tool for the OLTP system. The search utility allows the user to display and edit the transactional data. SRM7.x provides a search utility tool for the SRM documents and it is named as Advanced Search. Advanced Search is a very flexible and complex tool. It uses the Personalized Object Work List (POWL) framework. The POWL is a standard Web Dynpro framework offered by SAP Enterprise Portal. It delivers an overview of objects the user is working with, and it provides him or her with the ability to access individual objects for further processing. POWL allows users to modify queries and create personal variants if the user is authorized. Advanced Search is a Web Dynpro Configuration of the POWL

Advanced Search is a one point search utility provided for SRM documents. Advanced search is available from SRM 6.0. In the earlier version, for each SRM object, there is a separate UI program to do search. The activities on these search programs are limited and extension is required the extended technical development. Advanced Search is a great utility to search all SRM business objects and do specific actions.

This chapter explains the basics of POWL, SRM functionality, configuration and technical enhancements. POWL comprises a number of components. The basic of POWL provides you a good platform to understand Advanced Search and POWL. This chapter explains the integration of POWL and the Advanced Search. Also, the chapter explains what exit points (BADIs) are provided to enhance the Advanced Search functionality.

Introduction

In SRM6.0 or higher, the Advanced Search replaces all search objects into a single object for listing out the Selection criteria and do further activities on the SRM documents. The Advanced Search is a POWL based framework. In this section, you can see components of Advanced Search UI screen.

- Top and Bottom Button – Close button on top and bottom part of the screen.
- Extended Search – Choose the business object to search
- Query View – List of available queries for the user
- Search Screen – Search listing and Define Own query, Change Query and Personalize the output for the User
- Activity Toolbar – Activities can be applied on the Result document.
- Result Screen – List of the Objects based on the Selection Screen.

7.1 POWL Basics

The Web Dynpro application POWL_UI_COMP is a framework used by the POWL. The Advanced Search utility uses the Web Dynpro configuration /SAPSRM/WDA_ADV_SEARCH on the application POWL_UI_COMP. The POWL UI Application accesses the data from POWL Cache instead of database. The POWL Cache is nothing but the resultant data of the queries. The POWL Cache reduces the performance bottlenecks. There is an SAP standard load program to populate the POWL Cache for all queries. The load program information is discussed under the POWL Reports section.

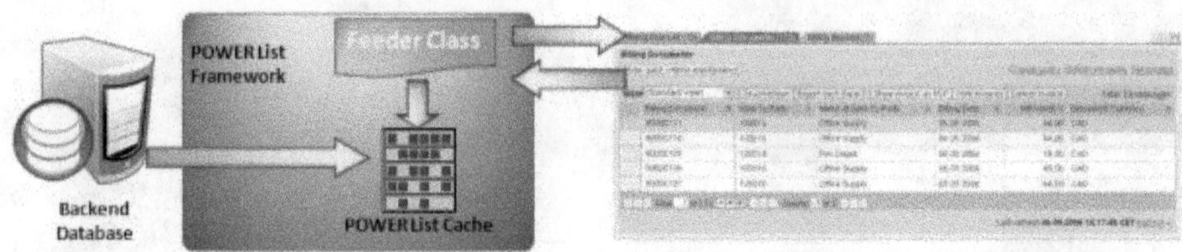

The Feeder Class is the base of the POWL and it communicates with the database based on the selection criteria and forwards the data to the POWL Cache. It refreshes the POWL List based on the user's demand. Also, the Feeder Class handles all activities defined on the application.

Technical Information

Each SRM object type uses a separate feeder class. All the feeder classes implement the interface IF_POWL_FEEDER. Interface IF_POWL_FEEDER has following methods:

Method	Description
GET_ACTIONS	define action meta data for represented object type
GET_ACTION_CONF	define an action confirmation message
GET_SEL_CRITERIA	define selection criteria meta data
GET_FIELD_CATALOG	define field catalog meta data
GET_OBJECT_DEFINITION	define data structure for represented object type
GET_OBJECTS	data retrieval for represented object type
GET_DETAIL_COMP	object-detail WD comp., implementing IFC_POWL_DETAIL
HANDLE_ACTION	handle actions for object type (c.f. GET_ACTIONS)

The ABAP class /SAPSRM/CL_CLL_POWL_POWL_BASE_AGENT is the base agent class for the Feeder. All the pre-defined feeder classes are inherited from this class. The base class defineds all BADIs where you can enhance your SRM POWL Advanced Search. SRM provides base agent classes for each SRM object type (overall, header and item level). The following are list of SRM object level agent classes:

BO Agent Class	Description
/SAPSRM/CL_CLL_POWL_A_BO_PO	BO base class for PO

/SAPSRM/CL_CLL_POWL_A_BO_PO_H	BO base class for PO header
/SAPSRM/CL_CLL_POWL_A_BO_PO_I	BO base class for PO Item

SAP provides a number of pre-defined feeder classes and configured with pre-defined POWL types. The following are few pre-defined feeder classes:

Feeder Class	**Description**
/SAPSRM/CL_CLL_PWL_A_CTR	POWL feeder class for Contract
/SAPSRM/CL_CLL_PWL_A_CTR_H	POWL feeder class for Contract Header
/SAPSRM/CL_CLL_PWL_A_CTR_I	POWL feeder class for Contract Items
/SAPSRM/CL_CLL_PWL_A_CONF	POWL feeder class for Confirmation
/SAPSRM/CL_CLL_PWL_A_CONF_H	POWL feeder class for Confirmation Header
/SAPSRM/CL_CLL_PWL_A_CONF_I	POWL feeder class for Confirmation Item
/SAPSRM/CL_CLL_PWL_A_PO	POWL feeder class for PO
/SAPSRM/CL_CLL_PWL_A_PO_H	POWL feeder class for PO Header
/SAPSRM/CL_CLL_PWL_A_PO_I	POWL feeder class for PO Item
/SAPSRM/CL_CLL_PWL_A_SC	POWL feeder class for Shopping cart
/SAPSRM/CL_CLL_PWL_A_SC_H	POWL feeder class for Shopping cart header
/SAPSRM/CL_CLL_PWL_A_SC_I	POWL feeder class for Shopping cart item

7.2 POWL Setup

POWL consist of a number of components and POWL construction comprises a number of building blocks. This section explains its components and how to configure each block. SRM provides the basic setup for POWL application and you can modify these configurations.

7.2.1 POWL Application ID

Each Feeder Class needs to be registered under a specific Application ID. The Application ID is associated with the SRM business object type. The definition includes the Application ID and its description. You can configure the POWL application ID by the transaction FPB_MAINTAIN_HIER.

7.2.2 POWL Type

The POWL Type is the Feeder Type according SRM Configuration. The POWL Type definition holds the Feeder Class information. Relationship between POWL Type and Application ID is base for the relationship between the Application ID and Feeder Classes. You can access the POWL Type definition by the transaction code POWL_TYPE.

7.2.3 Role Assignment

The Role Assignment is used to create a relationship between POWL Application ID and POWL type along with Role. These roles are part of the Basis Security roles. Most of SRM Role assignments involve only Application ID and POWL type not Role. The POWL Authorization object has been used to authentic the POWL Type and Query. You can configure the role assignment using the transaction code POWL_TYPER.

7.2.4 POWL Query

POWL Query consists of the query definition on the SRM object. The definition of POWL Query includes Query ID and its related POWL Type. Further Query Parameters and Settings can be configured. In this Query definition, you can set Layout variants. The POWL query can be done using the transaction code POWL_QUERY.

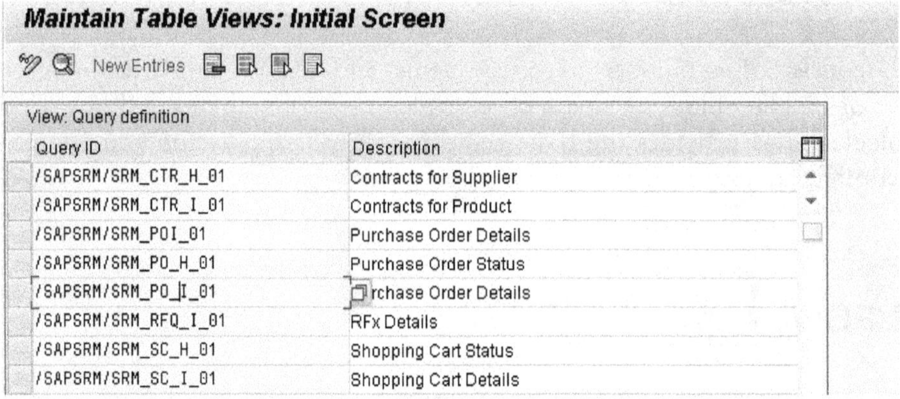

Maintain Table Views: Initial Screen

New Entries

View: Query definition

Query ID	Description
/SAPSRM/SRM_CTR_H_01	Contracts for Supplier
/SAPSRM/SRM_CTR_I_01	Contracts for Product
/SAPSRM/SRM_POI_01	Purchase Order Details
/SAPSRM/SRM_PO_H_01	Purchase Order Status
/SAPSRM/SRM_PO_I_01	Purchase Order Details
/SAPSRM/SRM_RFQ_I_01	RFx Details
/SAPSRM/SRM_SC_H_01	Shopping Cart Status
/SAPSRM/SRM_SC_I_01	Shopping Cart Details

The Query can be defined further in the following screen.

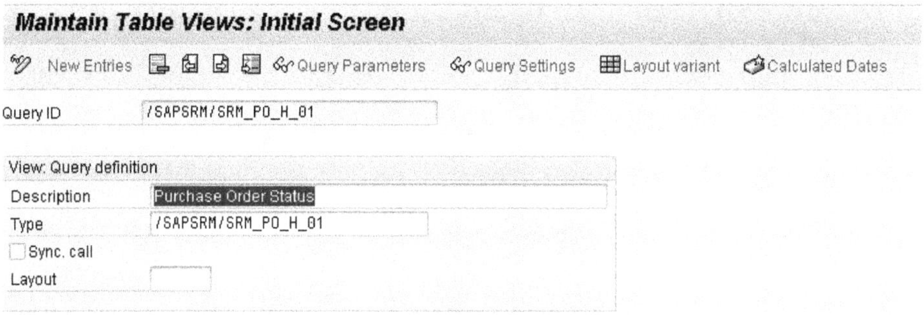

Maintain Table Views: Initial Screen
New Entries
Query Parameters
Query Settings
Layout variant
Calculated Dates
Query ID
/SAPSRM/SRM_PO_H_01
View: Query definition
Description
Purchase Order Status
Type
/SAPSRM/SRM_PO_H_01
Sync. call
Layout

The Query parameters can define the value of the Selection Criteria.

Parameters for query /SAPSRM/SRM_PO_H_01
Purchase Order Numb
to
Purchase Order Name
Status
Timeframe
3
Creation Date
to
Purchasing Organiza
to
Purchasing Group
to
Supplier
to
Company Code
Process Type
Check
Accept

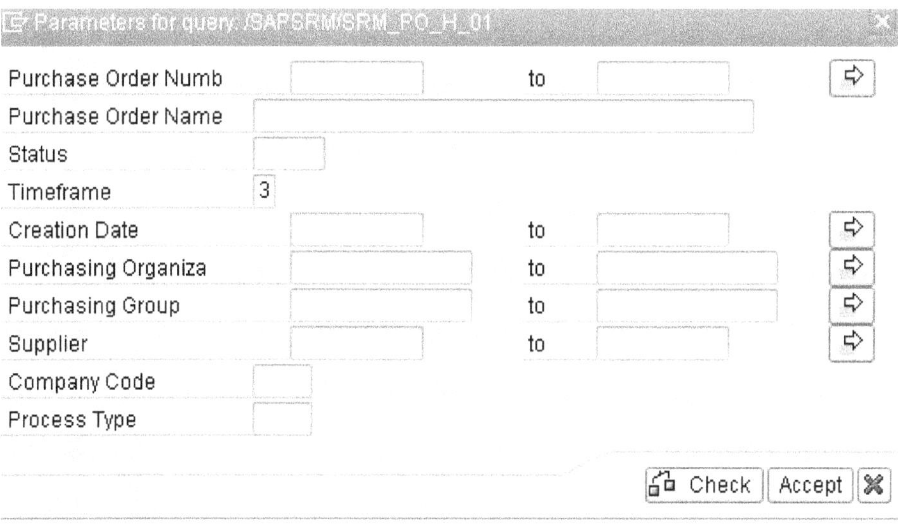

Also, Query parameters settings can be set on this transaction. The parameter settings like Mandatory, Read only and Hide.

Maintain Table Views: Initial Screen

Selection criteria settings

	Mandatory	Read only	Hidden	Quick search
Purchase ...	☐	☐	☐	☑
Purchase ...	☐	☐	☐	☑
Status	☐	☐	☐	☑
Timeframe	☐	☐	☐	☑
Creation D...	☐	☐	☐	☑
Purchasing...	☐	☐	☐	☑
Purchasing...	☐	☐	☐	☑
Supplier	☐	☐	☐	☑
Company ...	☐	☐	☐	☑
Process Ty...	☐	☐	☐	☑

Layout Setting is the basic ALV layout settings. Layout settings brings the portal page:

https://sever.com/sap/bc/webdynpro/sap/powl_master_query?QUERY= %2fSAPSRM%2fSRM_PO_H_01&TYPE=%2fSAPSRM%2fSRM_PO_H_01&SAP-CLIENT=100&***SAP-CONFIG-MODE=X.***

The SAP-CONFIG-MODE helps to administrator view layouts. See the following screen by clicking Settings link on top right side of ALV screen.

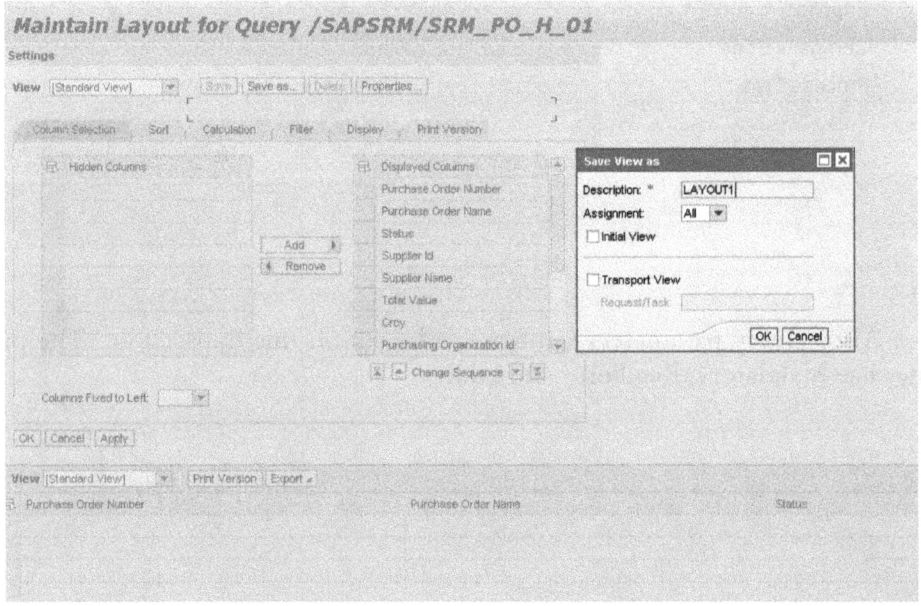

The layout view changes can be saved and create transport request by clicking Transport View check box. The transport can be moved to further system landscape and the layout views can be used. The layout view can be defaulted by clicking on the Initial View.

7.2.5 Query Role Assignment

Query Role Assignment relates Query and Application ID. You access this configuration by the transaction code POWL_QUERYR. Based on this definition, you can view the Query list in their screen for each SRM Object type. Also, on this step, Query can be categorized and sequenced. The category is meant to structure several queries for a POWL in a link matrix.

Change View "View: Query - Role assignment": Details

New Entries

Application	/SAPSRM/SRM_PO_H_01
Role	
Query ID	/SAPSRM/SRM_PO_H_01

View: Query - Role assignment

Category	SRM_PO
Description	Purchase Order Status
Category sequence no	
query sequence no	
Tab sequence no	
✓ Activate	

There is a check box to activate or de-activate the Query for the Application ID. The above steps provide the basic construction of POWL. The SRM extension explains the configuration and technical enhancements.

7.3 SRM Extension

SRM provides a set of configuration objects and Technical objects to use POWL for Advance Search Functionality. The technical object contains a set of Feeder Classes and Search engine integration to fetch the SRM documents.

The extended Search part of Advanced Search provides option to choose the object do the search. SRM supports multiple business objects and configuration helps to define what objects can be viewed. Advanced Search can show the list of Business Objects based on the configuration defined in the IMG configuration. The IMG Menu Path: SRM Server->Cross-Application Basic Settings->POWL and Advanced Search->Define Object Types for Advanced Search

Change View "Object Types for POWL-Based Advanced Search": Overview

New Entries

Object Types for POWL-Based Advanced Search

Object Type	Description	Description (Long)
BUS2000113	Contracts	SRM and ERP Contracts
BUS2013	Schedule Agreements	ERP Schedule Agreements
BUS2017	Goods Receipt	ERP Goods Receipt
BUS2091	Service Entry Sheet	ERP Service Entry Sheet
BUS2105	Purchase Requisition	ERP Purchase Requisition
BUS2121	Shopping Cart	SRM Shopping Cart
BUS2200	RFx	SRM RFx
BUS2201	Purchase Order	SRM Purchase Order
BUS2203	Confirmation	SRM Confirmation of Goods/Services
BUS2205	Incoming Invoice	SRM Incoming Invoice
BUS2206QA	Quota Arrangments	SRM Quota Arrangments
BUS2206VL	Supplier List	SRM Supplier List
BUS2208	Auction	SRM Auction
BUS2209	Purch.Order Response	SRM Purchase Order Response

7.3.1 SRM POWL Applications

SAP provides a set of POWL applications and POWL types. SRM associates the POWL application with SRM Business Objects. SRM provides an option to configure the default POWL application and POWL Query. The IMG Menu Path: **SRM Server->Cross-Application Basic Settings->POWL and Advanced Search->Define Default POWL Applications for Advance Search.**

Change View "Default POWL Application for Advanced Search": Overview

New Entries

Default POWL Application for Advanced Search

Object Type	Application	Query ID
BUS2000113	SAPSRM_AS_CTR	SAPSRM_AL_CONTRACT_01_01
BUS2013	SAPSRM_AS_OA	SAPSRM_AL_CONTRACT_04_01
BUS2017	SAPSRM_AS_GR	SAPSRM_AL_RECEIVING_02_01
BUS2091	SAPSRM_AS_SE	SAPSRM_AL_RECEIVING_04_01
BUS2105	SAPSRM_AS_PR	SAPSRM_AL_PURCHASING_01_01
BUS2121	SAPSRM_AS_SC	SAPSRM_AL_PURCHASING_02_01
BUS2200	SAPSRM_AS_RFX	SAPSRM_OP_SOURCING_01_01
BUS2201	SAPSRM_AS_PO	SAPSRM_AL_PURCHASING_03_01
BUS2203	SAPSRM_AS_CONF	SAPSRM_OP_PURCHASING_05_01
BUS2205	SAPSRM_AS_INV	SAPSRM_E_CHECKSTATUS_03
BUS2206QA	SAPSRM_AS_QTA	SAPSRM_SP_CONTRACT_03_01
BUS2206VL	SAPSRM_AS_ASL	SAPSRM_SP_BUSINESSPARTNER_01_01
BUS2208	SAPSRM_AS_AUC	SAPSRM_OP_SOURCING_02_01
BUS2209	SAPSRM_AS_POR	SAPSRM_AL_PURCHASING_04_01

Actual Feeder Types for SRM Object types can be identified by the transaction POWL_TYPE. Using this transaction, you can identify what Feeder Classes are used by the application.

7.3.2 SRM Feeder Types

Feeder Types are the backbone for SRM POWL Advanced Search. The Feeder Types are combination of Feeder Classes, Field Catalog, Selection Criteria and Action Listing. The Feeder types can be configured in IMG. Each SRM Feeder type has an equivalent POWL_TYPE definition. The Feeder Class is defined under the POWL type only.

The IMG Menu Path is SRM Server->Cross-Application Basic Settings->POWL and Advanced Search->Adjust POWL Layout Search criteria and Pushbuttons. Transaction code is /SAPSRM/POWL_CUST.

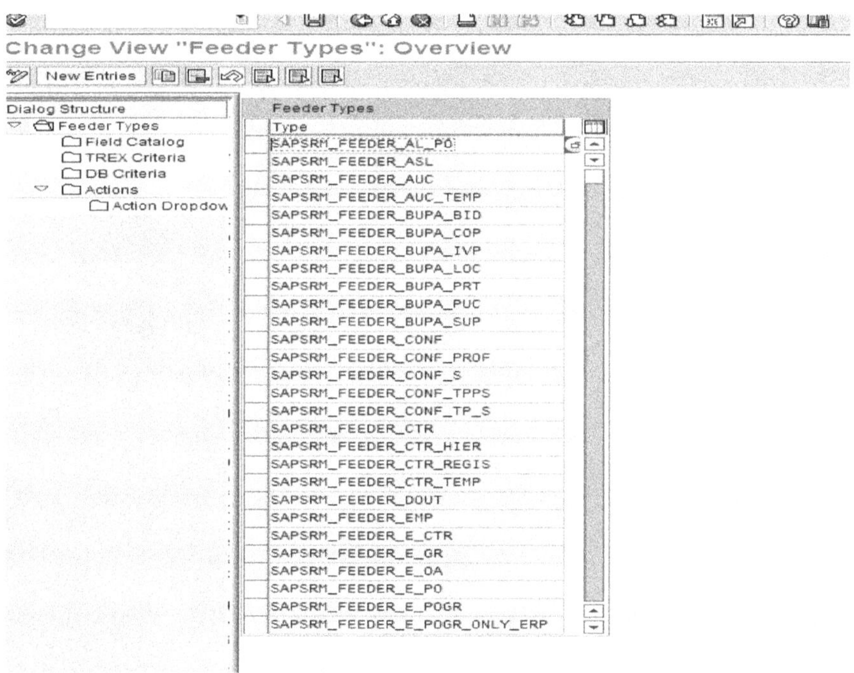

In this configuration, the user can configure the Field Catalog of the Feeder Type and its Field Catalog (list), Selection Criteria (which displays in selection criteria) and Actions. The name of SRM POWL Type (Feeder Type) starts with SAPSRM_FEEDER.

7.3.3 Action Buttons

Actions can be maintained for each Feeder Type and Dropdown values. Customization allows setting position, separator, text and Tooltip text. Also, you can maintain dropdown values for Actions.

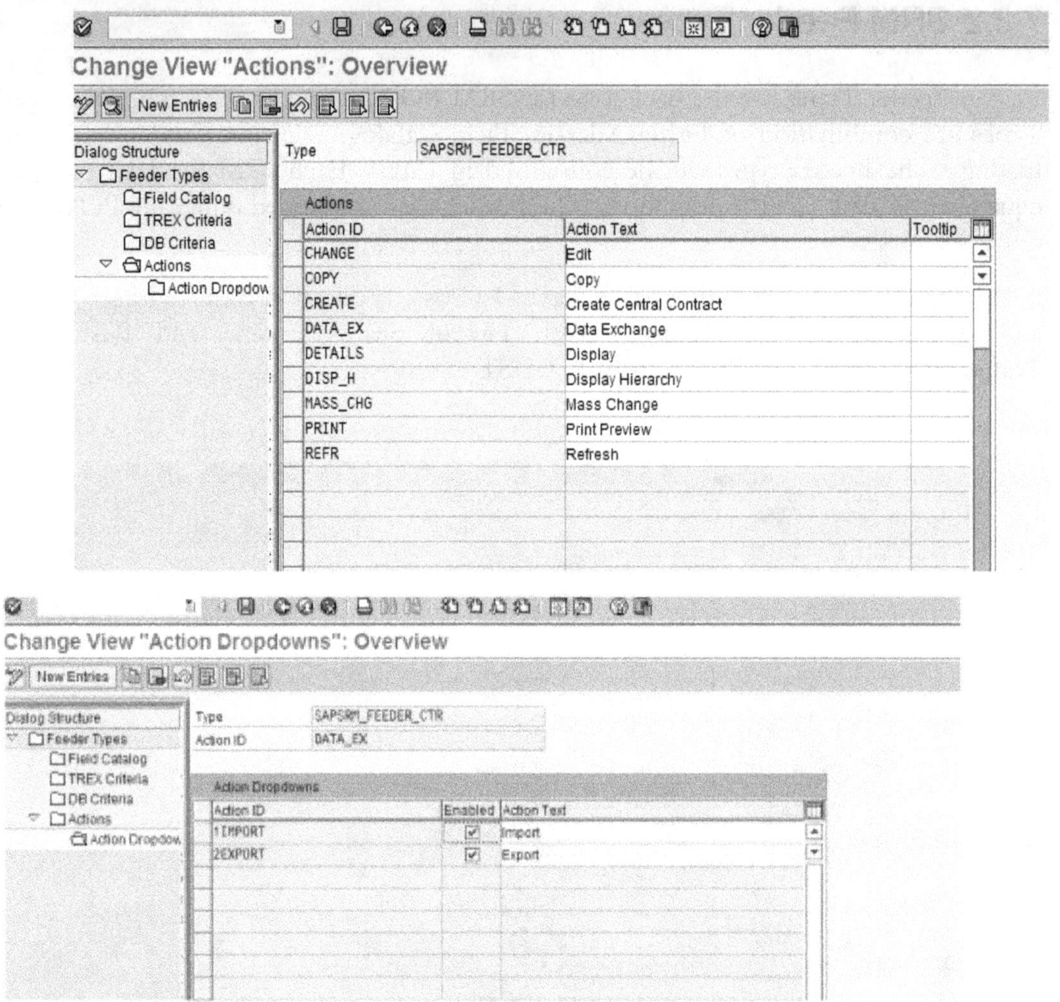

7.3.4 Technical Information

SRM provides the base class /SAPSRM/CL_CLL_POWL_BASE_AGENT for the Advanced Search Application. The base class implements the POWL Feeder interface IF_POWL_FEEDER. The GET_OBJECTS method implements the Search function of all SRM documents. SRM provides a Search engine class for each SRM business object type. SRM provides a number of Search Services for DB and TREX types.

Service Object	Description
/SAPSRM/CL_SRC_SRV_DB_ASL	Search Service for Approved Supplier List
/SAPSRM/CL_SRC_SRV_DB_AUC	Search Service for Auction
/SAPSRM/CL_SRC_SRV_DB_CONF	Search Service for Confirmation
/SAPSRM/CL_SRC_SRV_DB_CTR	Search Service for Contract
/SAPSRM/CL_SRC_SRV_DB_PO	Search Service for PO
/SAPSRM/CL_SRC_SRV_DB_POR	Search Service for PO Response
/SAPSRM/CL_SRC_SRV_DB_QTA	Search Service for Quota Arrangement
/SAPSRM/CL_SRC_SRV_DB_QTE	Search Service for Quote
/SAPSRM/CL_SRC_SRV_DB_RFQ	Search Service for Bid Invitation
/SAPSRM/CL_SRC_SRV_DB_SC	Search Service for Shopping Cart
/SAPSRM/CL_SRC_SRV_DB_SUPP	Search Service for Supplier

In the Search Engine service, SRM uses the standard its own SRM Search Objects. The following table lists few ABAP object classes.

Object	Description
/SAPSRM/CL_PDO_SO_SEARCH_AUC	Search Object for Auction
/SAPSRM/CL_PDO_SO_SEARCH_AVL	Search Object for Available Vendor List
/SAPSRM/CL_PDO_SO_SEARCH_CONF	Search Object for Confirmation
/SAPSRM/CL_PDO_SO_SEARCH_CTR	Search Object for Contract
/SAPSRM/CL_PDO_SO_SEARCH_INV	Search Object for Invoice
/SAPSRM/CL_PDO_SO_SEARCH_PO_2	Search Object for PO
/SAPSRM/CL_PDO_SO_SEARCH_POR	Search Object for PO Response
/SAPSRM/CL_PDO_SO_SEARCH_QTE	Search Object for Quote
/SAPSRM/CL_PDO_SO_SEARCH_RFQ	Search Object for Bid Invitation
/SAPSRM/CL_PDO_SO_SEARCH_SC_2	Search Object for Shopping cart

These entire ABAP object supports the BADI BBP_WF_LIST. The method BBP_WF_LIST is supported. The BADI can be used to override the search results. In POWL search object, you can add a new filter. But, you cannot add new records into the resultant data. The authority check is run on the resultant data after this BADI.

7.4 Configuration

The SRM POWL provides a number of IMG configurations to extend your Advanced Search options. The IMG configuration can be accessed by the menu SRM Server->Cross-Application Settings->POWL and Advanced Search.

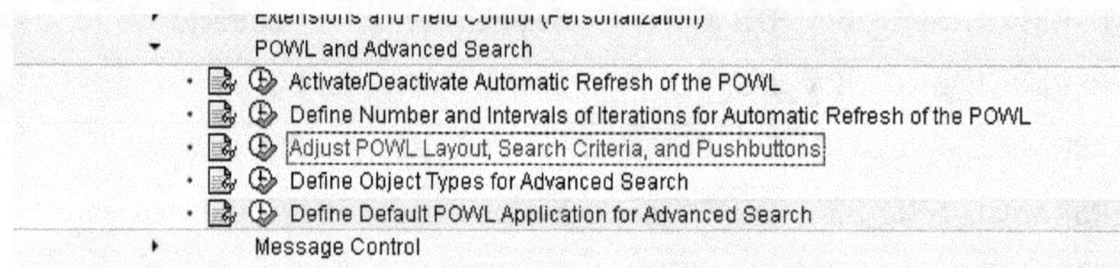

- Automatic Refresh – You can activate or deactivate refresh of POWL. By default, this automatic refresh is inactive.

- Define Number of Intervals of Iterations for Automatic Refresh – You can define number of iterations and time interval for Automatic Refresh. The automatic refresh may cause performance issue.

- Feeder Type definition – Discussed in the SRM Feeder Type section.

7.5 Enhancements

The Advanced Search is a Web Dynpro application designed using the POWL application. SRM provides a set of technical ABAP objects to support the Advanced Search. SRM provides a number of BADIs and supports Advanced Search Enhancements. This section explains Custom Fields addition and changing the search results.

7.5.1 Adding Custom Fields to Search Screen

In SRM project, Client adds a number of custom fields in SRM documents. Chapter 3 explains how to add new custom fields and how to add it into a SRM document screen to edit/display. This section will explain how to add these custom fields in the Selection Criteria screen. Note that custom fields are retrieved from FM BBP_PROCDOC_GETDETAIL. The custom fields can be either at Header or Item Level.

For the new selection criteria to appear on the UI, the method IF_POWL_FEEDER~GET_SEL_CRITERIA of the corresponding class must be enhanced accordingly with UI Meta data.

- Append the field to structure /SAPSRM/S_SEARCHFIELDS. To do so, create an append structure in SE11 and enter the new field there. This can be done either directly or by including another structure that contains the new field (recommended). You must make sure that custom fields must be part of Header or Item Level supported custom fields.

- SM30 view /SAPSRM/V_SRC_CR: enter the field for BO / BUS2000113 / DB. The Criterion Type must be suitable for the type of that field.

Maintain Table Views: Initial Screen
Find Maintenance Dialog
Table/View /SAPSRM/V_SRC_CR
Restrict Data Range
Determine Work Area: Entry
Work Area
Idx Object Type BO
Idx Object Name BUS2000113
Search Service Type DB
Further select cond Append

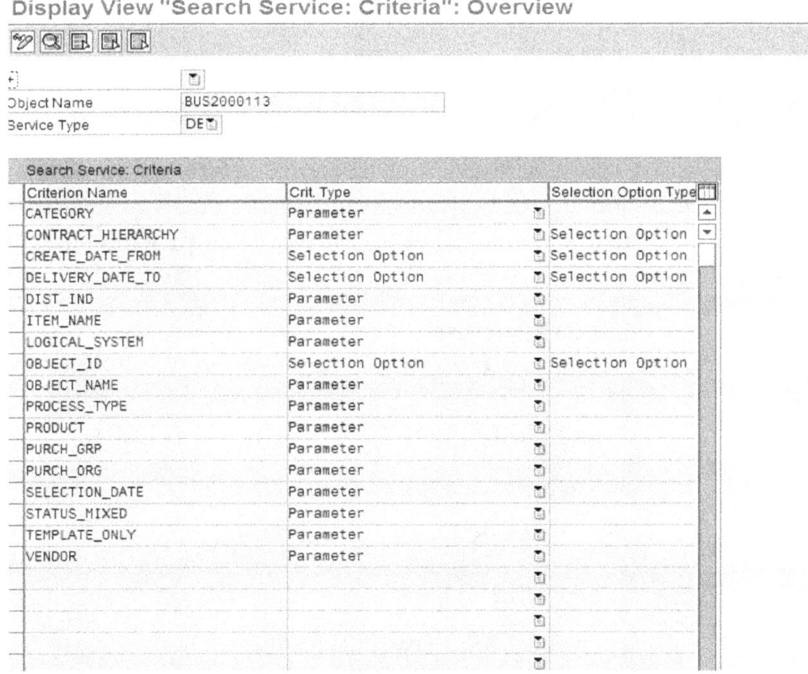

Criterion Name	Crit. Type	Selection Option Type
CATEGORY	Parameter	
CONTRACT_HIERARCHY	Parameter	Selection Option
CREATE_DATE_FROM	Selection Option	Selection Option
DELIVERY_DATE_TO	Selection Option	Selection Option
DIST_IND	Parameter	
ITEM_NAME	Parameter	
LOGICAL_SYSTEM	Parameter	
OBJECT_ID	Selection Option	Selection Option
OBJECT_NAME	Parameter	
PROCESS_TYPE	Parameter	
PRODUCT	Parameter	
PURCH_GRP	Parameter	
PURCH_ORG	Parameter	
SELECTION_DATE	Parameter	
STATUS_MIXED	Parameter	
TEMPLATE_ONLY	Parameter	
VENDOR	Parameter	

- Maintain your DB criteria in transaction /SAPSRM/POWL_CUST. The Criterion Type must be the same as in view /SAPSRM/V_SRC_CR (second step). The Parameter Type must be suitable for the type of that field - the input field is generally acceptable, but depending on the field's DDIC type. Parameter type allows only Input Field, Checkbox, Dropdown list or text-line.

The following screen shows Contract selection criteria. You can add user selection criteria name which matches with entry in/SAPSRM/V_SRC_CR.

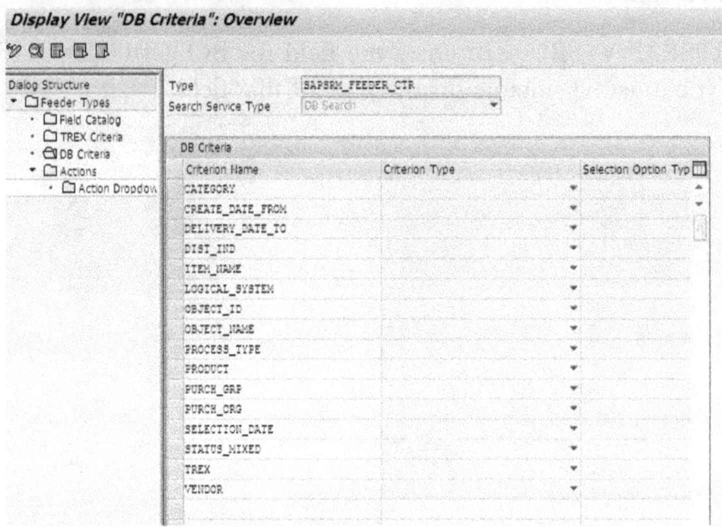

This will automatically changes selection criteria screen and filter the results based on selection criteria.

7.5.2 Changing Results

The advanced search result of the object refers to different data structure. The custom fields will not be included in the selection result screen. You need to enhance these structures to include custom fields. The following table provides the list of the data structure for each object.

Object	Data structure
PO	/SAPSRM/S_POWL_RESULT_PO
PO Item	/SAPSRM/S_POWL_RESULT_PO_ITEM
Shopping Cart	/SAPSRM/S_POWL_RESULT_SC
Shopping Cart Item	/SAPSRM/S_POWL_RESULT_SC_ITEM
Bid Invitation	/SAPSRM/S_POWL_RESULT_BID
Contract	/SAPSRM/S_POWL_RESULT_CTR
Contract Item	/SAPSRM/S_POWL_RESULT_CTR_ITEM
Quota Arrangement	/SAPSRM/S_POWL_RESULT_QUOT

Invoice	/SAPSRM/S_POWL_RESULT_INV

Table type structures are defined for all result structures. Each structure has a customer enhancement structure to include the custom fields. Make sure that data type matches with standard SRM table extension. The following table lists the custom field enhancement structures for the object.

Object	**Data structure**
PO	INCL_EEW_PD_SEARCH_HDR_CSF_PO
PO Item	INCL_EEW_PD_SEARCH_ITM_CSF_PO
Shopping Cart	INCL_EEW_PD_SEARCH_HDR_CSF_SC
Shopping Cart Item	INCL_EEW_PD_SEARCH_ITM_CSF_SC
Bid Invitation	INCL_EEW_PD_SEARCH_HDR_CSF_BID
Contract	INCL_EEW_PD_SEARCH_HDR_CSF_CTR
Contract Item	INCL_EEW_PD_SEARCH_ITM_CSF_CTR
Quota Arrangement	INCL_EEW_PD_SEARCH_HDR_CSF_QUT
Invoice	INCL_EEW_PD_SEARCH_HDR_CSF_INV

The SRM POWL provides an enhancement spot to manipulate the Changing Results. The enhancement can be used to add new filter that is not in selection criteria or you can change result values. There is a BADI /SAPSRM/BD_POWL_CHNG_SEL_RSL to change results. The BADI can be filtered based on Application ID and POWL Type.

Name: /SAPSRM/BD_POWL_CHNG_SEL_RSLT		Multiple Use: Yes	Filter: Yes
Description: Change POWL Search Result			
Method: CHANGE_SELECT_RESULT ***Description***: You can change your search result using POWL_TYPE, User name and SELCRIT_VALUES. The result table is based on the business object. Parameters:			
Name	Type	Data Type	Description
IV_FLT_POWL_TY PE	Import	POWL_TYPE_TY	POWL type ID
IV_FLT_APPLID	Import	POWL_APPLID_TY	Application ID
IV_USERNAME	Import	XUSER	User Name

IV_LANGU	Import	LANGU	Language Key
IT_SELCRIT_VALUES	Import	RSPARAMS_TT	Selection Criteria
IT_VISIBLE_FIELDS	Import	POWL_VISIBLE_COLS_TTY	Visible columns
CT_RESULT	Change	INDEX_TABLE	Selection Result
CT_MESSAGES	Change	POWL_MSG_TTY	Message

The Sample Code is as below:

```
* Note that result will be based on POWL TYPE.
  DATA: lt_result_po  TYPE /sapsrm/t_powl_result_po_item,
        ls_result_po  TYPE /sapsrm/s_powl_result_po_item,
        lt_result_ctr TYPE /sapsrm/t_powl_result_ctr,
        ls_result_ctr TYPE /sapsrm/s_powl_result_ctr,
        lt_result_sc  TYPE /sapsrm/t_powl_result_sc_itm,
        ls_result_sc  TYPE /sapsrm/s_powl_result_sc_itm.  "#EC NEEDED
  FIELD-SYMBOLS : <fs_result> TYPE ANY.
  LOOP AT ct_result ASSIGNING <fs_result>.
   IF <fs_result> IS ASSIGNED.
    CASE lv_object_type.
     WHEN 'BUS2201'.
      MOVE-CORRESPONDING <fs_result> TO ls_result_po.
* Do your validation based on GUID
      MOVE-CORRESPONDING <fs_result> TO ls_result.
      APPEND ls_result TO lt_result.
     WHEN 'BUS2121'.
* Do your validation based on GUID
      MOVE-CORRESPONDING <fs_result> TO ls_result.
     APPEND ls_result TO lt_result.
    ENDCASE.
   ENDIF.
   MOVE lt_result TO ct_result.
```

```
ENDLOOP.
```

Technical Challenges: External Requirements are transferred from the back-end ECC system to SRM system. The shopping cart with transaction type EXTRQ is created using the background user name rather than actual user name. The advanced search does not list out any shopping cart that is not created by the current user. The requirement is that the client wants to list out all the shopping cart line items created under their purchasing group and selection criteria entered in the selection screen.

Solution: Copy ABAP Object /SAPSRM/CL_SRC_SRV_DB_SC into a new ABAP object ZC_NEW_SRC_DB_SC. Change the method EXECUTE_SEARCH_INTERNAL_ITEM & EXECUTE_SEARCH_INTERNAL_HEADER to under the user created by background user name.

```
* do the search
CLEAR: ms_search_criteria-requestor, ms_search_criteria-requestor_guid.
* Assign your purchase group in the variable ms_search_criteria-purch_grp
* Note that Purchase group should be HR one not EKGRP set search parameters
 CALL METHOD lo_object_item->set_search_values
  EXPORTING
   is_search_criteria_sc = ms_search_criteria
   is_search_cuf_h      = ms_search_cuf_header
   is_search_cuf_i      = ms_search_cuf_item.
* do the search
 CALL METHOD lo_object_item->execute_search
  EXPORTING
   iv_user          = 'BACKGROUNDUSER'
  IMPORTING
   et_guid_list     = lt_guid_list
  CHANGING
   co_message_handler = lo_message_handler.
* message handling
 IF lo_message_handler IS BOUND.
  me->map_handler_mess_to_mess_tab(
   EXPORTING
```

```
      io_message_handler = lo_message_handler
    IMPORTING
      ev_contains_errors = lv_contains_errors
    CHANGING
      ct_search_messages = et_messages ).
  ENDIF.
* do the search – normal one
  CALL METHOD lo_object_item->execute_search
    EXPORTING
      iv_user          = iv_user
    IMPORTING
      et_guid_list     = lt_guid_list1
    CHANGING
      co_message_handler = lo_message_handler.

  APPEND LINES OF lt_guid_list1 TO lt_guid_list.
```

The search service object must be configured. The configuration can be done using the table maintenance tool (SM30) of the table /SAPSRM/C_SRC_SV.

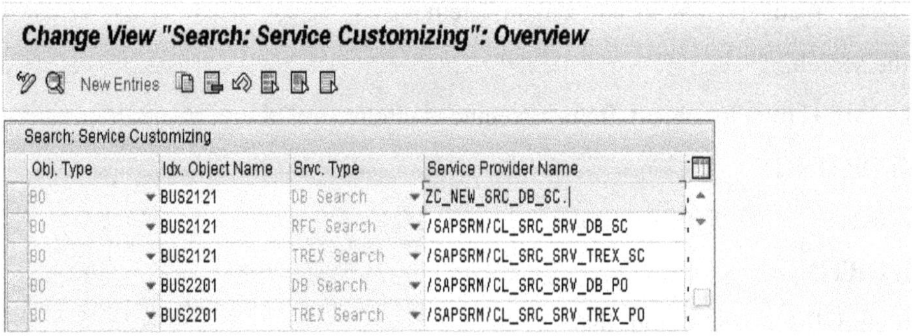

Change View "Search: Service Customizing": Overview

New Entries

Search: Service Customizing

Obj. Type	Idx. Object Name	Srvc. Type	Service Provider Name
BO	BUS2121	DB Search	ZC_NEW_SRC_DB_SC.
BO	BUS2121	RFC Search	/SAPSRM/CL_SRC_SRV_DB_SC
BO	BUS2121	TREX Search	/SAPSRM/CL_SRC_SRV_TREX_SC
BO	BUS2201	DB Search	/SAPSRM/CL_SRC_SRV_DB_PO
BO	BUS2201	TREX Search	/SAPSRM/CL_SRC_SRV_TREX_PO

Once the search engine is configured, the search object will be part of the SC and DB search. Make sure that the new ABAP object follows all required search engine needs. Also, the standard search engine covers all BADI provided by SRM POWL. A better option is to copy from the base SRM ABAP class.

7.6 Authorization Objects

CA_POWL is an authorization object for POWL object. There is an ABAP object CL_POWL_UTIL and there is a method DO_AUTHORITY_CHECK to do an authority check on POWL authorization. The authorization fields of the authorization object are as follows:

Fields	Comments
POWL_APPID	Application ID
POWL_CAT	Activity
POWL_LSEL	Authorization status: allowed or not allowed
POWL_QUERY	Query activity
POWL_RA_AL	Refresh status: allowed or not allowed
POWL_TABLE	Query result table

POWL_QUERY – Determines authorization on POWL Query creation. The activities on the authorization object are:

- 01 – Allowed user to create/change/delete own queries for all POWL object types
- 02 – Allowed user to create own queries on the basis of admin queries assigned
- 03 – Allowed user to change own queries on the basis of admin queries assigned

POWL_CAT - Determines the authorities of a user with respect to query categories. The activities are:

- 01: the user is allowed to create/change/delete own categories and assign queries to them
- 02: the user is only allowed to assign queries to the existing categories and change the order of queries
- 03 (and other values): the user is not allowed to re-assign queries or change the query order.
- Note: if field POWL_QUERY is set to 01 or 03, setting POWL_CAT to 03 is not sensible. Therefore, the value will be set to '02' implicitly in that case.

POWL_LSEL - Determines if the user is allowed to select the layout style (either one entry in a hyper-link matrix or one tabstrip per query) for the POWL iView

POWL_TABLE - Determines if the user is allowed to personalize the query result table settings (define column order, hide columns, etc.).

POWL_RA_AL - Determines if the user gains access to a "Refresh all" button, which triggers a parallelized refresh for all queries which are active on the POWL iView identified by POWL_APPLID. Note this may cause high system load on the application server group used for refreshes on this POWL iView.

7.7 Troubleshooting

POWL provides a number of standard administrative reports to handle POWL application and queries.

POWL_D01 - POWL_D01 is the utility program to delete the queries from the database.

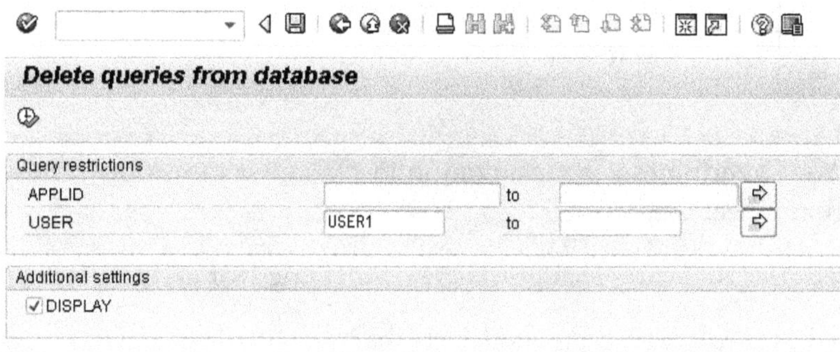

POWL_WLOAD - POWL_WLOAD is the utility program to refresh active POWL queries. The program can be used to increase performance by scheduling refresh at nighttime to avoid morning refreshes at morning by users.

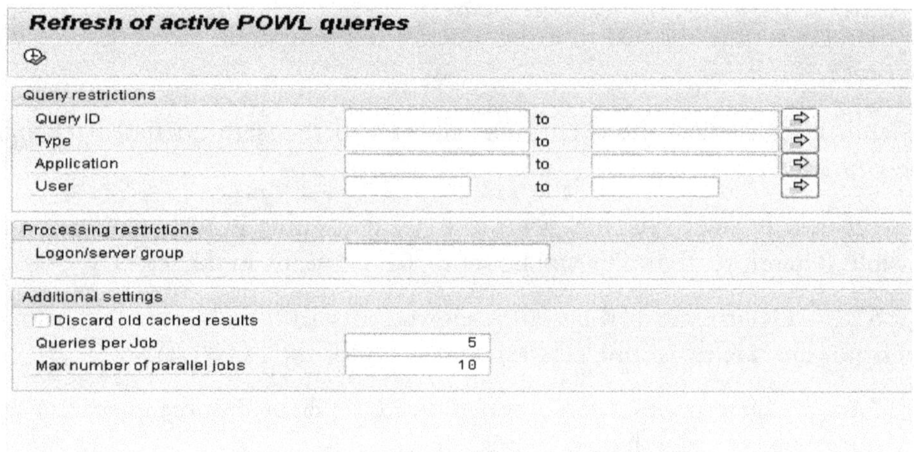

POWL_D02 - This is a utility program to list out Query details. The program can have two select options viz., by Roles or by Application Id.

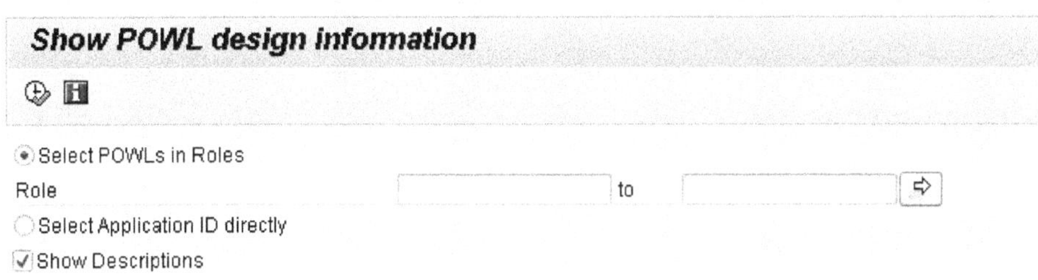

The result screens:

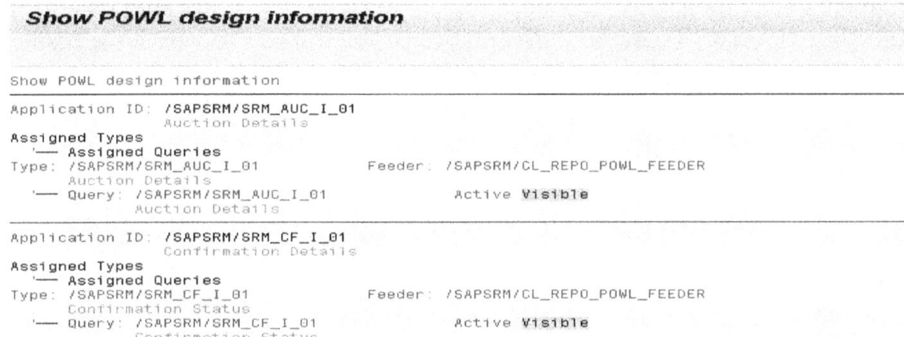

POWL_D03 – The utility program is to check consistency of the Query. This report also compares check results generated at difference instances, displaying the differences in POWL table entries between them. This report can be scheduled at regular basis and run as a background job.

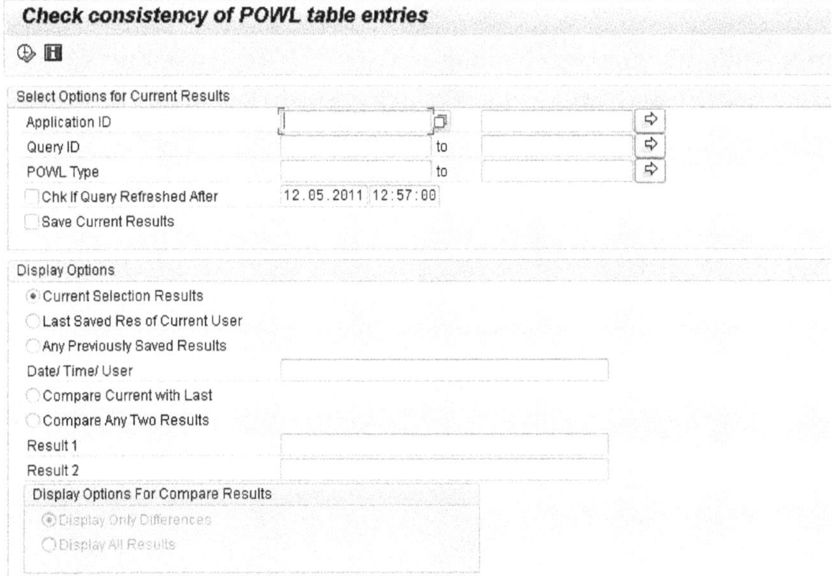

POWL_D04 – The report can be used to delete selection criteria. This is one of reports used by Administrator to delete query criteria.

7.7.1 Performance

The SRM POWL involves a number of queries and high volume of data. The performance is a challenge for POWL Advanced Search. You need to exercise caution in the design of the queries.

Unrestricted Queries - The execution of unrestricted queries is very time consuming and, in most cases, unwanted. Hence, SAP delivers most of the queries with default timeframe 'last 30 days'. To avoid performance problems due to very large result sets, we recommend restricting user to administrate the queries. In some cases, we can restrict the use of few queries from the users. Use the transaction POWL_QUERY to restrict the query results. At least, the performance problem for the initial refresh can be avoided this way.

Refresh - The POWL_WLOAD report can be scheduled to refresh the queries nightly, based on POWL application, query, user or feeder type. It will update the POWL Cache for the queries. This avoids the 'morning refresh'.

We strongly recommend restricting user access to the 'Refresh all' button. This can be done via authority object CA_POWL – Field POWL_RA_AL (determines if the user gains access to a "Refresh all" button, which triggers a simultaneous refresh for all queries which are active on the POWL iView identified by POWL_APPLID). Note that this may cause high system load on the application server group used for refreshes on the POWL iView.

Active Queries - We recommend limiting the number of active queries per POWL. Only queries relevant to the user's daily work should be defined. Since POWL caches queries per user, too many unnecessary queries could lead to unnecessarily high memory consumption. It is possible to restrict user authorization to create new queries via the authority object CA_POWL - Field POWL_QUERY.

Locking Issue - One of common issues is the locking issue. If the same query is executed in multiple instances, you will get this issue.

Advanced Search

Advanced Search

Query 'Last 7 Days' is already open in another session Display Help

Close

Search For: Shopping Cart

You can resolve this issue by clearing the lock on POWL_RESULT of the query if the query is not used by another instance. Use transaction SM12, to clear the locks on POWL_RESULT. POWL shadowing can be utilized to avoid this lock issue.

7.7.2 POWL Shadowing

The POWL shadowing is option to allow the same query to be opened in multiple sessions. You need to set the parameter 'allowShading' in the configuration. If you turn on the parameter, it will allow opening the same query in multiple instances.

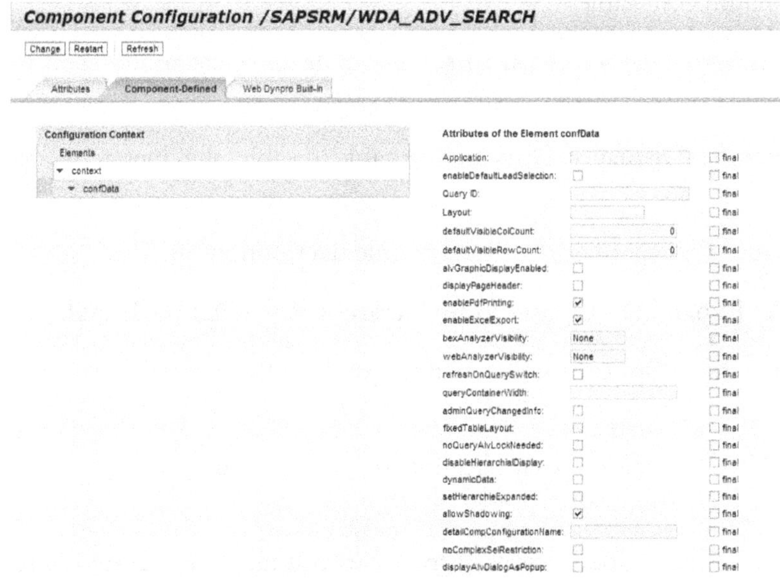

The POWL UI other configuration parameters are as follows:

- Application - The POWL will load this application ID.
- Query ID - Default query and it will be loaded.

- Layout - Layout of the POWL and allowed are: Link Matrix and Tab strip.
- Default Visible Count - Option to set the default number of columns to load.
- Default Visible Row Count - Option to set the default number of rows to load.
- ALV Graphic Display Enabled -> Option to set ALV graphic Option in settings of table when POWL load.
- Display Page Header - Option to display page header
- Enable PDF Printing - Enable the button to print PDF button
- Enable Excel Export - Enable the button to enable the excel export button
- Bex Analyzer Visibility - Option to enable BEX Analyzer.
- Web Analyzer Visibility - Option to WEB Analyzer.
- Refresh On Query Switch - Option will refresh the query whenever there is a query switch.
- Query Container Width - Option will set the query container width for matrix Data.
- Admin Query Change Info - Option to set the admin Query Changed info on UI.
- Fixed Table Layout - Option to set the Table layout fixed that allows the user to resize the columns on Table.
- No Query ALV needed - Option to set the table in select mode even if there is lock is applied.
- Disable hierarchy Display - Option to enable/disable the hierarchy option for table.
- Dynamic Data - Option to enable the dynamic data option on ALV.
- Set Hierarchy Expanded - Option to set hierarchy expanded by default.
- Allow Shadowing - Option to allow same query to be opened in more than one session.
- Error Page URL - Option for application to give customization error page to be displayed.
- No Complex Selection Restriction - Option to not allow any complex restriction for select Options.
- No Underline for Links - Option will enable/Disable underlines from the links.

- Include Category Info In Query- Option to include category info with query by default on UI.
- Query without Count - Option to display Queries without count.
- Display Alv Dialog as Popup - Display Alv Dialog as a POPUP in place on Detail component.
- Enable Alv Cell Action - Option will enable ALV cell option.
- Enable Default Lead Selection - Option to enable initial lead selection by default.
- Popup Comp Configuration Name- Default configuration for POPUP component.
- Display Powl Pers As Popup - Option to open POWL personalization window as a POPUP.
- Force Sync Refresh - Option to refresh POWL Queries in Synchronous mode.
- Selection Mode - Option to set the selection modes for ALV table.
- Last Hierarchy as Leaf - Display last hierarchy node as a leaf. If this flag is set, then the last hierarchy column is displayed next to the DOT in the hierarchy display. If you only have ONE hierarchy column defined, like in this example, then you only have the root hierarchy node and the DOTs. For the last hierarchy column which is to be displayed as leaf no subtotals will be calculated.
- Fire Event for Every Row Selection - Option to fire event for every row selection.
- Toolbar Refresh Button - Option to show the toolbar button
- POWL Default Focus - Set the default Focus on POWL when a number of elements are there on View.
- Hide Settings Link - Hide the settings link from Table.
- Enable New Ui - Option to switch on UI based on new BTC Guidelines.

7.8 Summary

In this chapter, you have learned about the basics of SRM POWL and its integration with Advanced Search tool. The chapter discussed the POWL Advanced Search configuration in detail. You have learned to how to add custom fields in the selection criteria, resultant data and how to add it search filter.

The SRM Approval process is based on SRM Workflow. SRM7.x uses Process Controlled Workflow and uses the Business Rule Framework to define the business processes and rules.

8 SRM Workflow

SAP Workflow is a workflow engine that enables the design and execution of business process within SAP application systems. Workflow may be a simple release or approval procedures or a complex business processes like Multi-Step Approval associated with multiple agents. The audit trail and history of system-based workflow helps the organization in a transparent manner. Workflow processes are delivered as a part of standard SAP. The standard SAP workflow can be enhanced and you can create a new custom workflow. The number of workflow templates and tasks has been defined for a specific SRM object type like Shopping Cart, Purchase Order, etc. The business workflow process is known as Application Controlled Workflow.

Also, a set of common workflow templates and tasks are defined for a specific process (not by SRM object type). This new type of business workflow is known as process controlled workflow. This new workflow concept with Business Rules Framework (BRF) was introduced in SRM version 6.0. The BRF is a part of standard SAP components. In SRM, the BRF is used to enhance the Business Workflow. SRM supports the older version of the application controlled workflow processes also. The process-controlled workflows use a type of workflow template that can be used for all application objects.

This chapter will explain details about the process-controlled workflows in detail. The chapter discusses Business Rule Framework and its technical guidance to create a BRF event function module. You can understand how to configure the SRM workflow and how to extend and enhance the process workflow. The last section provides the possible methods to troubleshoot the workflow issues. You will learn about the technical details of the SRM process oriented workflow and its usage.

Process-controlled workflows are available for the following SRM business objects:

- Shopping Cart
- RFQ
- Quotation
- Contract

- Purchase Order
- Confirmation
- Invoice

8.1 Business Rule Framework

The Business Rule Framework (BRF) is an SAP NetWeaver component. The BRF is a standard SAP tool to evaluate the business rules and executes the actions. The BRF is an independent framework and it does not have any business logic on its own. It evaluates complex logical expressions and rules into a single value. The result can be any type of values like Boolean Result, String, etc. You can use the BRF for a variety of purposes to due to evaluating the complex expressions. The SRM7.x process-controlled workflows use BRF for their approval process. BRF is used to control specific aspects of the standard implementation for approval processes. Note that the BRF is not a workflow or workflow engine.

BRF comprises a runtime environment and a maintenance environment. BRF is an event-controlled environment for processing rules. Note that any number of rules can be assigned to an event. The event consists of a Boolean expression and an action. The BRF maintenance environment provides options to create Rules, Events, Expressions and Actions.

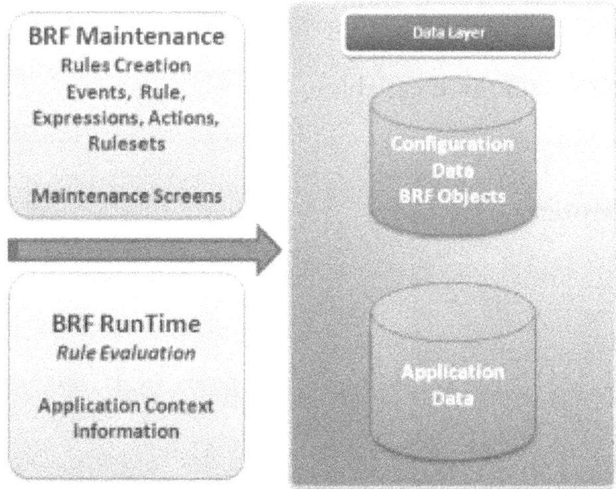

The BRF runtime environment evaluates the defined rules and expressions and provides application context information. The framework was implemented using ABAP Objects and utilizing the concept of persistent classes.

8.1.1 Main Objects of BRF

This section explains main components of BRF and technical information with respect to SRM. SRM does not use all of the components of BRF. SRM uses BRF to derive process schema for the document instance.

- **Application Class -** The application class is the base class of BRF for every application. There must be only one application class for each application. The application class for SRM is SRM_WF.

- **Event -** The BRF Event is the basic entry point of BRF. BRF Event is a term used within BRF. The linkage of the event is fixed and synchronous. So, the event should not be viewed as an ABAP Object Oriented event or the Observer Pattern. This event represents loose linkage between two components. There are a hundreds of pre-defined SRM BRF events. BRF event carries the contextual information that can be used in the expression to resolve the return value.

- **Expression –** Expression returns a result for BRF. The result can be any one of data types supported by BRF. Expression uses expression type to determine how an expression is calculated. The supported expression types are:

    - Constant
    - Field of a structure
    - Field of a line of an internal table
    - Call function module/ABAP Object method
    - Boolean expressions with three variables
    - Simple formula
    - SAP Formula interpreter
    - Truth Table
    - Case Expression
    - Date Interval
    - Random generator
    - Simple Decision tree

You can choose the expression type based on the requirement. A truth table is one of the discrete mathematics formulae used to identify Boolean expressions. You can use a function module to handle a complex BRF Boolean expression. The function module requires the developer knowledge and authorization. Other expression can be configured without the programming.

- **Action** – Action is manipulation of any data sets to support the business requirements and can be performed technically. The action is executed based on Action Type. Note that SRM does not use Actions.

- **Rule** – Rule is used to execute one or more actions based on a condition. If condition returns true then it execute related actions. The rule is not used in SRM perspective.

- **Rule Set** – Rule set is grouping of rules from a business point of view. The supported rule set types are Normal rule set, Rule Pool and Enhanced Rule Pool. The rule set is not used in SRM Workflow.

You can access BRF using the transaction code BRF. The transaction is the design environment for BRF. SRM_WF is the BRF object for SRM process controlled workflow.

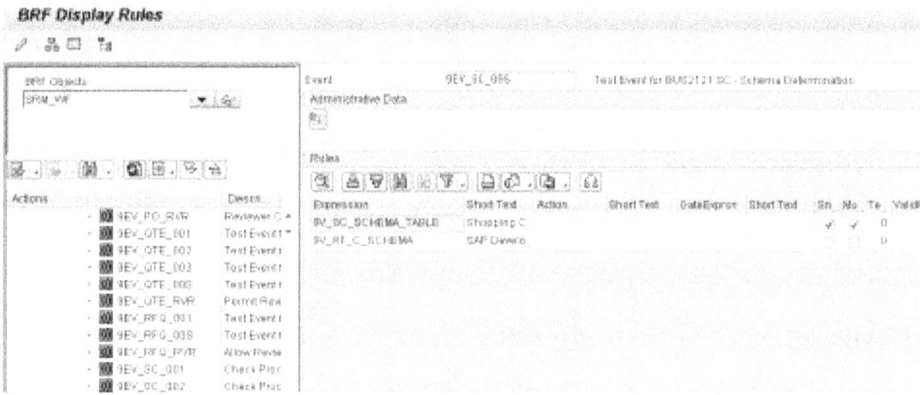

Technical Info

The ABAP Object /SAPSRM/IF_WF_RULE_C has all BRF Rule Evaluation Constants. All main components of BRF can be viewed in database tables and the following are the list of important transparent tables used in BRF application.

Table Name	Description
TBRF000	Application Class
TBRF001	Application Class Customer specific
TBRF110	Events
TBRF150	Expressions
TBRF170	Actions
TBRF171	Concrete actions
TBRF200	Where used List of BRF objects

TBRF210	BRF: Assignment of Event, Expression, Action
TBRF280	Rule sets
TBRF310	BRF Rule Assignment of Events, Expressions and Actions.
TBRF320	Version Information
BRFWB*	Related to BRF Workbench data

The ABAP class /SAPSRM/CL_WF_BRF_EVENT is a BRF event class. BRF event programming is discussed in later chapter.

8.1.2 BRF Event Function Module Programming

Most of SRM implementation uses the BRF event function module to support complex derivation rules for process schema. The following section discusses how to define a function module that can be used in the BRF expression. You can see a number of function modules provided by SRM that are used in the expression. You must follow the following interfaces to define a custom BRF event function.

```
*"*"Local Interface:
*" IMPORTING
*"    REFERENCE(IT_EXPRESSIONS) TYPE  SBRF260A_T
*"    REFERENCE(IO_EVENT) TYPE REF TO  IF_EVENT_BRF
*"    REFERENCE(IO_EXPRESSION) TYPE REF TO
IF_EXPRESSION_BRF
*" EXPORTING
*"    REFERENCE(EV_VALUE) TYPE  BRF_RESULT_VALUE
*"    REFERENCE(EV_TYPE) TYPE  BRF_RESULT_TYPE
*"    REFERENCE(EV_LENGTH) TYPE  BRF_RESULT_LENGTH
*"    REFERENCE(EV_CURRENCY) TYPE  BRF_CURRENCY
*"    REFERENCE(EV_OUTPUT_LENGTH) TYPE
BRF_RESULT_OUTPUT_LENGTH
*"    REFERENCE(EV_DECIMALS) TYPE  BRF_RESULT_DECIMALS
*"    REFERENCE(EV_DATA_MISSING) TYPE  BRF_DATA_MISSING
```

Make sure that you are assigning the appropriate values to the exporting parameters EV_TYPE, EV_LENGTH, etc. The sample code explains preset return values and writes your own logic to derive the exact value. The following sample code is code snippet and you can see that it returns the Boolean value.

```
* preset return values
  ev_type        = /sapsrm/if_wf_rule_c=>type_char.
  ev_length      = 1.
  CLEAR ev_currency.
  ev_output_length = 1.
  ev_decimals    = 0.
  CLEAR ev_value.
  ev_value       = /sapsrm/if_wf_rule_c=>brf_result_bool_ok. " no processing
*  ev_data_missing  = /sapsrm/if_wf_rule_c=>brf_data_missing.
  CLEAR ev_data_missing.
```

Context Information

In the runtime environment, the BRF event is associated with a complex data structure and ABAP object. You can retrieve the SRM document information from the BRF event's contextual object. The BRF event contextual object is referred by the ABAP class /SAPSRM/CL_WF_BRF_EVENT. The following code explains how to get the document GUID and its object type.

```
 DATA lo_wf_brf_event   TYPE REF TO /sapsrm/cl_wf_brf_event.
  DATA lo_context_provider   TYPE REF TO
/sapsrm/if_wf_context_provider.
lo_wf_brf_event ?= io_event.
lo_context_provider = lo_wf_brf_event->get_context_provider( ).
  CALL METHOD lo_context_provider->get_document
    IMPORTING
      ev_document_guid = lv_document_guid
      ev_document_type = lv_document_type.
```

The document GUID can be used to fetch SRM document information to resolve the expression. The following code will fetch base WF_PDO for a given GUID and type. You can use the PDO object to get related information and write your logic to derive the process scheme and return the value.

```
DATA lo_pdo_sc TYPE REF TO /sapsrm/if_pdo_bo_sc.
* get instance
lo_wf_pdo ?= /sapsrm/cl_wf_pdo_impl_factory=>get_instance(
iv_document_guid = lv_document_guid
iv_document_type = lv_document_type
).
lo_pdo_sc ?= io_wf_pdo->get_pdo( ).


----* Implement logic to determine Scheme
*-------------ev_value = 'YOUR_PROCESS_SCHEME'.
```

/SAPSRM/WF_BRF_0EXP00 - This is standard SRM BRF function that can execute a particular BRF class method to get exporting parameters. You must pass the BRF class and its methods in parameters as constant expressions.

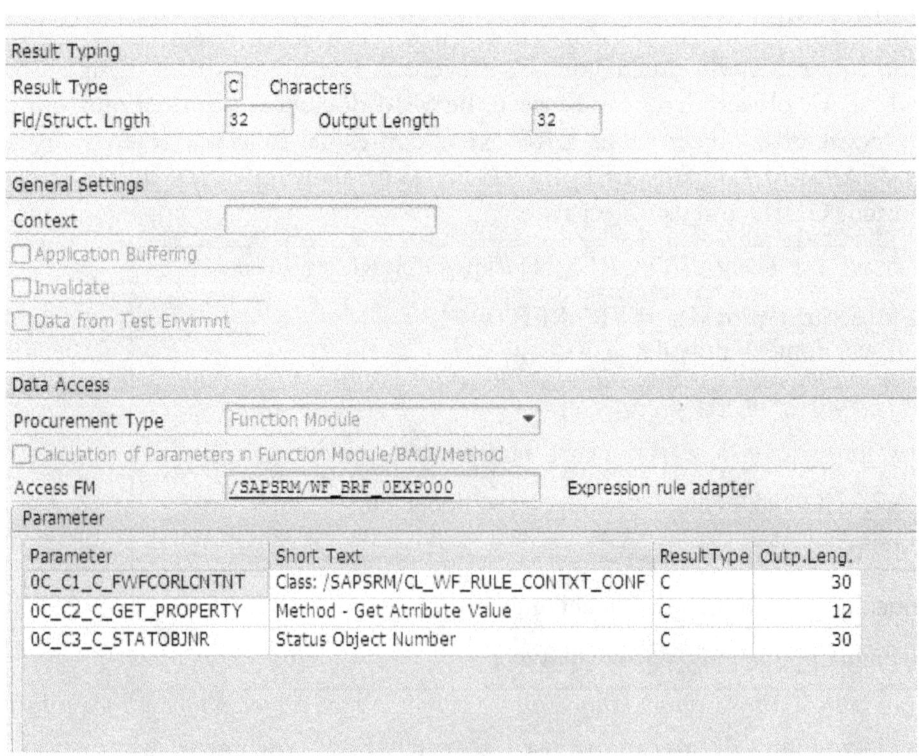

Result Typing

Result Type: C Characters

Fld/Struct. Lngth: 32 Output Length: 32

General Settings

Context:

☐ Application Buffering

☐ Invalidate

☐ Data from Test Envirmnt

Data Access

Procurement Type: Function Module

☐ Calculation of Parameters in Function Module/BAdI/Method

Access FM: /SAPSRM/WF_BRF_0EXP000 Expression rule adapter

Parameter

Parameter	Short Text	ResultType	Outp.Leng.
0C_C1_C_FWFCORLCNTNT	Class: /SAPSRM/CL_WF_RULE_CONTXT_CONF	C	30
0C_C2_C_GET_PROPERTY	Method - Get Atrribute Value	C	12
0C_C3_C_STATOBJNR	Status Object Number	C	30

The above is an example of using BRF FM /SAPSSRM/WF_BRF_0EXP00. It will execute the method GET_PROPERTY of the BRF class /SAPSRM/CL_WF_RULE_CONTXT_CONTR. It passes the parameter value as STATOBJNR.

Also, you should pass parameters in a sequence (Class, Method, property, and property values). The expressions used should comply with the following restrictions:

- BRF class constant expression name should contain 'C1_C'
- BRF method constant expression name should contain 'C2_C'.
- BRF property constant expression name should contain 'C3_C'.
- BRF property value constant expression name should contain 'C4_C'.
- BRF currency key constant expression name should contain 'C5_C'.
- BRF business object expression name should contain 'C6_C'.

A good example for custom BRF class constant expressions is ZC_C1_CMYCLASS. Note that the class used in the expression must inherit from /SAPSRM/CL_WF_RULE_CONTEXT and the method should have the following interface parameters:

Ty.	Parameter	Type spec.	Description
	IV_DOCUMENT_GUID	TYPE /SAPSRM/WF_DOCUMENT_GUID	GUID of SRM purchasing document
	IV_PROPERTY	TYPE CHAR255 OPTIONAL	
	IT_EXPRESSIONS	TYPE SBRF260A_T OPTIONAL	BRF: Structure Parameter + Other Fields (Table Category)
	EV_VALUE	TYPE /SAPSRM/WF_BRF_VALUE	Char255
	EV_TYPE	TYPE /SAPSRM/WF_BRF_TYPE	Single-Character Flag
	EV_DATA_MISSING	TYPE CHAR1	Single-Character Flag
	EV_CURRENCY	TYPE /SAPSRM/WF_BRF_CURRENCY	BRF Return Value Currency
	/SAPSRM/CX_WF_RULE_ERROR		Basis Exception (in BRF rule eval): SRM workflow engine
	/SAPSRM/CX_WF_RULE_ABORT		Basis Exception (in BRF rule eval): SRM workflow engine

8.2 Configuration

A new approval process implementation requires the IMG customization, BRF configuration with programming tasks if any and also implements standard BADIs. Before starting the implementation, check the following:

- Identify that how to evaluate the correct process schema. If there is more than one process schema used for a business object type and the determination is complex then derive the BRF event using the function module. If the derivation is simple, BRF provides a number of expression types and uses the appropriate expression type to derive the process schema.

- Need to configure process levels for each process schema. When the process level is varied based on the data then use the dynamic determination of the process level. Otherwise, you use the standard IMG configuration.
- Implement BADI implementations for agent determination and reviewer determination.

Make sure that you have configured at least one process schema containing a sequence of all possible completion and approval levels.

8.2.1 Define Reviewer

You can configure the list of reviewers. The reviewer BADI uses configured reviewers as a part of the filter. The IMG menu Path is SRM Server->Cross-Application Basic Settings->Business Workflow->Process Controlled Workflow->Define Filter Values for BADI 'Define Reviewer'.

Change View "Reviewer Determination Rules": Overview

New Entries

Reviewer Determination Rules

Reviewer Rule	Text
RV_EMPLOYEE	Specify Employee as Reviewer
RV_REPORTING_LINE_UNIT	Get all Employees of Specified Department as Reviewers
RV_ROLE	Get all Users of Specified Role as Reviewers
RV_SOURCE_DOCUMENT_RESPONSIBLES	Get Source-Document Responsibles as Reviewers

8.2.2 Responsibility Resolver

The IMG configuration is used to define the list of the Responsibility Resolvers (Agents). The resolver name can be used as a filter in BADI. The IMG Menu path is SRM Server->Cross-Application Basic Settings->Business Workflow->Process Controlled Workflow->Define Filter Values for BADI 'Define Agents'.

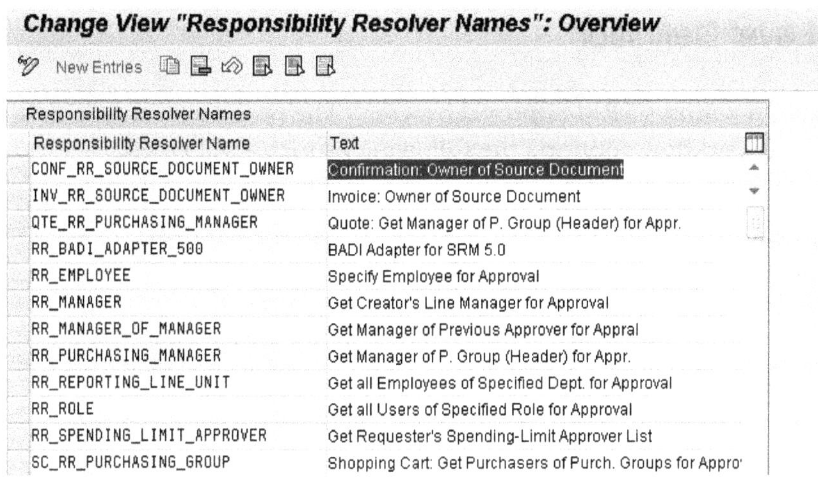

Change View "Responsibility Resolver Names": Overview

New Entries

Responsibility Resolver Names

Responsibility Resolver Name	Text
CONF_RR_SOURCE_DOCUMENT_OWNER	Confirmation: Owner of Source Document
INV_RR_SOURCE_DOCUMENT_OWNER	Invoice: Owner of Source Document
QTE_RR_PURCHASING_MANAGER	Quote: Get Manager of P. Group (Header) for Appr.
RR_BADI_ADAPTER_500	BADI Adapter for SRM 5.0
RR_EMPLOYEE	Specify Employee for Approval
RR_MANAGER	Get Creator's Line Manager for Approval
RR_MANAGER_OF_MANAGER	Get Manager of Previous Approver for Appral
RR_PURCHASING_MANAGER	Get Manager of P. Group (Header) for Appr.
RR_REPORTING_LINE_UNIT	Get all Employees of Specified Dept. for Approval
RR_ROLE	Get all Users of Specified Role for Approval
RR_SPENDING_LIMIT_APPROVER	Get Requester's Spending-Limit Approver List
SC_RR_PURCHASING_GROUP	Shopping Cart: Get Purchasers of Purch. Groups for Appro'

8.2.3 Recipient Notification

The configuration helps you to define which user will get notification for the application scenario. If there are no settings for a specific application scenario then no notification is sent. The notification will be sent to Inbox of the receiver.

The IMG Menu Path is SRM Server->Cross-Application Basic Settings->Business Workflow->Process Controlled Workflow->Define Recipient of Notifications.

Change View "Define Recipient of Notifications": Overview

New Entries

Define Recipient of Notifications

Scenario	User Role
Approve Bid	Contact Person (in most cases
Approve Goods Receipt or Return	Approver
Approve Goods Receipt or Return	Contact Person (in most cases
Approve Goods Receipt or Return	Reviewer
Approve Invoice or Credit Memo	Approver
Approve Invoice or Credit Memo	Contact Person (in most cases
Approve Invoice or Credit Memo	Reviewer
Approve Shopping Cart	Approver
Approve Shopping Cart	Contact Person (in most cases
Approve Shopping Cart	Reviewer
Approve Vendor	Approver
Approve Vendor	Contact Person (in most cases
Approve Vendor	PU

8.2.4 Process Level Definition

A Process Level is a level within a SRM approval process. The process level type defines the process level. SRM Workflow supports the following process level types:.

- o Approval with Completion
- o Approval
- o Automatic (system user)

The process level type 'Automatic' comes at end of the approval process. It is only activated when no more additional preceding process levels have been activated at runtime.

Decision Sets

A decision set is a group of purchasing items in an approval process. For example, if the lines of a purchasing document belong to different product categories, the system can create a number of separated decisions sets. For each set, there is one work item created. The decision set is based on the decision types into four types.

- TYPE1 – Decision on entire document: The document is approved by a single agent as a single decision.

- TYPE2 – Item based decision for an entire document: The document is approved by a single agent and the decision is made individually for each line item.

- TYPE3 – Overall decision for a partial document: The items of the documents grouped into the decision sets. Each decision set is approved by a single agent and decision applies to the entire decision set.

- TYPE4 – Item based decision for a partial document: The items of the documents grouped into decision sets. Each decision set is approved by a single agent and decision is made individually for each line item of the decision.

For each level of the decision, the system determines the process level type, assignment of the document or items to responsibility areas and the agents based on the responsibility areas.

Each business object is associated with an evaluation ID. The evaluation ID must be a BRF event defined under the SRM_WF application class. The BRF Event will return the process schema. The BRF Event uses the expression to derive the process schema. This is one of BRF's vital roles in the workflow. The workflow is controlled by the process schema that is determined at runtime by the evaluation ID (BRF event).

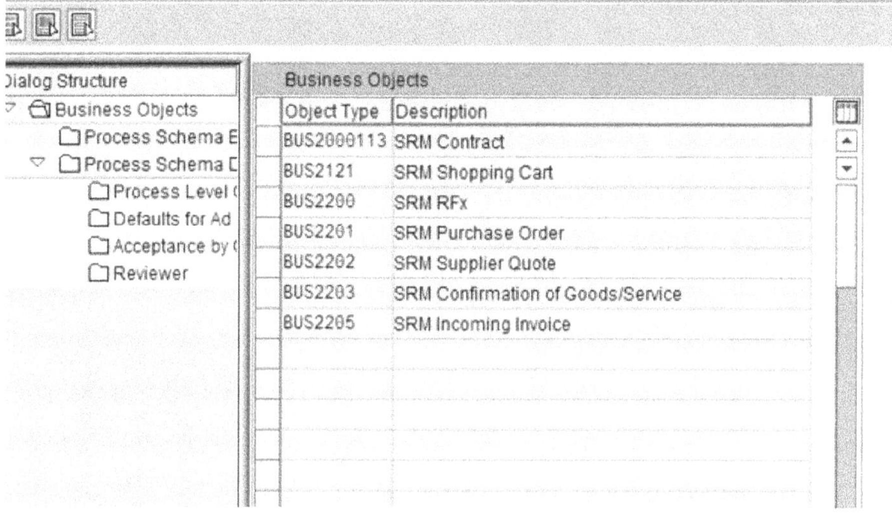

Display View "Business Objects": Overview

Object Type	Description
BUS2000113	SRM Contract
BUS2121	SRM Shopping Cart
BUS2200	SRM RFx
BUS2201	SRM Purchase Order
BUS2202	SRM Supplier Quote
BUS2203	SRM Confirmation of Goods/Service
BUS2205	SRM Incoming Invoice

Dialog Structure
- Business Objects
  - Process Schema Eva
  - Process Schema De
    - Process Level Cc
    - Defaults for Ad H
    - Acceptance by Cc
    - Reviewer

Object Type BUS2201

Process Schema Evaluation

Evaluation ID ZEV_PO_001

The process schema for each business objects can be configured with the process levels. You can define all possible process schema definition for each SRM business object type. Note that BRF event should return one of these process schemas.

Change View "Process Schema Definition": Overview of Selected Set

Dialog Structure
- Business Objects
  - Process Schema Eva
  - Process Schema De
    - Process Level Cc
    - Defaults for Ad H
    - Acceptance by Cc
    - Reviewer

Process Schema Definition

Object Type	Process Level Schema
BUS2201	9C_BUS2201_EX01
BUS2201	9C_BUS2201_EX02

Process level Configuration

The configuration of the process level at schema level is vital for the workflow. This is important have multiple level definition. The level type, Response Resolver (Defined in IMG and used in resolver BADI filter), Task, and decision set definition are configured at this level.

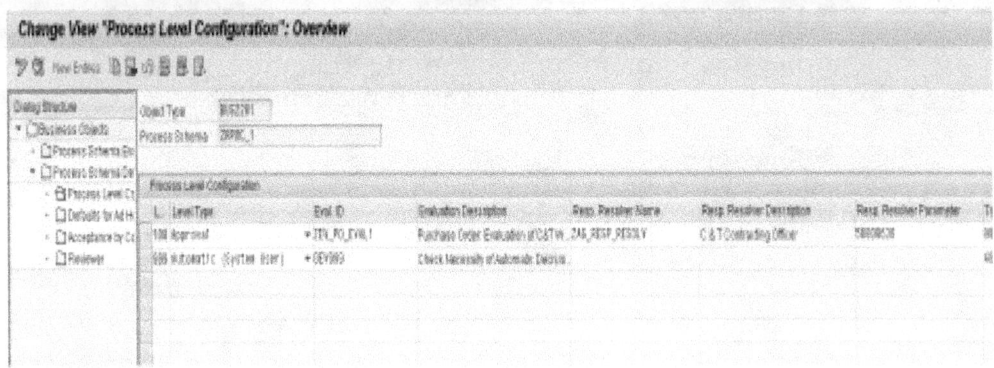

SRM provides standard process level types as follows:

- Approval with completion
- Approval
- Automatic

8.3 Enhancements

SRM Workflow has provided a number of enhancement spots to enhance the system by technical development. All enhancements are BADI based. These enhancements provide more dynamic changes of the configuration and business processes.

8.3.1 Process Level Enhancement

The process level can be added dynamically for a process schema. This can be done using BADI /SAPSRM/BD_WF_PROCESS_CONFIG. The BADI is called each time the workflow evaluates the process levels and checks whether to start a new process level. In standard SRM system, two BADI implementations are provided and active by default.

- /SAPSRM/BD_WF_CONFIG_SC_SL – Dynamic Process Schema for SC Spending Limit and RR_EMPLOYEE as resolver.

- /SAPSRM/BD_WF_CONFIG_PO_SL – Dynamic Process Schema for PO spending Limit and RR_SPENDING_LIMIT_APPROVER as resolver.

You can define spending limits and approval limits for individual users, organizational units or roles.

8.3.2 Define Agents

The approval process requires determination of the appropriate agents. The determination depends on the current decision set since the context of each decision set might be different. The responsible agents are determined in the following steps.

- Each item assigns to an area of responsibility and the same area of responsibility forms a decision set. A new sub-workflow is started for each decision set.
- For each area of responsibility, the agents of the decision set are determined. For example, if the area of responsibility is a cost center, the person responsible for cost center could be returned as an agent. If the area of responsibility is a department then all employees of the department could be returned as agents.
- If there is no agent found then fallback agents can be returned as agents to avoid workflow getting stuck.
- The BADI /SAPSRM/BD_WF_RESP_RESOLVER can be implemented in order to ensure actual strategy and correct agent assignment. The BADI can be accessed using the IMG path SRM Server->Business Add-Ins->SAP Business Workflow (New)->Define Agents. There is a number of enhancement implementations defined for each business object type and they are listed in the following table.

Resolver	**Enhancement Implementation**
RR_EMPLOYEE	/SAPSRM/BD_WF_<BO>_RR_EMPLOYEE
RR_MANAGER	/SAPSRM/BD_WF_<BO>_RR_MANAGER
RR_ MANOFMA	/SAPSRM/BD_WF_<BO>_RR_MANOFMA
RR_PURMGR	/SAPSRM/BD_WF_<BO>_RR_PURMGR
RR_RLUNIT	/SAPSRM/BD_WF_<BO>_RR_RLUNIT
RR_SL	/SAPSRM/BD_WF_<BO>_RR_SL
RR_PGRP	/SAPSRM/BD_WF_<BO>_RR_PGRP
RR_P_OWNER	/SAPSRM/BD_WF_<BO>_RR_P_OWNER

Supported <BO>s are CTR (Contract), CONF (confirmation), INV (Invoice), PO (Purchase order), QTE (RFx Response), RFQ (Bid Invitation), and SC (Shopping Cart). The BADI must be implemented for each custom Resolver configured. The BADI has the following four methods:

- GET_RESP_RESOLVER_PARAMETER_F4 – Search Help for Responsibility Resolver Parameter
- GET_APPROVERS_BY_AREA_GUID – This method gets the list of approvers for the responsibility area. This method is called in the task TS40007943.
- GET_AREA_TO_ITEM_MAP – This method assigns areas of responsibility to the items in the document. This method is called when the document is split into decision sets.
- GET_FALLBACK_AGENTS – This method is executed when there is no agent returned in the get_approvers_by_area_guid method. The fallback agents can approve or reject the work item. This method is optional.
- CHECK_RESP_RESOLVER_PARAMETER – Check Responsibility Resolver Parameter

You can write a common function module to determine the fallback agent. It can be used in all custom implementation. The fallback agents will be used when get approver method fails. In standard, SAP uses the workflow administrator as a fallback agent.

8.3.3 Define Reviewer

The approval process allows reviewers to be added in the process. The receivers will get the work item. The reviewers can note and add an attachment to the object. The review process can be executed parallel with the approval process. The BADI /SAPSRM/BD_WF_REVIEWER_RULE can be implemented to execute dynamic reviewer determination. SRM provides a number of implementations like Responsible Resolver.

Reviewer	**Enhancement Implementation**
RV_EMPLOYEE	/SAPSRM/BD_WF_<BO>_RV_EMPLOYEE
RV_MANAGER	/SAPSRM/BD_WF_<BO>_RV_MANAGER
RV_ MANOFMA	/SAPSRM/BD_WF_<BO>_RV_MANOFMA
RV_PURMGR	/SAPSRM/BD_WF_<BO>_RV_PURMGR
RV_RLUNIT	/SAPSRM/BD_WF_<BO>_RV_RLUNIT

RV_SL	/SAPSRM/BD_WF_<BO>_RV_SL
RV_PGRP	/SAPSRM/BD_WF_<BO>_RV_PGRP
RV_P_OWNER	/SAPSRM/BD_WF_<BO>_RV_P_OWNER

BADI provides the following three methods:

- GET_REVIEWER_BY_DOCUMENT – This method determines the agents for a given area of responsibility for each decision set in the document.
- CHECK_REVIEWER_RULE_PARAM – It validates the value of RULE_PARAMETER. The method is optional.
- GET_REVIEWER_RULE_PARAM_F4 – This method provides option to F4 help for the field RULE_PARAMETER. The method is optional.

8.3.4 Define Deadline

The deadline monitory is a workflow runtime system function that monitors the start and end deadlines for the processing of work items in an approval process. You can configure the deadline alerts in alert management. You can use BADI /SAPSRM/BD_WF_DEADLINES to compute your deadline dynamically. There is a method DETERMINE_DEADLINE with input parameters GUID, document type, work item ID and changing parameters deadlines. BADI supports filter type for process type.

8.3.5 Process Re-start

The re-start of approval process is required when the requestor or responsible agent changes the document. You can override the standard behavior of process restarts using the BADI /SAPSRM/BD_WF_PROCESS_RESTART. Note that in case of complete restart, any ad-hoc agents and approvers added are not taken into account. You need to add them again. If the process restarts, all existing work items are called back and deleted. The BADI is called after the document has been changed and saved. BADI provides the following two methods:

- VALIDATE_RESTART - The method is used when a process restart is to take place or not. The export parameter EV_RESTART (True - restart and False - no restart).
- SUPPRESS_PROCESS_RESTART - Not used.

8.4 SRM Technical Information

This section provides technical objects and tips to handle real time programming. You can understand BRF event programming, PDO layers, Workflow Areas, and Workflow objects. The section covers workflow objects and PDO technical layer for workflow.

8.4.1 Workflow Objects

The approval process is the major SRM process oriented workflow. All documents use same workflow objects. The main workflow template for a process-oriented workflow is WS40000014 (Main SRM Approval Process Template). The template is associated with the event READY_FOR_WORKFLOW of the class /SAPSRM/CL_WF_PDO. The main list of workflow templates and tasks are listed below:

Workflow Object	Description
WS40000014	Main workflow template
WS40000015	n-Level Approval Loop workflow template
TS40007935	Get reviewers
TS40007937	Get next process level
TS40007938	Create Decision set
TS40007957	Get current process level
TS40007961	Email notification after document change

The decision sets are determined in task TS40007938. Task TS40007943 is used for the assignment of agents. The ABAP object /SAPSRM/CL_WF_PROCESS is used for handling Workflow processes.

8.4.2 Responsibility Area

SRM provides a number of ABAP Classes for Workflow Area. All these classes are inherited from the base class /SAPSRM/CL_WF_AREA. You can use these ABAP objects in Agent and Reviewer determination BADIs.

ABAP Class	Description
/SAPSRM/CL_WF_AREA_COST_CENTER	Cost Center Workflow Area
/SAPSRM/CL_WF_AREA_EMPLOYEE	Employee Workflow Area
/SAPSRM/CL_WF_AREA_EMPLO_LIST	Employee List Workflow Area
/SAPSRM/CL_WF_AREA_MANAGER	Manager Workflow Area
/SAPSRM/CL_WF_AREA_PURCH_GRP	Purchase Grp Workflow Area
/SAPSRM/CL_WF_AREA_RL_UNIT	RL unit Workflow Area

8.4.3 PDO Layer

SRM Workflow provides PDO technical objects. The PDO objects are used in BRF event and workflow BADIs. For each SRM object type, there is a PDO object. The PDO object implements the interfaces /SAPSRM/IF_WF_PDO and IF_WORKFLOW.

Object Type	PDO Class
Confirmation	/SAPSRM/CL_WF_PDO_CONF
Contract	/SAPSRM/CL_WF_PDO_CTR
Invoice	/SAPSRM/CL_WF_PDO_INV
Purchase Order	/SAPSRM/CL_WF_PDO_PO
Quote	/SAPSRM/CL_WF_PDO_QTE
Bid Invitation	/SAPSRM/CL_WF_PDO_RFQ
Shopping Cart	/SAPSRM/CL_WF_PDO_SC

These PDO object uses SRM Business objects. These entire PDO objects inherit from /SAPSRM/CL_WF_PDO. The PDO object can be used to instantiate using the factory class /SAPSRM/CL_WF_PDO_IMPL_FACTORY. The PDO layer can be used to access procurement document information.

To access a SRM procurement document instance in Workflow BADIs, use the following code snippet.

```
DATA lo_wf_pdo TYPE REF TO /sapsrm/if_wf_pdo.
lo_wf_pdo ?= /sapsrm/cl_wf_pdo_impl_factory=>get_instance(
```

```
iv_document_guid = is_document-document_guid
iv_document_type = is_document-document_type ).
```

- /SAPSRM/CL_WF_PROCESS_MGR_SBWF – ABAP object used in the workflow standard tasks.
- /SAPSRM/CL_WF_CONFIG_USER – ABAP Object to get use account configuration parameters. The ABAP object can be used get Spending Limit, Approval Limit, Spending Limit Approver and Get Manager List. The Spending Limit and Approval Limit can be found at the User level (SU01) personalization tab.

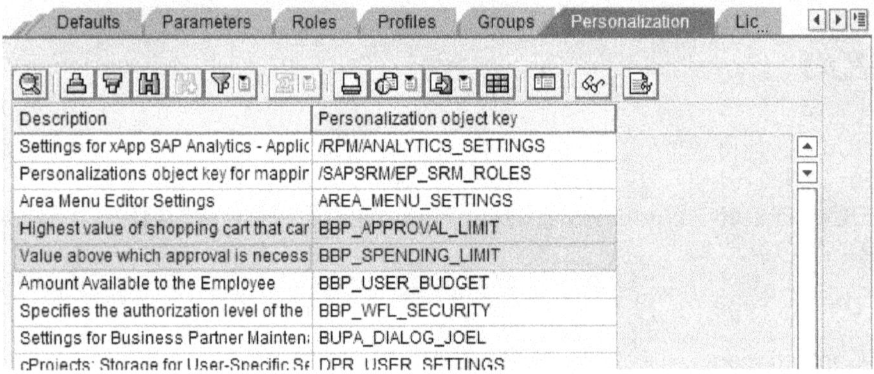

The object /SAPSRM/CL_WF_CONFIGURATION can be used to get workflow configuration information. The following list provides to get workflow version for a given document type. There are multiple methods to get the workflow version.

```
 CALL METHOD
/sapsrm/cl_wf_configuration=>get_apf_version_by_botype
   EXPORTING
     iv_document_type = gc_po
     iv_user_id       = sy-uname
   RECEIVING
     rv_apf_version   = lv_workflow_version.
```

8.5 Process Flow

The process-controlled workflow process flow is listed below.

1. Determine process schema based on evaluation (BRF event).
2. SRM workflow starts new instance of workflow template WS4000014 that controls overall process control.
3. The subworkflow WS40000015 (process level evaluation) determines whether the process schema contains further process levels to be carried out. The process level evaluation runs in the loop and repeated each time a process level has been finished. If there is no level then restart has been requested. Based on by configuration or BADI, the system checks whether or not a specific process level must be activated.
4. Depending on the process level type, the sysem starts the following subtemplates:
    a. WS40000015 - for level type 'approval'
    b. WS40000016 - for level type 'approval with completion'
5. The system determines the agent for the current process level and generates work items. The agent determination is based on the agent BADI. The agent will receive the work item in UWL/inbox
6. The agent can process work item by accepting or rejecting the work item.

- Repeat steps 3 through 6 for each process level of the process schema.

8.6 SRM Workflow step-by-step

In this section, you can see the step-by-step procedure to setup the basic SRM7.x workflow. This procedure is applicable only to the process-controlled workflow.

- Identify the business objects for process-controlled workflow. Define custom evaluation IDs for each business objects.
- Define all process schemas based on your requirements for each business object type.

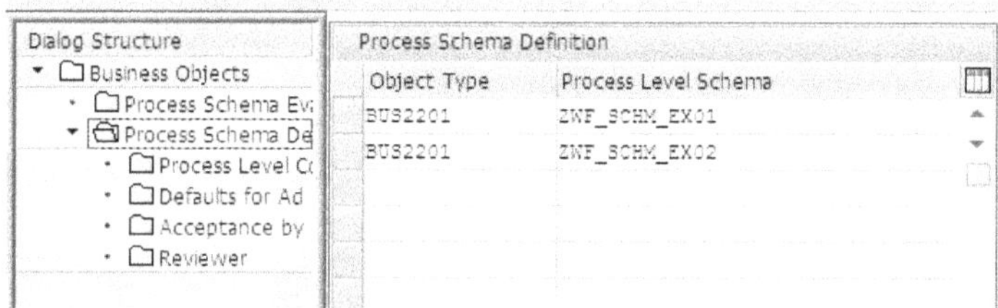

- Create function module ZF_GET_SCHEMA with BRF Event FM programming interfaces. You can copy the standard SRM BRF function module **/SAPSRM/WF_BRF_0EXP001. This function module will be used for all business objects.**

```
DATA lo_wf_brf_event   TYPE REF TO /sapsrm/cl_wf_brf_event.
  DATA lo_context_provider  TYPE REF TO
/sapsrm/if_wf_context_provider.
lo_wf_brf_event ?= io_event.
lo_context_provider = lo_wf_brf_event->get_context_provider( ).
  CALL METHOD lo_context_provider->get_document
    IMPORTING
      ev_document_guid = lv_document_guid
      ev_document_type = lv_document_type.
DATA lo_pdo_po TYPE REF TO /sapsrm/if_pdo_bo_po.
CASE lv_document_type.
WHEN lc_po.
* get instance
lo_wf_pdo ?= /sapsrm/cl_wf_pdo_impl_factory=>get_instance(
iv_document_guid = lv_document_guid
iv_document_type = lv_document_type
).
lo_pdo_po ?= io_wf_pdo->get_pdo( ).
----* Implement logic to determine Scheme  Process schema can be based
on
* trsnaction type, business partner or customer fields.
 ------------- ev_length = 32.
------------- ev_type = ‘C’.
*-------------ev_value = 'YOUR_PROCESS_SCHEME’.
WHEN lc_sc
…..
….
WHEN lc_contract.
```

```
WHEN OTHERS.
ENDCASE.
```

- Repeating following steps for each business object and evaluation ID. The following step is an example for the PO business object.
  - Create an expression ZV_PO_SCHEMA with implementation class 0CF001 (BADI and function module) and associate the function module ZF_GET_SCHEMA with the expression. Make sure that result type is character and length is set to 32.

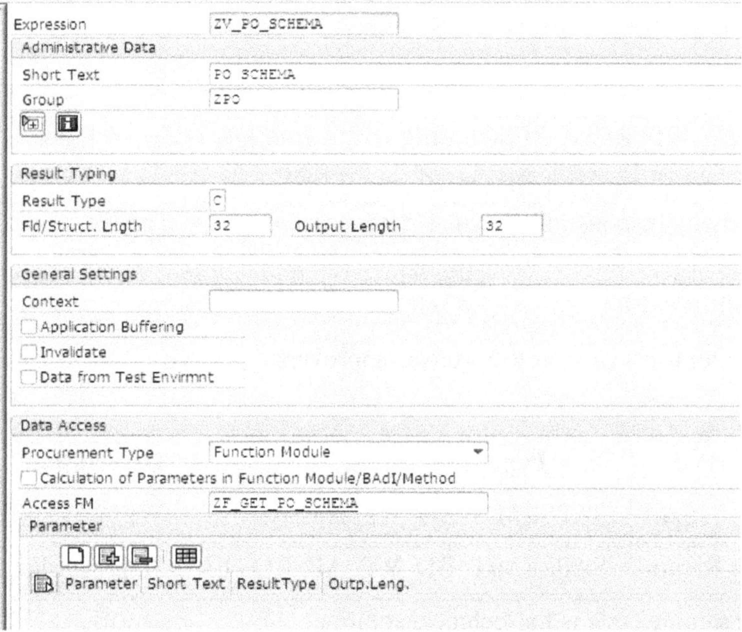

  - Create a BRF event. The event is defined in process schema configuration as evaluation id.

- The BRF event will return process schema for the business object based on the data. SRM uses corresponding process schema and its process levels.

- Configure the Approver agents. You can configure new approvers if SRM predefined approval agents do not fulfill your requirements. For each new approver, you need to implement the BADI /SAPSRM/BD_WF_RESP_RESOLVER. You can implement logic to get approver list in the method GET_APPROVERS_BY_AREA_GUID. The approver list logic can be written directly in BADI method or you can create new custom WF area class by inheriting the base class /SAPSRM/CL_WF_AREA. You should redefine constructor method and GET_RESPONSIBLE_APPROVERS method.

Name:/SAPSRM/BD_WF_RESP_RESOLVER		Multiple Use: No	Filter: Yes
Description: Resolving responsibility areas for item assignment and agent determination.			
Method: GET_APPROVERS_BY_AREA_GUID Description: Return all users of your user role as approvers. Parameters:			
Name	**Type**	**Data Type**	**Description**
IS_AREA	Import	/SAPSRM/S_BD_WF_AREA	WF Area
RT_APPROVER	Return	/SAPSRM/T_BD_WF_APPROVER	Approver list
Sample code: The sample code is for technical solution.			

```
 DATA lo_area TYPE REF TO /sapsrm/if_wf_area.
 CONSTANTS: gc_yr_wf_area TYPE swf_clsname value ‘ZCL_WF_AREA’.
* Input checks
 ASSERT ID /sapsrm/wf_cfg CONDITION(NOT is_area IS INITIAL).
 IF is_area IS INITIAL.
   RETURN.
 ENDIF.
* Get responsibility area reference for given area GUID
 lo_area = /sapsrm/cl_wf_area=>/sapsrm/if_wf_area~get_instance_by_guid(
   iv_area_type = gc_yr_wf_area
   iv_area_guid = is_area-area_guid
   ).

* Return all responsible users assigned to that area
 rt_approver = lo_area->get_responsible_approvers( ).
```

- You can define fallback users if your get approver list does not return any approver. This is one of recommended practice. So, the document approval will not be struck in the middle.

- Create process levels for each process level schema. You can define any number of process levels. You need to define Level type, Evaluation ID, Responsible agent resolver and parameter, Task ID and Decision Type. The responsible resolver parameter can be fetched by the following ABAP statement.

```
lv_parameter = me->/sapsrm/if_wf_area~get_leading_object_id( ).
```

- Last process level should be "Automatic (System User)“. This is controlleld by the standard event 0EV999, which ensures that the process step gets invoked when if none of the previous process levels are invoked.

- If you require any custom evaluations in the process level then you must define custom BRF events (same as evaluation id) and its corresponding expressions. Note that BRF expression should have result type as Boolean. You can use the BRF function module if any expression requires complex derivation logic. If the evaluation return true then it will execute the process level and get all approvers as in the process level. The work item will be sent to approvers to approve or reject it.

8.7 Troubleshooting

Since the workflow is executed in background and if there is any issue on the workflow, identifying the issue and cause of the issue requires some troubleshooting techniques. This section will explain how to troubleshoot the workflow and its component. SAP provides a number of tools to view the log and analyze the workflow.

You can use the report /SAPSRM/WF_CFG_ANALYSIS_001 to analysis the workflow of the SRM document in SAP back-end GUI. You can view the agent groups and items information.

Analysis of Process-Level Configuration

Document

Document Type	BUS2201	SRM Shopping Cart
Document ID	8500003494	
Document GUID	00000000000000000000000000000000	

Analysis of Process-Level Configuration

Seq. No.	Lvl Type	Resolver	Parameter	Evaluation ID	WF Task ID	Approval Task Description
100	A	ZRR_KO	50000638	ZEV_PO_0_000	TS90707935	SRM Purchase Order Approval

Analysis of Process-Level Configuration

Level Number: 100
Level Status: Inactive
Document Type: SRM Purchase Order
Document ID: 8500003494
Document GUID: 4AD378FDAE262DE7E100000083461630

Object List	GUID
SRM Purchase Order	4AD378FDAE262DE7E100000083461...
Responsibility Area	4DDCABCB5A12278DE10000008346...
Agent Group	
Item List	
Item	All Items

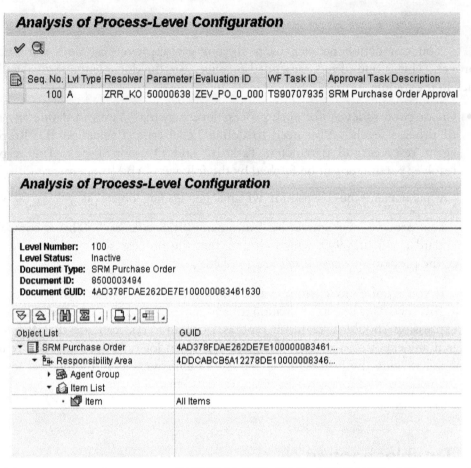

You can use the report /SAPSRM/WF_CFG_ANALYSIS_002 to analysis derivation of the process levels.

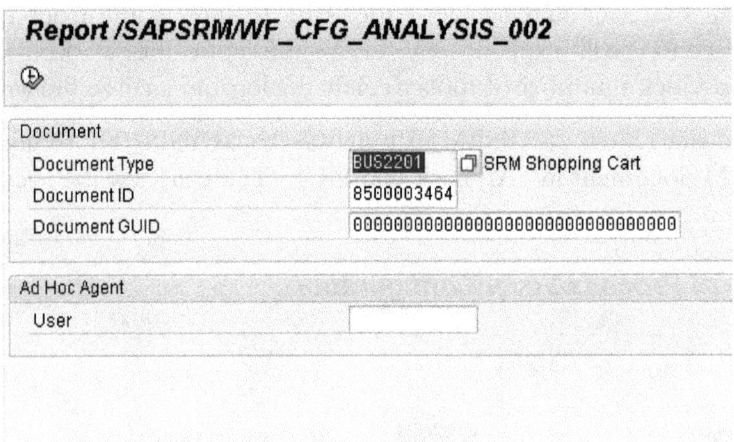

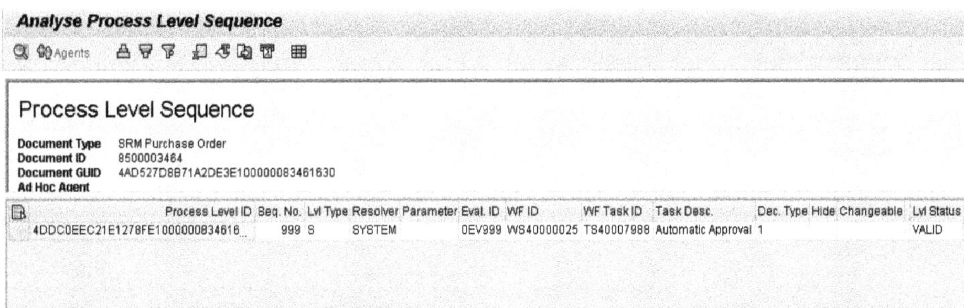

Document Approval Process Analysis

The analysis document approval process can be viewed using the Web Dynpro application /SAPSRM/WDC_WF_ANCFG_MAIN. The tool provides the analysis of workflow for a particular SRM document. The document can be identified by the GUID or Object ID. The selection has few parameters as you case see in the following screen shot.

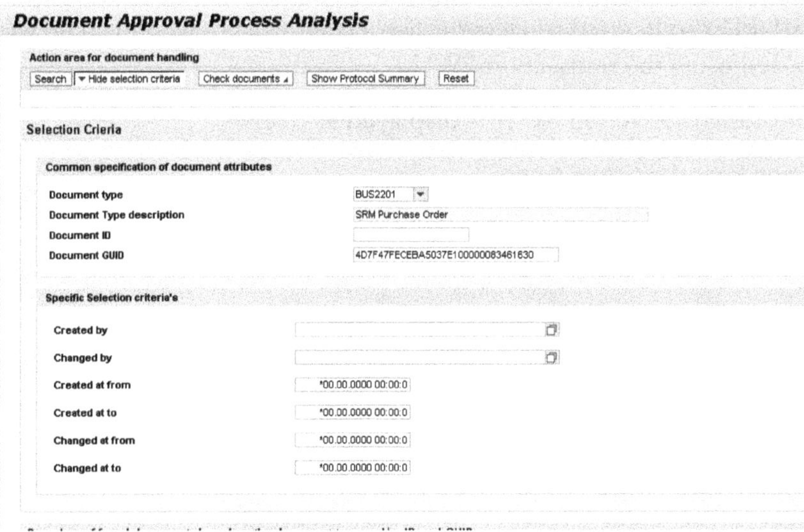

Based on the selection, the found documents are listed. The check documents can provide further information.

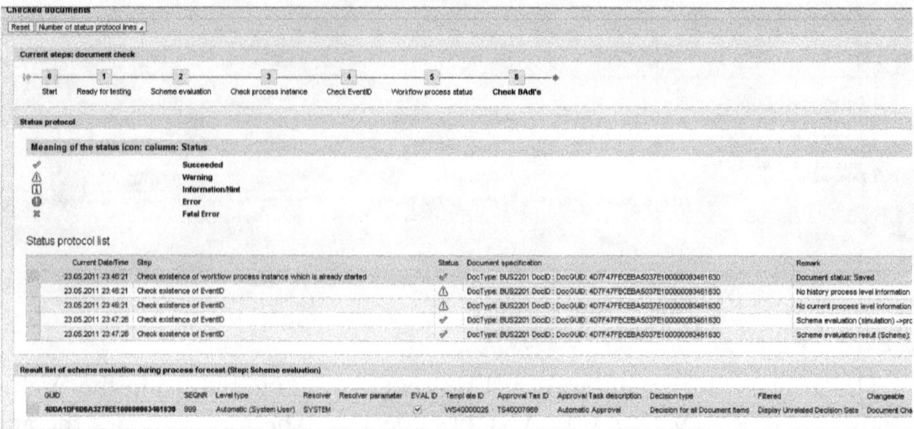

Workflow Log

All workflow items in SRM are associated with a SRM document. As we see the document display in the chapter 2 (Procurement Document – Document Display), the transaction BBP_PD can be used to view the associated workflow item. The workflow item can be viewed using the transaction SWI1.

The screenshot of the transaction SWI1 is displayed as below:

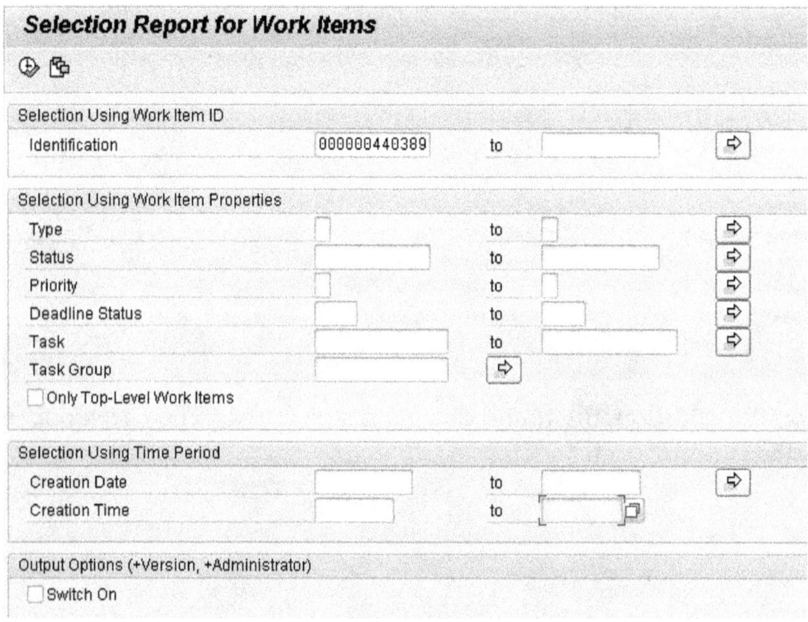

If you execute the report, it will display the workflow item.

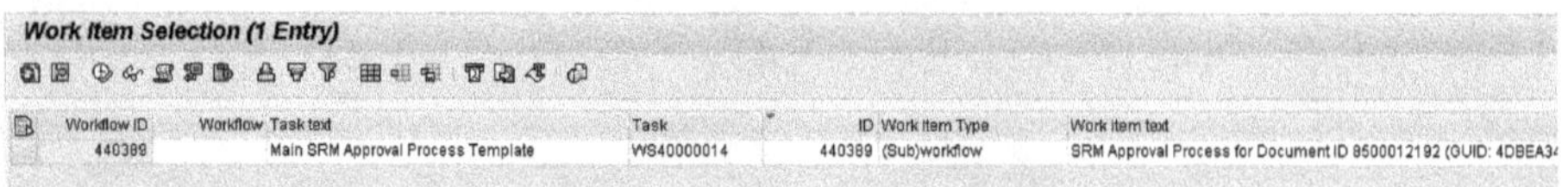

The report provides the workflow log. The workflow provides the detail of each step. Also, the technical list option (Menu GoTo->List with technical details) lists all the steps with technical details like Container information and status of each step. The report also provides option to see the workflow log in the graphics mode.

Application Log

SRM BRF trace is stored in the application log object /SAPSRM/. You can view the application log using the transaction code SLG1. Make sure enter /SAPSRM/ in Object. You can provide sub-object also to filter the application log further. You can provide GUID of the object in External ID to see only application log of the SRM document.

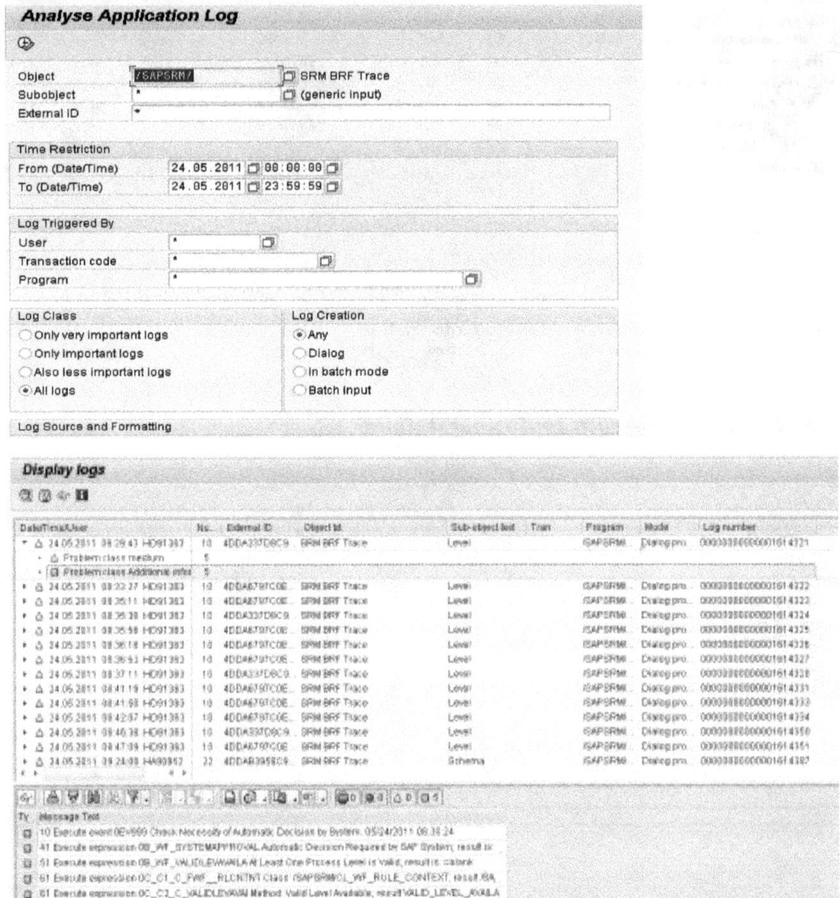

Issue: No Workflow Triggered

When there is no workflow triggered for the object, you need to check the event linkage type for the class /SAPSRM/CL_WF_PDO and its event READY_FOR_WORKFLOW to workflow task WS40000014. Make sure that event linkage for this has been activated. This event linkage is very basic for the process-controlled workflow.

Solution: To release the Workflow status of the business object, you can use the function module BBP_PDO_<BO>_STATUS_CHANGE_WF. This is one of useful function module to fix the Awaiting for Approval Issue.

8.8 Event Linkage

Event linkage is part of the SAP workflow process. Event linkage table is a database table which defining connection between events and their associated receiver programs. The event linkage table is populated for the triggering event of the workflow. Also, you can create own subscribe receiver type to handle the event by your own function module. This functionality provides a great flexibility for the developer to provide a simple follow-on action for an event. You can activate or de-activate the linkage table. The event linkage can be viewed using the transaction SWE2. The event linkage supports only the events defined in workflow business objects (defined in SWO1) and ABAP Class events. The ABAP class event linkage makes ABAP class definition more versatile. The receiver call can be either Function module or ABAP Class method.

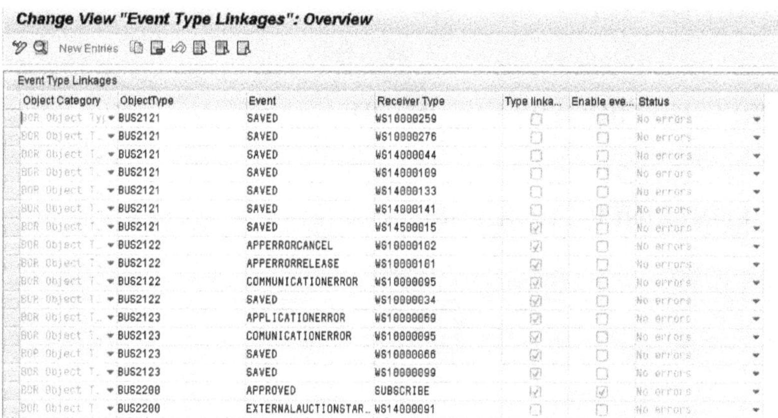

Change View "Event Type Linkages": Overview

New Entries

Event Type Linkages

Object Category	ObjectType	Event	Receiver Type	Type linka...	Enable eve...	Status
BOR Object Typ	BUS2121	SAVED	WS10000259	☐	☐	No errors
BOR Object T...	BUS2121	SAVED	WS10000276	☐	☐	No errors
BOR Object T...	BUS2121	SAVED	WS14000044	☐	☐	No errors
BOR Object T...	BUS2121	SAVED	WS14000109	☐	☐	No errors
BOR Object T...	BUS2121	SAVED	WS14000133	☐	☐	No errors
BOR Object T...	BUS2121	SAVED	WS14000141	☐	☐	No errors
BOR Object T...	BUS2121	SAVED	WS14500015	☑	☐	No errors
BOR Object T...	BUS2122	APPERRORCANCEL	WS10000102	☑	☐	No errors
BOR Object T...	BUS2122	APPERRORRELEASE	WS10000101	☑	☐	No errors
BOR Object T...	BUS2122	COMMUNICATIONERROR	WS10000095	☑	☐	No errors
BOR Object T...	BUS2122	SAVED	WS10000034	☑	☐	No errors
BOR Object T...	BUS2123	APPLICATIONERROR	WS10000069	☑	☐	No errors
BOR Object T...	BUS2123	COMUNICATIONERROR	WS10000095	☑	☐	No errors
BOR Object T...	BUS2123	SAVED	WS10000066	☑	☐	No errors
BOR Object T...	BUS2123	SAVED	WS10000099	☑	☐	No errors
BOR Object T...	BUS2200	APPROVED	SUBSCRIBE	☑	☑	No errors
BOR Object T...	BUS2200	EXTERNALAUCTIONSTAR...	WS14000091	☐	☐	No errors

New event type linkage is created for the event Reject of the PO.

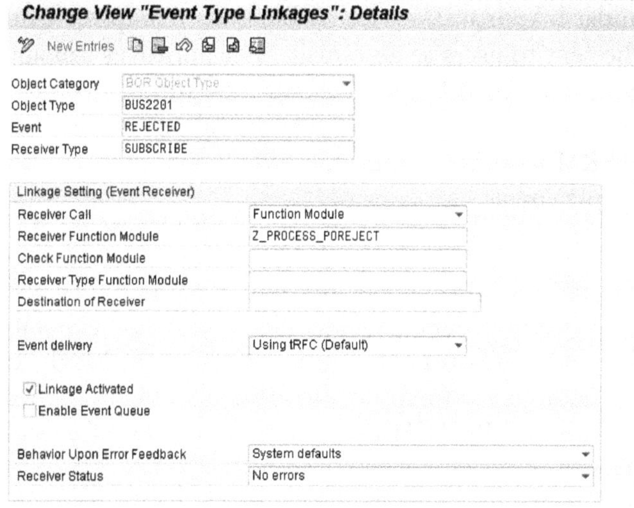

Change View "Event Type Linkages": Details

New Entries

Object Category	BOR Object Type
Object Type	BUS2201
Event	REJECTED
Receiver Type	SUBSCRIBE

Linkage Setting (Event Receiver)

Receiver Call	Function Module
Receiver Function Module	Z_PROCESS_POREJECT
Check Function Module	
Receiver Type Function Module	
Destination of Receiver	
Event delivery	Using tRFC (Default)

☑ Linkage Activated
☐ Enable Event Queue

Behavior Upon Error Feedback	System defaults
Receiver Status	No errors

The event linkage provides option to enable use of Queue for the event processing. If the indicator is set, then the event queue is active else the receiver is started immediately. If you define a custom function module or ABAP class method is defined in the configuration then it must follow the event linkage interfaces.

```
*"----------------------------------------------------*"*"Local Interface:
*" IMPORTING
*"    VALUE(EVENT) LIKE  SWETYPECOU-EVENT
*"    VALUE(RECTYPE) LIKE  SWETYPECOU-RECTYPE
*"    VALUE(OBJTYPE) LIKE  SWETYPECOU-OBJTYPE
*"    VALUE(OBJKEY) LIKE  SWEINSTCOU-OBJKEY
*"    VALUE(EXCEPTIONS_ALLOWED) LIKE  SWEFLAGS-
EXC_OK DEFAULT SPACE
*" EXPORTING
*"    VALUE(REC_ID) LIKE  SWELOG-RECID
*" TABLES
*"     EVENT_CONTAINER STRUCTURE  SWCONT
*"----------------------------------------------------
```

8.9 Offline Approval

SRM provide options to users to approve the work items without SRM system access. It will not use the standard Approval service or Business workplace of the SRM system. The work items will be sent to users as an e-mail. The approver can approve or reject the work item by replying the email by just clicking on Approval or Reject link provided in the email. The replied email containing the approval or rejection decision is received and processed by the SRM workflow. Inbound SMTP configuration is required to handle the offline decision reply emails.

The program RBBP_NOTIFICATION_OFFAPP is used to generate and sending e-mails for offline approval. The emails are sent only to those users with FORWARD_WI flag is set. Also, the program picks only work items generated since the last run with Ready or Waiting status. The program RBBP_OFFLINE_EVAL is used to process inbound mail and approve or reject the SRM document. Schedule this program as a background job with WF-BATCH user. The frequency of execution can be determined by your requirement.

The BADI BBP_OFFLINE_APP_BADI is used to adapt and extend SRM standard functionality for offline approval. The BADI has the following methods:

- WORKITEMS_SELECT – You can use this method to define the work items that are sent as e-mail for offline approval. The program RBBP_NOTIFICATION_OFFAPP is used to generating and sending e-mails for the offline-approval. This program is available from SRM5.0.

- RECIPIENTS_GET – You can this method to determine the recipients per work item. The recipients will receive e-mail for offline approval.

- MAIL_DATA_GET – This method can be used to define the mail contents.

- MAIL_CREATE – This BADI is used as an alternative method for EXECUTE of the default offline message class CL_BBP_MESSAGE_CREATE_OFFAPP.

- DETERMINE_CLASS_NAME – This method is used to override the default class to your own transfer class.

- SMTP_INBOUND_ADDR_GET – This method is used to change e-mail address for the decision e-mail that is sent when the approval links in the HTML emails are selected.

- CHK_SENDER_IND_SET – You can override the parameter sender Indicator from the processing report RBBP_OFFLINE_EVAL in order to validate whether the sender of reply and the owner of the work item match.

You need to define exit rules for the inbound processing. This can be done using the transaction SO50 (or you can access the transaction SCOT). SRM provides exit class CL_BBP_SMTP_INBOUND_OFFAPP to process the incoming messages.

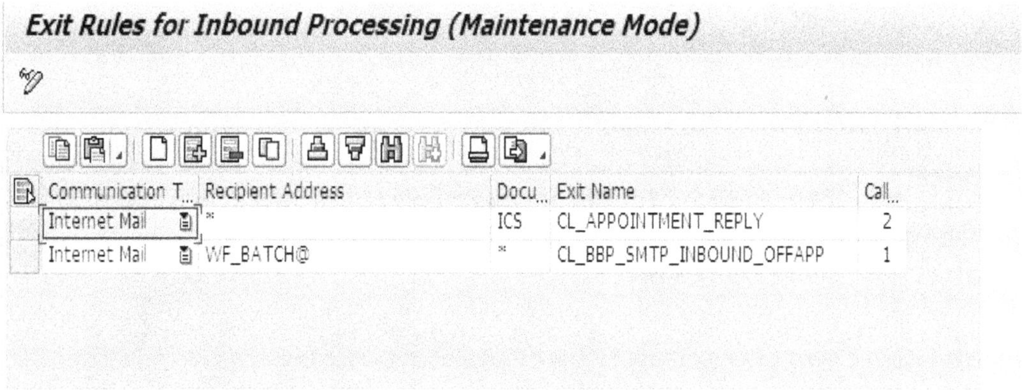

Exit Rules for Inbound Processing (Maintenance Mode)

Communication T...	Recipient Address	Docu...	Exit Name	Call...
Internet Mail	*	ICS	CL_APPOINTMENT_REPLY	2
Internet Mail	WF_BATCH@	*	CL_BBP_SMTP_INBOUND_OFFAPP	1

8.10 Application Controlled Workflows

SRM7 uses the process-controlled workflow but it still supports the application-controlled workflows. The SRM configuration allows you to set what kind of workflow framework (Application or Process controlled workflow) for the business objects. You can access this IMG activity by the IMG path SRM Server->Cross-Application Basic Settings->Business Workflow.

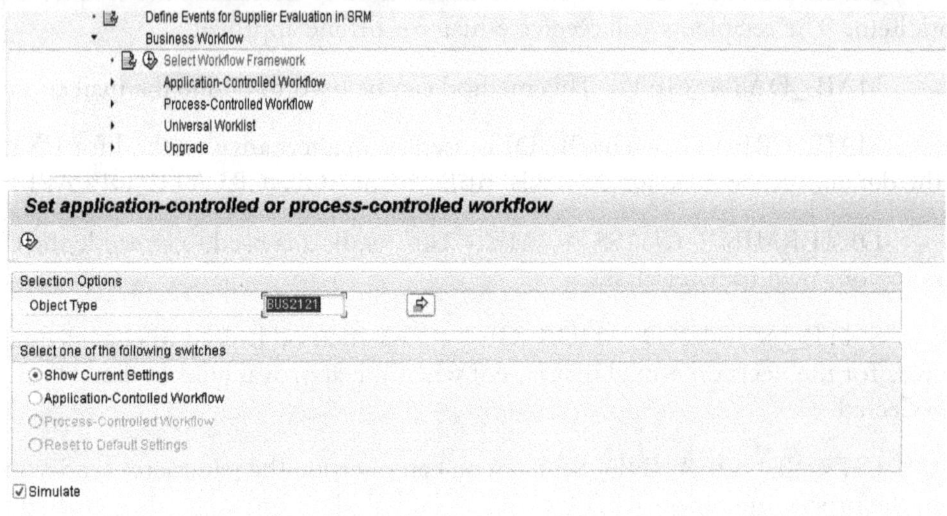

The process-controlled workflow is set by default in SRM7. Note that once you switch to application-controlled workflow to process controlled workflow and/or once a process-controlled workflow has been run, it is not supported to switch back to application-controlled workflow. The configuration can be used to see current settings of SRM object types.

8.11 Summary

In this chapter, you have learned the basic concept of BRF and usage of BRF in SRM. The BRF programming is discussed in detail and its usage. You have also learned about process controlled workflow.

Appendices

Flexible Message Control

Flexible message control allows you control the message type of the message. You can switch off some messages so that they do not appear at all. This is very useful when some of standard SAP hard error check is not applicable for your business requirements. So, you can ignore or neglect the error message. You can configure flexible message control using the IMG path SRM Server-> Cross-Application basic settings->Message Control.

You can use Influence Message Control IMG activity to control the class message type. You can change the message type from E(rror) to W(arning). The warning message will be displayed and you can carry out further actions on the document. Also, you can change the message type W(arning) to E(rror). So, it will prevent the document from further actions. The message flexible message is based on the SRM business objects.

Display View "Business Objects": Overview

Dialog Structure
- Business Objects
  - Message Control

Business Objects

Business Object	Description
BUS2121	EC Requirement Coverage Request
BUS2200	Bid Invitation EC
BUS2201	EC Purchase Order
BUS2202	EC Vendor Bid

Business Object BUS2121 EC Requirement Coverage Request

Message Control

Message cl	No.	Text	Type	Standard
/SAPSRM/PDO_SC	035	Item price in SC has been modifie...	W	E
BBP_PD	584	Preferred delivery date cannot be...	W	E

The activity Influence incoming message control allows you to control message type when XML inbound process. You can ignore certain messages with type E(rror). The document remains incomplete but it is created as an error-free document and follows workflow process.

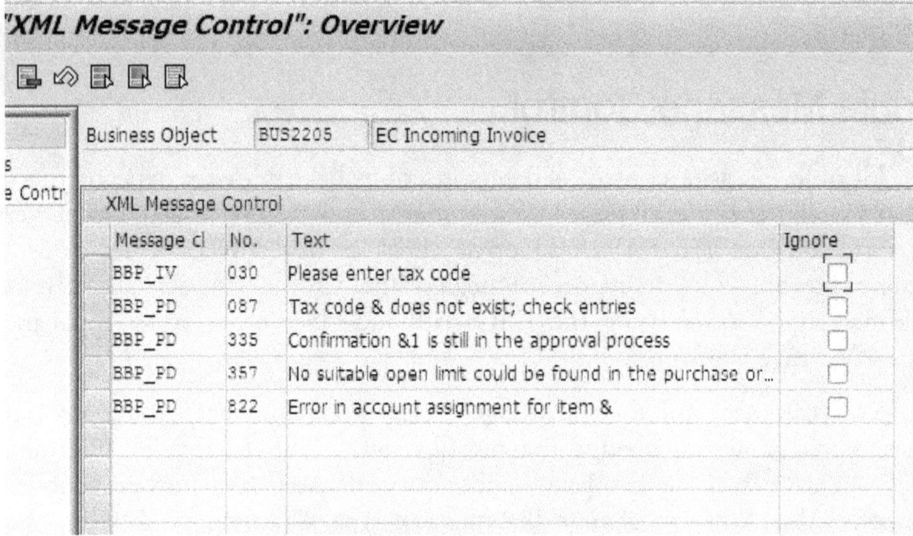

Debug Tip

The error/warning messages in the SRM UI screen will not show the message ID and number. You can get the information by placing debug point at the function module BBP_PD_MSG_ADD.

INDEX